Learning Microsoft Azure

A comprehensive guide to cloud application development using Microsoft Azure

Geoff Webber-Cross

PUBLISHING

BIRMINGHAM - MUMBAI

Learning Microsoft Azure

First published: October 2014

Production reference: 1091014

Published by Packt Publishing Ltd.
Livery Place
35 Livery Street
Birmingham B3 2PB, UK.

ISBN 978-1-78217-337-3

www.packtpub.com

Credits

Author
Geoff Webber-Cross

Reviewers
Debarchan Sarkar

Jignesh Gangajaliya

Zhidong Wu

Commissioning Editor
Amarabha Banerjee

Acquisition Editor
Sonali Vernekar

Content Development Editor
Anila Vincent

Technical Editor
Mrunal M. Chavan

Copy Editors
Sayanee Mukherjee

Alfida Paiva

Project Coordinator
Neha Bhatnagar

Proofreaders
Mario Cecere

Maria Gould

Lawrence A. Herman

Indexers
Mariammal Chettiyar

Monica Ajmera Mehta

Rekha Nair

Tejal Soni

Graphics
Ronak Dhruv

Valentina D'silva

Disha Haria

Abhinash Sahu

Production Coordinators
Aparna Bhagat

Manu Joseph

Shantanu N. Zagade

Cover Work
Manu Joseph

About the Author

Geoff Webber-Cross has over 10 years' experience in the software industry, working in manufacturing, electronics, and other engineering disciplines. He has experience of building enterprise and smaller .NET systems on Azure and other platforms. He also has commercial and personal experience of developing Windows 8 and Windows Phone applications. He has authored *Learning Windows Azure Mobile Services for Windows 8 and Windows Phone 8, Packt Publishing*.

I'd like to thank my wife and two boys for keeping me motivated throughout the book-writing process.

About the Reviewers

Debarchan Sarkar is a Support Escalation Engineer in the Microsoft HDInsight team and a technical author of books on SQL Server BI and Big Data. His total tenure at Microsoft is 7 years, and he was with the SQL Server BI team before diving deep into Big Data and the Hadoop world. He is an SME in SQL Server Integration Services (SSIS) and is passionate about the present-day Microsoft self-service BI tools and data analysis, especially social-media brand sentiment analysis. He hails from the "City of Joy" Kolkata, India, and is presently located in Bangalore, India, for his job in Microsoft Global Technical Support Center. He owns and maintains his *Big Data Learnings* group on Facebook and is a speaker at several of Microsoft's internal and external community events. His Twitter handle is @debarchans.

He is the author of *Microsoft SQL Server 2012 with Hadoop*, Packt Publishing and *Pro Microsoft HDInsight: Hadoop on Windows*, Apress Media LLC.

I want to thank my father, Mr. Asok Sarkar, for his continued encouragement and all the hard work he has done throughout his life to see us happy. I feel better today because I'm able to acknowledge that I'm proud to have you as my father, from the core of my heart.

Jignesh Gangajaliya is a principal technical architect with over 11 years of core technology and global business leadership experience in defining solutions and technology architectures.

His expertise is in design, development, and deployment of large-scale software systems and solutions across various industry verticals. His core strengths are wide and deep hands-on technological expertise, strategic thinking, comprehensive analytical skills, creativity in solving complex problems, and the ability to quickly understand complex business problems and come up with pragmatic solutions.

He is passionate about creating a strategic vision, and building and transforming organizations to accelerate growth and value creation by leveraging new technologies, trends, and emerging opportunities.

He specializes in enterprise architecture, solution architecture, Microsoft server products and technologies, cloud computing, SaaS, Microsoft Azure, and Amazon Web Services.

Zhidong Wu received his M.S. degree in Computer Science from Brown University. He has worked at Microsoft Corporation and Baidu in the past. He is an enthusiast in Big Data and has experience in Apache Hadoop, Microsoft Azure HDInsight, and Microsoft Cosmos. He can be contacted at `zhidong_wu@brown.edu`. You can find out more about him at `http://www.linkedin.com/in/wuzhidong1122`.

www.PacktPub.com

Support files, eBooks, discount offers, and more

You might want to visit www.PacktPub.com for support files and downloads related to your book.

Did you know that Packt offers eBook versions of every book published, with PDF and ePub files available? You can upgrade to the eBook version at www.PacktPub.com and as a print book customer, you are entitled to a discount on the eBook copy. Get in touch with us at service@packtpub.com for more details.

At www.PacktPub.com, you can also read a collection of free technical articles, sign up for a range of free newsletters and receive exclusive discounts and offers on Packt books and eBooks.

http://PacktLib.PacktPub.com

Do you need instant solutions to your IT questions? PacktLib is Packt's online digital book library. Here, you can access, read and search across Packt's entire library of books.

Why subscribe?

- Fully searchable across every book published by Packt
- Copy and paste, print and bookmark content
- On demand and accessible via web browser

Free access for Packt account holders

If you have an account with Packt at www.PacktPub.com, you can use this to access PacktLib today and view nine entirely free books. Simply use your login credentials for immediate access.

Instant updates on new Packt books

Get notified! Find out when new books are published by following @PacktEnterprise on Twitter, or the *Packt Enterprise* Facebook page.

Table of Contents

Preface	**1**
Chapter 1: Getting Started with Microsoft Azure	**9**
An overview of cloud computing	**9**
Microsoft Azure overview	**10**
Selecting a Microsoft Azure solution	**11**
Infrastructure capabilities	12
Platform capabilities	13
Cost	13
Decision flow diagrams	14
Administration of Microsoft Azure systems	**16**
Choosing a subscription	**17**
Creating a Microsoft Azure account	**18**
Adding a subscription	**20**
Exploring the portal	**22**
The top toolbar	22
The side toolbar	25
The bottom toolbar	25
Examining Microsoft Azure Services	**27**
Compute services	27
Websites	27
Virtual machines	28
Mobile services	28
Cloud services	29
Data services	29
SQL Server Database	30
Storages	30
HDInsight	31
Cache	31
Recovery services	32
App services	32

Media services	32
Service Bus	32
Visual Studio Online	33
BizTalk Services	33
Scheduler	33
Active Directory (AD)	34
Network services	**34**
Virtual Network	34
Traffic Manager	35
Summary	**35**
Questions	**35**
Answers	**36**
Chapter 2: Designing a System for Microsoft Azure	**37**
Designing scalable and resilient systems	**38**
Systems architecture	**40**
A case study of a small business system	**41**
System requirements	41
Identifying subsystems	42
Customer website design	42
Administration system design	44
System integration	45
Identifying critical systems	46
Selecting services	46
Conclusion of the small business case study	47
A case study of an enterprise system – Azure Bakery	**47**
System requirements	48
Sales requirements	48
Production requirements	49
Supply requirements	49
Identifying subsystems	49
Sales subsystems	49
Production subsystems	50
Supply subsystems	50
System design	50
System design – the sales customer phone app	51
System design – sales order processor	52
Sales system integration	52
Identifying critical services	53
Selecting Microsoft Azure Services	54
Selecting common services	54
Selecting sales services	54

Selecting production services	56
Selecting supply services	57
Conclusion of an enterprise system case study – Azure Bakery	57
Designing platform environments	**59**
Common environment roles	59
Example environment sets	60
Using website deployment slots	62
Using cloud service staging environments	63
Summary	**64**
Questions	**64**
Answers	**65**
Chapter 3: Starting to Develop with Microsoft Azure	**67**
Preparing our development environment	**67**
Setting up software	67
Mobile development	68
The Microsoft Azure SDK	69
Checking for Visual Studio updates	**69**
Creating a website	**70**
Configuring a website in the portal	**72**
Creating a Visual Studio Online project	**77**
Creating a Visual Studio Online account	78
Creating a Visual Studio Online project	79
Setting up continuous deployment	**80**
Adding a solution to source control	80
Configuring continuous deployment	84
Examining the build definition	87
Setting up alerts	**89**
Summary	**91**
Questions	**92**
Answers	**92**
Chapter 4: Creating and Managing a Windows Azure SQL Server Database	**93**
Creating a database using the Azure management portal	**94**
Building a database using Entity Framework (EF) Code First Migrations	**96**
Creating the data model	97
Configuring a database context	101
Linking an authenticated user to the model	102
Configuring the connection string	103
Enabling migrations and updating the database	104

Publishing with migrations   109
Managing SQL Azure Servers and databases   **112**
  Managing a database through the portal   113
    Features of the management portal   115
  Managing a database using SSMS   116
  Managing a database through Visual Studio   119
    Using the table designer   122
  Using Azure PowerShell   123
  Choosing a management tool   124
Backing up and restoring databases   **125**
  Automated exports   125
Summary   **128**
Questions   **128**
Answers   **129**

Chapter 5: Building Azure MVC Websites   **131**
Implementing OAuth authentication   **131**
  Creating a Twitter application   132
  Modifying the external login   133
  Testing the Twitter login   136
Completing the customer sales website   **138**
  Modifying the user account panel   138
  Temporary PayConfirm action   140
  Final activities   141
Adding a custom domain name to a website   **142**
Implementing an SSL certificate   **144**
  Creating CER files   146
  Using OpenSSL to create a PFX certificate   148
  Uploading the certificate   149
  Redirecting all HTTP traffic to HTTPS   150
Adding Azure AD single sign-on to a website   **151**
  Configuring AD   151
  Configuring an MVC website for AD single sign-on   152
  Publishing the website with AD single sign-on   154
Implementing Azure AD group authorization   **156**
  Creating an AD group   157
  Modifying the application service principal   158
  Implementing AzureAdAuthorizeAttribute   159
Completing the admin sales website   **163**
Summary   **165**
Questions   **166**
Answers   **167**

Chapter 6: Azure Website Diagnostics and Debugging   **169**

  Enabling diagnostics   **170**
    Working with logfiles   171
    Viewing logfiles in Visual Studio   171
    Streaming logs   172
      Filtering stream logs   174
    Downloading logs   174
    Accessing files using FTP   175
  Application logging   **175**
    Implementing tracing in the application   177
    Application logging to table storage   181
      Querying table data   183
    Application logging to blob storage   184
    Diagnosing a real bug   185
      Setting up the website   186
      Producing an error   187
  Site diagnostics   **188**
    Extra filesystem settings   188
    Site diagnostics using blob storage   189
  Kudu   **190**
  Remote debugging   **192**
    When to use remote debugging   195
  Summary   **195**
  Questions   **196**
  Answers   **197**

Chapter 7: Azure Service Bus Topic Integration   **199**

  Introducing Azure Service Bus and topics   **200**
  Dead-letter queues   **201**
  Creating a Service Bus topic   **202**
  Connecting a website to the Service Bus topic   **206**
    Preparing the website   207
    Creating messaging logic   208
    Sending a message from the controller   211
  The messaging simulator   **212**
    Setting up the project   213
    Creating a data service   214
    Creating a messaging service   216
    Completing the simulator   220
    Running the simulator   220
  Exploring the topic workspace   **222**
    The MONITOR tab   223

The CONFIGURE tab   224
The SUBSCRIPTIONS tab   225
Summary   **226**
Questions   **227**
Answers   **228**

Chapter 8: Building Worker Roles   **229**
Introducing cloud services   **229**
Exploring worker roles   **230**
Creating a worker role   230
Examining the worker role   233
Examining the cloud service   234
Running locally   **235**
The compute emulator UI   236
The storage emulator UI   237
Publishing a worker role   **238**
Building the production order processor   **241**
Adding an entity model   242
Preparing the Service Bus topic   243
Adding an order processor task   244
    Creating TopicProcessorBase   244
    Implementing TopicProcessorBase   247
    Using OrderTopicProcessor in the worker role   248
Creating a scheduled work activity   **250**
Creating a scheduled job and queue   251
Configuring a connection string   253
Adding batch processor tasks   255
    Creating a storage queue processor base   255
    Implementing StorageQueueProcessorBase   257
Completing the worker role   **258**
Testing the production order processor   **260**
Testing a single instance   261
Testing multiple instances   262
Deleting idle cloud services   **263**
Summary   **263**
Questions   **264**
Answers   **264**

Chapter 9: Cloud Service Diagnostics, Debugging, and Configuration   **267**
Configuring diagnostics   **267**
Adding local diagnostics   269
Configuring Azure storage diagnostics   271

Remote debugging	**272**
Stopping the debugger	275
Examining how remote debugging works	276
Debugging with IntelliTrace	**276**
Remote desktop connection	**279**
Downloading a Remote Desktop Protocol (RDP) file	279
Establishing an RDP connection	280
Firewall issues	282
Detecting configuration changes in code	**283**
Start-up tasks	**284**
Creating a batch script	284
Adding the task	286
Environmental variables	287
Summary	**288**
Questions	**288**
Answers	**289**
Chapter 10: Web API and Client Integration	**291**
Introducing a Web API	**292**
Introducing SignalR	**293**
Building a Web API service	**293**
Creating a Web API project	294
Creating API controllers	298
Creating a SignalR hub	**302**
Publishing a Web API	**305**
Modifying the Web API AD manifest	**307**
Adding a client application to AD	**308**
Building a client application	**310**
Preparing the WPF project	311
Creating an authentication base class	313
Creating a data service	315
Creating a SignalR service	316
Completing the application	318
Testing the application	319
Summary	**320**
Questions	**320**
Answers	**321**
Chapter 11: Integrating a Mobile Application Using Mobile Services	**323**
Introducing Azure mobile services	**326**
Creating the customer Azure mobile service	**327**

Creating a mobile services project	328
Exploring the mobile service sample project	**329**
The sample table controller	330
The sample data entity	331
A sample scheduled job	331
Mobile service DbContext	331
WebApiConfig	332
Cleaning up the project	332
Integrating with the sales database	333
Configuring development app settings	333
Integrating authentication with the sales website	334
Adding a channel registration API controller	336
Adding an order controller	338
Publishing the mobile service	339
Creating a Windows Phone application	**342**
Adding data services	343
The DataServiceBase class	343
The DataService class	346
Setting up push notifications	347
Modifying the manifest	347
Adding a channel helper	348
Notifications debug	348
Completing the app	349
Updating the order processor	**349**
Updating the admin website	**351**
Creating the supply mobile service	**352**
Configuring a mobile service for Azure AD auth	353
Creating the barcode controller	355
Creating the order controller	356
Creating the supply Windows Store application	**358**
Configuring the Store app for AD authentication	359
Creating a DataServiceBase class	361
Summary	**361**
Questions	**361**
Answers	**362**
Chapter 12: Preparing an Azure System for Production	**365**
Project configurations for multiple environments	**365**
Adding build configurations to a solution	367
Website configuration transforms	369
Application configuration transforms	370
Cloud configuration	372

Building website deployment packages   **374**
   Manually publishing websites to the filesystem   374
   Building web packages on a build server   375
Building cloud service deployment packages   **381**
   Building cloud service deployment packages manually   381
   Building cloud service deployment packages on a build server   382
Deploying web packages to Azure   **385**
Deploying cloud packages to Azure   **387**
Creating database scripts from Entity Framework Code
First Migrations   **389**
The go-live checklist   **389**
Monitoring live services   **390**
   The Microsoft Azure portal   390
   The Service Management REST API   390
   Management services alerts   390
   Azure PowerShell   392
Azure daily service checks   **392**
Azure periodic service activities   **392**
Azure tool list   **393**
Summary   **394**
Questions   **395**
Answers   **395**
Index   **397**

Preface

Learning Microsoft Azure is a practical, hands-on book for learning how to build systems for Microsoft Azure. This book is themed around an enterprise case study based on a fictional industrial bakery called Azure Bakery, which spans three business units: sales, production, and supply. The entire system is built on the Microsoft Azure technology that utilizes a broad range of services.

The sales business unit is responsible for selling products to customers through the MVC 5 customer website, where customers can place orders and view their status as the order moves through the system. Products are managed through another administrator website that implements Azure Active Directory authentication. A Windows Phone app with .NET mobile service and Twitter authentication integrated with the customer website allows customers to view the order status on their phone and receive push notifications via the notifications hub when the order status changes and new products are created. The sales system has its own dedicated SQL Azure Database and communicates with the other systems via a Service Bus topic. A worker role is implemented to keep the sales system updated as orders are processed through the enterprise system.

The production business unit is responsible for manufacturing the products for the customer orders and has a worker role at the core of it, which consumes customer orders from the Service Bus topic, enters the orders into the production SQL Azure Database, creates batch schedules to bake products, and allocates stock in the system. Production staff uses an on-premises WPF client application with Azure Active Directory authentication to view batch schedules and manage stock via a Web API 2 service with SignalR hub and Azure Service Bus backplane, allowing client applications to update in real time.

The supply business unit is responsible for picking up and packing orders from the production business unit and delivering them to customers. A worker role consumes orders from the Service Bus topic and stores customer details in a table storage, and automatically creates barcode labels stored in a blob storage. Supply staff interacts with the system via an Enterprise Windows Store app, which is authenticated with Azure Active Directory and has a .NET mobile service backend.

As we're building the system, we learn about the topic we're exploring and apply it to our system with detailed walk-throughs and relevant code samples. There are complete working code samples for the entire system that are broken down chapter-wise.

What this book covers

Chapter 1, *Getting Started with Microsoft Azure*, gives an introduction to cloud computing and Microsoft Azure followed by how to choose a subscription and signing up for a subscription. We finish this chapter by taking a look around the portal, and then start looking at the different services Microsoft Azure has to offer.

Chapter 2, *Designing a System for Microsoft Azure*, covers designing scalable, resilient systems for Microsoft Azure by looking at methodologies for breaking systems into subsystems and selecting appropriate Azure services to build them. This process will be applied to design a small system for an independent station that requires a website and a basic administration system; it is then extended to a full enterprise system, where will we introduce the Azure Bakery case study.

Chapter 3, *Starting to Develop with Microsoft Azure*, gives you the first taste of developing for Microsoft Azure, where you will prepare their development environment with the required tools and sign up for a Visual Studio Online account. We'll create the foundations of the sales customer website and publish it to the cloud, and then set up continuous deployment using the Visual Studio Online Team Foundation build server.

Chapter 4, *Creating and Managing a Windows Azure SQL Server Database*, creates a database for the sales business unit and builds it using Entity Framework Code First Migrations. This chapter will examine different tools for working with the database from a developer and administrator point of view, and look at options for database backup.

Chapter 5, *Building Azure MVC Websites*, builds the sales customer website and administrator website, with Twitter authentication for the customer site and Azure Active Directory authentication for the administrator site. We will learn how to apply custom domain names and SSL certificates to Azure websites and learn how to perform Azure AD group authorization in an MVC website.

Chapter 6, Azure Website Diagnostics and Debugging, follows on from the previous chapter, exploring techniques and tools to help diagnose problems and debug Azure websites. We'll look at enabling diagnostics in websites, working with logfiles, and examining application logging and site diagnostics. Finally, we'll look at the Kudu service and remote debugging Azure websites.

Chapter 7, Azure Service Bus Topic Integration, starts with an overview of the Service Bus topics and creates a topic for handling order messaging between the three business tiers. We'll integrate the sales customer website into the topic with a subscription, allowing the newly-created orders to be sent across the system, where they will be collected by the production system for manufacturing, and the supply system for producing address labels and planning deliveries. We'll also create a messaging simulator to allow the topic to be loaded up with high volumes of orders to help test the scalability and capacity of the system. Finally, we'll look at the features in the portal to help us monitor and manage our Service Bus topic.

Chapter 8, Building Worker Roles, gives an introduction to cloud services and creating a worker role. Then, we'll create and run a basic cloud service locally on the compute emulator, and publish and run it in the cloud. The production order processor is created next, which is responsible for receiving orders from the Service Bus topic, saving them to the production database, creating product batch schedules, and allocating stock. Finally, we'll test the cloud service in a scaled deployment using the simulator created in *Chapter 7, Azure Service Bus Topic Integration*.

Chapter 9, Cloud Service Diagnostics, Debugging, and Configuration, continues on from the previous chapter and covers diagnostics, remote debugging, and IntelliTrace. We'll learn how to deal with configuration changes made in the portal at runtime and implement start-up tasks for performing customizations to prepare the server environment for the service.

Chapter 10, Web API and Client Integration, provides an introduction to the Web API and SignalR with an Azure Service Bus backplane followed by building a Web API service and a SignalR hub, to allow the production management application to interact with the production database and Service Bus topic. The system will be authenticated with Azure AD authentication, allowing production staff to log in to the WPF client application using their Azure AD credentials.

Chapter 11, Integrating a Mobile Application Using Mobile Services, brings the whole system together with the addition of a mobile service and a Windows Phone 8 application for the sales system, which allows users to log in with the same credentials as the customer website, view orders, and receive order updates and product news via the notifications hub. The sales mobile service provides APIs for the admin website and order processor to interact with the notifications hub. Finally, the chapter looks at building an Azure AD authenticated mobile service for the supply Windows Store application to view orders and retrieve address labels from a blob storage created by the supply order processor.

Chapter 12, Preparing an Azure System for Production, is the final chapter, and looks at configuring systems for various environments including production, and creating publishing packages using the Visual Studio Online Team Foundation build server and producing database scripts in order to manage the system deployments in a controlled way by systems administrators or developers. We'll learn how to monitor the different services implemented throughout the book once they are live, and also cover guidelines for publishing web-connected mobile applications.

What you need for this book

You need a good spec machine with Windows 8.1 installed as a starting point. A premium version of Visual Studio 2013 is ideal but not necessary as multiple versions of Visual Studio Express (which are free) can be used instead. You will sign up for a Microsoft Azure subscription at the start of the book if you have not already got one; there are various paid options, but a free 3-month trial is available. To work on Windows Store applications, a Store account is needed, which is covered in *Chapter 11, Integrating a Mobile Application Using Mobile Services*.

Who this book is for

This book is aimed at .NET developers interested in building systems for Microsoft Azure. Good knowledge of Microsoft .NET is essential; knowledge of building websites, Windows applications, and Windows Phone or Windows 8 applications is helpful but not essential.

Conventions

In this book, you will find a number of styles of text that distinguish between different kinds of information. Here are some examples of these styles, and an explanation of their meaning.

Code words in text, database table names, folder names, filenames, file extensions, pathnames, dummy URLs, user input, and Twitter handles are shown as follows: "In the website project, open the `Views/Home/Index.cshtml` file and make some changes to the markup."

A block of code is set as follows:

```
public class AuthHelper
{
    public static async Task<Customer> GetCustomer(ServiceUser
      serviceUser, CustomerMobileServiceContext ctx)
    {
        // Find Twitter Id, of form Twitter:123456789
        var idParts = serviceUser.Id.Split(':');
        var key = idParts[1];
        var provider = idParts[0];
```

When we wish to draw your attention to a particular part of a code block, the relevant lines or items are set in bold:

```
public class AuthHelper
{
    public static async Task<Customer> GetCustomer(ServiceUser
     serviceUser, CustomerMobileServiceContext ctx)
    {
        // Find Twitter Id, of form Twitter:123456789
        var idParts = serviceUser.Id.Split(':');
        var key = idParts[1];
        var provider = idParts[0];
```

Any command-line input or output is written as follows:

```
Install-Package WindowsAzure.MobileServices
```

New terms and **important words** are shown in bold. Words that you see on the screen, in menus or dialog boxes for example, appear in the text like this: "Enter **Project name** and **Description** and select the **Team Foundation Version Control** option (this is the default option), and then click on **Create project**."

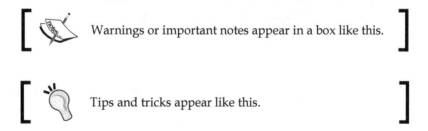

Warnings or important notes appear in a box like this.

Tips and tricks appear like this.

Reader feedback

Feedback from our readers is always welcome. Let us know what you think about this book—what you liked or may have disliked. Reader feedback is important for us to develop titles that you really get the most out of.

To send us general feedback, simply send an e-mail to `feedback@packtpub.com`, and mention the book title via the subject of your message.

If there is a topic that you have expertise in and you are interested in either writing or contributing to a book, see our author guide on `www.packtpub.com/authors`.

Customer support

Now that you are the proud owner of a Packt book, we have a number of things to help you to get the most from your purchase.

Downloading the example code

You can download the example code files for all Packt books you have purchased from your account at `http://www.packtpub.com`. If you purchased this book elsewhere, you can visit `http://www.packtpub.com/support` and register to have the files e-mailed directly to you.

Errata

Although we have taken every care to ensure the accuracy of our content, mistakes do happen. If you find a mistake in one of our books—maybe a mistake in the text or the code—we would be grateful if you would report this to us. By doing so, you can save other readers from frustration and help us improve subsequent versions of this book. If you find any errata, please report them by visiting `http://www.packtpub.com/submit-errata`, selecting your book, clicking on the **errata submission form** link, and entering the details of your errata. Once your errata are verified, your submission will be accepted and the errata will be uploaded on our website, or added to any list of existing errata, under the Errata section of that title. Any existing errata can be viewed by selecting your title from `http://www.packtpub.com/support`.

Piracy

Piracy of copyright material on the Internet is an ongoing problem across all media. At Packt, we take the protection of our copyright and licenses very seriously. If you come across any illegal copies of our works, in any form, on the Internet, please provide us with the location address or website name immediately so that we can pursue a remedy.

Please contact us at copyright@packtpub.com with a link to the suspected pirated material.

We appreciate your help in protecting our authors, and our ability to bring you valuable content.

Questions

You can contact us at questions@packtpub.com if you are having a problem with any aspect of the book, and we will do our best to address it.

1
Getting Started with Microsoft Azure

This chapter introduces Microsoft Azure, the process of implementing it, and the features and services it can offer us. We will cover the following topics:

- A brief overview of cloud computing and Microsoft Azure
- Selecting a Microsoft Azure solution
- Administration of a Microsoft Azure system
- Choosing a subscription
- A walk-through of creating a Microsoft Azure account
- Exploring the Microsoft Azure Management portal
- Examining all the Microsoft Azure service options

An overview of cloud computing

Cloud computing is a term for computing resources and services such as server and network infrastructure, web servers, and databases, hosted by cloud service vendors, rented by tenants, and delivered via the Internet.

Cloud computing companies such as Microsoft and Google offer a variety of computing services built on top of their own infrastructure, which are managed in dedicated globally distributed data centers that offer high availability, resilience, and scalability.

There are three types of cloud service models, **Infrastructure as a Service (IaaS)**, **Platform as a Service (PaaS)**, and **Software as a Service (SaaS)**. IaaS is the lowest service tier that offers server, storage, and networking infrastructure, which users can build their own systems on. PaaS allows users to create and deploy applications without having to worry about the infrastructure that's hosting it using services and tools designed to streamline the development and deployment processes. SaaS offers on-demand software products, which remove the infrastructure and software installation and setup overhead; web mail providers are an example of SaaS, where users can send and receive mails using a website rather than having to install a mail client on their machine.

Cloud services are often a cost-effective alternative to traditional on-premises infrastructure, which requires an initial investment in hardware and licenses and requires continual maintenance and expansion as required as well as utility costs such as premises' rent, electricity, and ISP.

There are four main cloud deployment models: public cloud, private cloud, hybrid cloud, and community cloud. Public cloud services are hosted by a vendor and made available to the public for use. Private cloud services emulate public cloud services in terms of features but are only available within a company's domain. Community cloud is a private cloud shared between a number of users. Hybrid cloud is a mixture of the other three.

Microsoft Azure overview

Microsoft Azure is the collective name for Microsoft's cloud computing services that provide IaaS and PaaS service models. In terms of deployment models, Azure services would be classed as public; however, it's possible to install Azure Pack (`http://www.microsoft.com/en-us/server-cloud/products/windows-azure-pack/`) in a private data center that offers a private cloud model.

Microsoft Azure IaaS comprises of a number of globally distributed data centers that host virtualized servers controlled by the **Azure Fabric Controller**. When we host systems on Azure, we become tenants and pay for our share of processing and network resources that we use through the subscription we choose. In this layer, we can make use of services such as virtual machines, disk storage, and network services.

Microsoft Azure PaaS services are the main entry point for most developers, where we are offered a set of tools and services that allow us to develop and deploy scalable and robust systems such as websites, worker roles, and mobile services.

Microsoft Azure (formerly known as Windows Azure) was first announced in 2008 and was available as **Community Technical Preview (CTP)**; then, it became commercially available from 2010. Since then, the number of services and features has continually grown to where we are now.

At the time of this writing, Windows Azure has been renamed Microsoft Azure as part of a rebranding exercise to move the services away from being tightly associated with Windows server operating systems, databases, and platforms, as Azure can support operating systems such as Linux that run on virtual machines, Oracle databases, Node.js, and PHP websites, to name a few. You may see the term Windows Azure still being used in documentation and resources for quite a long time. It's the same product, just with a different name, so it's likely to be still valid.

Selecting a Microsoft Azure solution

Before we start looking at everything Microsoft Azure can offer us, we need to take a step back and think about the reasons for choosing it in the first place. The first question is actually whether you should be using a cloud platform rather than your own infrastructure (if you have any); the second question, once you've decided to use a cloud platform, is whether to use Microsoft Azure or an alternative.

The main factors in choosing to deploy systems on a cloud platform are as follows:

- **Infrastructure capabilities**: If your business doesn't currently own infrastructure for hosting your solution, or it doesn't have sufficient capacity, or the business simply doesn't want to invest in its own infrastructure, then a cloud-based solution might be the best

- **Cost**: If a cloud-based solution is more cost-effective than a self-hosted solution irrespective of whether your business owns its own infrastructure or not, it may be a good option

The main reasons for choosing to deploy systems on Microsoft Azure in particular are as follows:

- **Platform capabilities**: If you've decided to build a cloud-based system using .NET, then Microsoft Azure is the obvious choice. If you are building a system on a different platform and Microsoft Azure can support it, it might be a good option.

- **Cost**: If Microsoft Azure can offer the right capabilities and is more cost-effective than other suitable competing platforms, then it's the best choice.

Choosing to host systems on the cloud is not a straightforward decision. You may find that you have to go through the decision-making process on a project-by-project basis rather than having a policy where you always do the same thing for all systems.

Infrastructure capabilities

There is an overhead in managing infrastructure of any scale. The following are the activities that must be performed frequently:

- Patch management
- Operating system migrations
- Platform migrations
- Provision for expansion
- Maintaining utilities (power, Internet, cooling, and so on)

The different scenarios for managing the infrastructure of a business are as follows:

- If your business runs internal systems on just a single server, this may not be a full-time job for someone, but it still needs to be done and may be time-consuming periodically
- If your business is on the other end of the spectrum and has two data centers that host hundreds of servers, you will need a team of people to manage them, which will obviously be very costly
- If your business doesn't want to invest in its own infrastructure, irrespective of whether it needs enough servers to justify building a data centre, or just a single server with a website and database, it might be your best option to host your systems on a cloud platform
- If your business' current infrastructure doesn't have the capacity for your system or it can't meet the required **Service Level Agreement (SLA)**
- If your business has a heavy investment in its own infrastructure and can support future expansion on a variety of platforms, you may be less likely to want to use a cloud platform, but even then, there may be a service your infrastructure can't provide, or a platform it simply can't support, so it may be cheaper and faster to implement it in the cloud

Platform capabilities

If your business builds systems using Microsoft technologies, then Azure would be the logical choice, because although it now supports a number of platforms, Windows Servers, SQL Server Databases, and .NET platform tooling have been established long ago and have a fantastic toolset.

If, for example, your company does own its own infrastructure, but it's designed for running Java websites on Linux operating systems, and you have a requirement to build and host some .NET systems, you may want to choose to build your system on Microsoft Azure instead of provisioning more servers.

If Microsoft technologies are not your normal choice and you want to build a system on a cloud platform, you may choose Azure if it is more cost-effective than a competitor cloud service provider for a comparable design and SLA.

Cost

Cost can be one of the main drivers behind most decisions in a business; it has come up in both decision-making steps for choosing to use a cloud solution, then Microsoft Azure, so it's clearly important. I'd love to get straight down to talking about coding and deciding which bits of Microsoft Azure to use for what; we still have a responsibility to make the best decisions for our business and that includes designing a cost-effective system.

If you're working on a personal project, you may want to pick up a technology for reasons such as it being new or looking interesting; everyone does this and we might not mind if it costs us a few pounds (dollars or whatever), but in a business, we need to make the right choice ourselves or convince other people of the right choice, especially in the case of larger organizations, and that means choosing a solution that is cost effective.

We can use the pricing calculator to help us work out how much a system will cost once we have designed it; it is available at `http://www.windowsazure.com/en-us/pricing/calculator/`.

Decision flow diagrams

I've tried to distil all this into two flow diagrams to help you with the decision-making process. You can use the following flow diagram to decide whether to implement a cloud-based system:

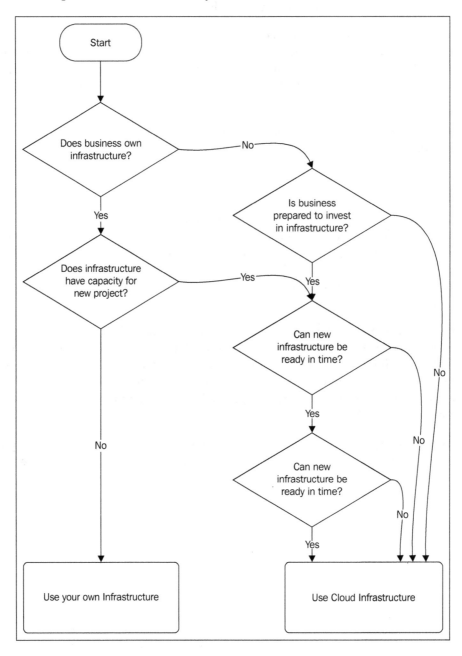

Once we've decided that building a cloud-based system is the right thing to do, we can use the following flow diagram to help us decide whether Microsoft Azure is the best platform:

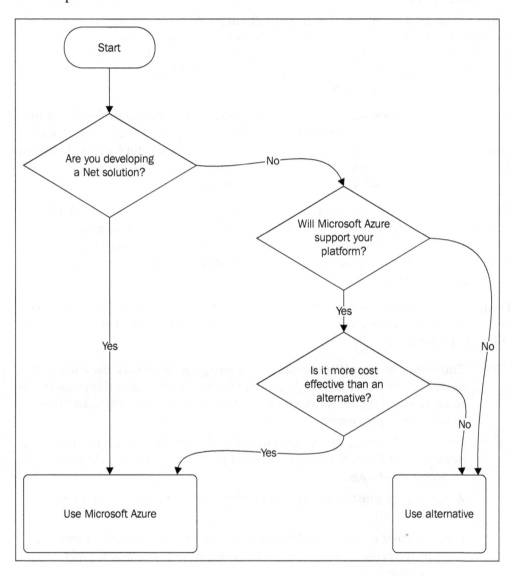

Administration of Microsoft Azure systems

We've talked a lot about whether to use a cloud platform or not, and if your business decides to, whether it will be Microsoft Azure or whether to use your business' infrastructure; so now, we'll look at the administration overhead in looking after a cloud-based system and incorporating it into your business' maintenance and support procedures.

If you have a small organization or you are working on personal projects, you may choose to manage your environments yourself (you may not have a choice) and you may deploy applications to the cloud straight from your development machine. This is fine, but it's worth thinking about managing this process to make things easy for you and save yourself from accidently causing loss of service.

If you work in a larger organization with some governance in place, which dictates how systems should transition from a development environment to a live system and then how they are managed and maintained after that, you may need to put some new procedures in place or modify the existing procedures for handling cloud-based systems.

Using a cloud platform, we don't completely get away from systems management and maintenance overhead. The following are examples of administrative tasks we still need to consider:

- **Training**: The people responsible for managing cloud systems will need to know how to manage and maintain them. This includes things such as understanding the different environments, using the portal, and how to perform deployments.

- **Error logs**: Error logs need to be monitored so that problems can be detected and fixed. Error logs will need pruning to avoid paying for unnecessary storage.

- **Alerts**: Alerts must be set up and configured for the appropriate set of support staff.

- **Database maintenance**: Databases need to be reindexed and statistics must be recalculated from time to time so that performance doesn't degrade over time.

- **Data backup**: Microsoft Azure does not automatically back up data, so this needs to be set up.

- **OS updates**: It's actually possible to disable automatic updates on Azure OSes (this is not the default option), so if your IT policy is to have staged updates, you may wish to disable automatic updates and include Microsoft Azure systems in your update process.

- **Billing**: Somebody needs to remember to pay the bill for the services the businesses are using. This is especially important if you pay your subscription by invoice and not credit card.

- **Password management**: Usernames and passwords for Microsoft Azure portals and databases must be securely recorded and made available to the administrative staff.

- **Release management**: Typically, in medium-to-large organizations, it's not normal for developers to deploy systems for staging or for live environments themselves, so this must be coordinated between developers and system administrators.

- **Renew SSL certificates and domain names**: If we use custom domain names on our websites or implement SSL security, we will need to renew these periodically.

It's important to think about these things when deciding to implement a cloud-based system, because although there is certainly a huge reduction in administration overhead, particularly on the infrastructure side of things, they aren't completely administration-free.

Choosing a subscription

The subscription you choose will depend on the type of project you are doing and its scale. If you are doing some experimentation or prototyping a system, which may never go into production, you may just want to use a free trial, which is time- and usage-limited, or go for a **Pay-as-you-go** option, where you pay for what you use rather than committing to a fixed payment. If you're a university student, your university may apply for a 5-month Educator Grant at http://www.microsoftazurepass.com/azureu.

To get started, you may need to do some design work to get some idea of the services you may require, what service tier you want, and how many instances of each service you may use, then go to the pricing calculator and start working out how much your monthly expenditure might be. There is a complete chapter dedicated to designing a system, and this whole book will help you choose which services you require, but we need a subscription to get started, so we'll talk about it now.

Once we have an idea about what our monthly expenditure might be, we can take a look at the purchase options page at `http://www.windowsazure.com/en-us/pricing/purchase-options/`.

The following table taken from the purchase options page shows us the discounts based on the base **Pay-as-you-go** rate and monthly commitment to spend in USD (there is a picker on the left-hand side of the page to change the currency):

Monthly Committed Spend	6-Month Monthly Pay	12-Month Monthly Pay	6-Month Pre-Pay	12-Month Pre-Pay
$500 TO £14,999	20%	22.5%	22.5%	25%
$15,000 TO £39,999	23%	25.5%	25.5%	28%
$40,000 AND ABOVE	27%	29.5%	29.5%	30%

As with most commodities, the more you commit to spend, the better discount you get, and you save even more committing to pay for the whole term in one go.

You can pay by invoice as well as by credit card; the page at `http://www.windowsazure.com/en-us/pricing/invoicing/` has details about requesting invoiced payments.

Creating a Microsoft Azure account

Before we go into all the different things Microsoft Azure has to offer us, we'll create an account so that we can use the portal to help us explore the services.

 There is a new portal (`https://portal.azure.com/`), which was introduced earlier in 2014 during the Build conference. Unfortunately, at the time of writing this book, it was not complete enough for the majority of the services we're covering, so this book uses the old portal (`https://manage.windowsazure.com/`), which will continue to be available for some time to come.

If you already have a Microsoft Azure account, continue to the next section; otherwise, click on the **Portal** tab (`https://manage.windowsazure.com/`). It will take you to log in using your Microsoft account if you are not already logged in. Once you have logged in, you will see a big page saying you have no subscription:

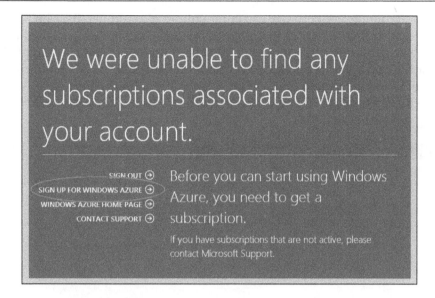

Click on the **SIGN UP FOR WINDOWS AZURE** link (`https://account.`
`windowsazure.com/SignUp`), and you should end up at the **Sign up** page (there are
a number of routes to get to this page through the website, but this seemed to be the
least clicks for me!). Your personal details should appear from your account info,
and you'll need to verify it's you with an SMS or call verification:

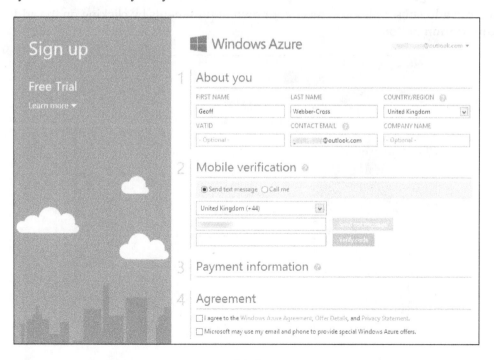

Once your account is verified, you can enter your credit card details. Don't panic if you want a free trial or pay as you go; you don't get automatically signed up for any premium subscriptions; however, $1 will be charged to you for credit card verification. Accept the agreement and click on the **Purchase** button; your card details will be validated, and you will be taken to the **subscriptions** page, where you'll be pleased to find that you already have a free trial! This is shown in the following screenshot:

Adding a subscription

You can add subscriptions to meet your own requirements by clicking on the **add subscription** button:

I chose the **Pay-As-You-Go** option for writing this book as I will not be leaving the system I'm building in production. Once you have selected your option, you get a purchase confirmation on your screen, as shown in the following screenshot:

Once the payment information is confirmed, we're taken back to the **subscriptions** page, where we can see our new subscription being listed:

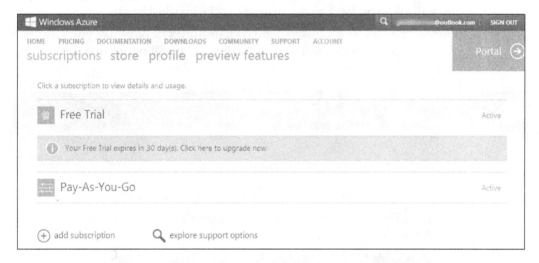

If you have chosen to use a trial subscription, there is a spending limit feature so that you don't incur any costs; once you reach the offer limits, services will be disabled and data will be available as read-only.

Exploring the portal

Now that we have a subscription, we can go and start exploring the portal at `https://manage.windowsazure.com/`. When you go into the portal for the first time, you'll be presented with a nice tour wizard, which is a really good way of learning about the portal's features; step through the wizard, and then we'll look at these features and more without the wizard.

The top toolbar

The top toolbar allows us to access some of the top-level options for the portal; there are six buttons:

The various options available in the top toolbar are as follows:

- **Home button (1)**: Wherever you are in the portal, clicking on the home button will take you back to the main **ALL ITEMS** dashboard.

- **Top menu (2)**: This drop-down menu contains links, which take you out of the portal to Microsoft Azure's web resources; you'll notice that the same menu appears on all Microsoft Azure websites:

The menu available inside the top menu is as follows:

- ○ **HOME**: This links to the main Microsoft Azure site.

- ○ **PRICING**: This links to the price calculator for all Microsoft Azure services.

- ○ **DOCUMENTATION**: This links to the Microsoft Azure documentation home page; from here, you can find a large amount of reference material, code samples, and tutorials.

- ○ **DOWNLOADS**: This links to the downloads page, where you can find links to SDKs for all platforms and command-line tools.

- ° **COMMUNITY**: This links to the community page from where we can find links to recent Microsoft Azure team blogs, links to other Azure blogs, and useful information to help us be up-to-date with what's going on with Microsoft Azure services. This is helpful because the platform is continually growing and changing, so it's good to be able to see what's going on.

- ° **SUPPORT**: This links to the support page, which lists various support options for technical and billing issues, and contains links to MSDN forums.

- **Credit status flyout (3)**: If you have a subscription with a credit allowance, this displays the remaining credit for the month and number of days until the end of the month:

- **Subscriptions menu (4)**: This menu allows you to adjust which subscriptions and their associated services are displayed in the portal; if you have a lot of subscriptions, you can even search for them! At the bottom of the page, there are also some useful links for managing your account:

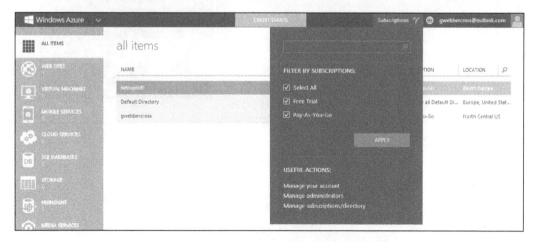

- **Language menu (5)**: The language menu allows you to change the portal's display language to a number of supported languages:

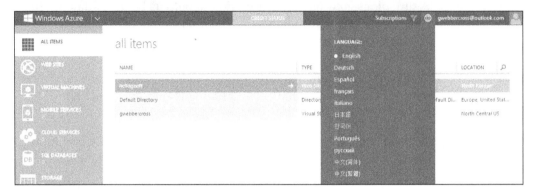

- **Main menu (6)**: Clicking on your username at the top-right corner of the screen opens the main menu, which allows you to sign out, change password, view your bill, contact support, and access some other legal bits:

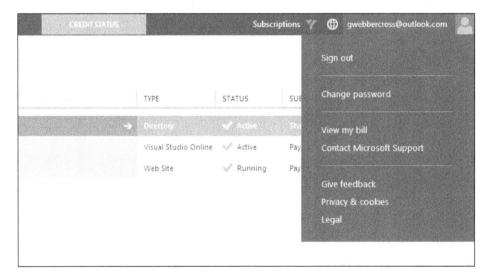

The side toolbar

The toolbar at the left-hand side allows you to view all items and navigate to service workspaces such as **WEB SITES, VIRTUAL MACHINES,** and **MOBILE SERVICES**:

The bottom toolbar

The bottom toolbar allows you to create new services, control the current service selected in a workspace, and view notifications:

The various options available in the bottom toolbar are as follows:

- **Create new (1)**: Clicking on the **+ NEW** button on the bottom toolbar opens the **Create New** menu from where you can create new services:

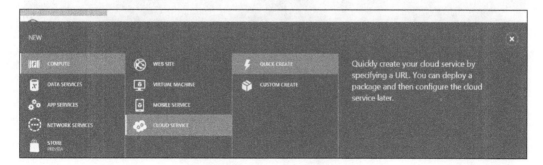

- **Commands (2)**: The command bar provides contextual commands for controlling the currently selected service; in the preceding example screenshot, the controls are used for running a website, allowing you to browse, stop, restart, and delete it, and also allowing you to install WebMatrix, which is a lightweight web development tool.

- **Notifications (3)**: The notifications bar will appear at the bottom of the portal to alert you of any issues you may need to address; they have three levels:

    ◦ Error

    ◦ Warning

    ◦ Information

    Clicking on an alert symbol opens the alert banner showing more information:

- **Completed operations (4)**: A number of activities in the portal can take a while to complete and run asynchronously; once they complete, the completed operations' count indicator gets incremented, and clicking on this button shows you the completed operations' banners:

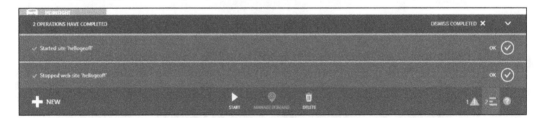

Individual operations can be dismissed by clicking on **OK**, or all of them can be dismissed by clicking on **DISMISS COMPLETED** at the top of the page.

- **Help (5)**: Clicking on the help button displays a contextual help menu that provides help information about the current service:

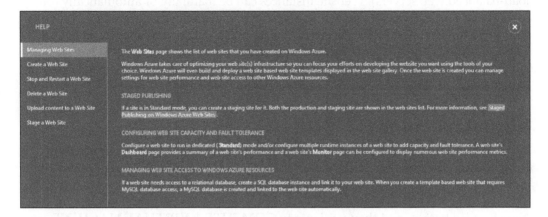

Examining Microsoft Azure Services

We'll start taking a look at all the Microsoft Azure services available to us; while we do this, it's helpful to refer to the portal, and use the **+NEW** button to see the different options for each category. Don't be afraid to create a service to take a closer look; you can always delete it afterwards.

Compute services

Compute services are a collection of services used for building different types of scalable, resilient applications on Microsoft Azure. We'll take a look at these now and see what they can offer us.

Websites

Microsoft Azure websites are a secure, scalable platform for publishing websites on a number of platforms (ASP.NET, PHP, Node.js, Python, and Classic ASP) with SQL Server and MySQL databases; there is also a large gallery of website templates for building websites on app frameworks such as Django, blog sites such as WordPress, and forums such as phpBB; to see the full list, click on the **New Service** button, and then navigate to **COMPUTE | WEB SITE | FROM GALLERY**.

Websites support SSL certificates for secure HTTPS sessions and custom domain names with **A** and **CNAME** records (for supporting a single domain name for a number of load-balanced web servers). Website instances can be manually or automatically (on schedule or on CPU metrics) scaled up and down to meet business demands. Websites can run in three modes, **FREE**, **SHARED**, or **STANDARD**, where **FREE** and **SHARED** run on a multitenant environment (a shared web server), but the **SHARED** mode has a higher resource quota than **FREE**. **STANDARD** runs on a dedicated virtual machine (small, medium, large size options similar to virtual machines).

Virtual machines

Virtual machines offer you a scalable server infrastructure to build your systems from scratch. They are available as Windows Server or Linux operating systems, and there are a number of images available with server software such as SharePoint, SQL Server, and Oracle preinstalled. To take a look at the complete list, click on the **New Service** button, and then navigate to **COMPUTE | VIRTUAL MACHINE | FROM GALLERY**.

There are currently eight image sizes ranging from extra small (shared core, 768 MB RAM) to A7 (eight cores, 56 GB RAM) and default (one core, 1.75 GB RAM); obviously, the bigger the image, the higher the cost. You can see the prices in the pricing calculator at `http://www.windowsazure.com/en-us/pricing/calculator/?scenario=virtual-machines`. Virtual machines are charged at compute hours and have a monthly value in the calculator; Windows Server and Linux images cost the same, but the price increases with additional server software due to the extra licensing cost.

Mobile services

Mobile services are designed for mobile app developers so that they have a simple platform to quickly create secure (OAuth2 and key-based authentication over SSL) database and custom APIs and easily make push notification requests on all major mobile platforms (Windows Store, Windows Phone, iOS, and Android). Backend services can be created on Node.js or .NET; Node.js, which is the original platform, can be scripted in the portal directly or locally, and can be pushed using Git version control, whereas .NET backends, which are a relatively new addition, are created locally and published in a similar way to other web applications.

There's a complete set of SDKs for integrating mobile applications and other backend services for a growing number of platforms including Windows Store, Windows Phone, iOS, Android, Xamarin, HTML, and Sencha.

I recently wrote an entire book on this subject, which is available from Packt Publishing at `http://www.packtpub.com/learning-windows-azure-mobile-services-for-windows-8-and-windows-phone-8/book`.

Cloud services

Cloud services allow you to create scalable applications that have a high availability (99.95 percent monthly SLA). There are two main types of cloud services: web role and worker role. Web roles are web applications hosted on IIS in their own environment. They are different from normal websites as they have extra capabilities listed in the following bullet list (although websites can now be staged too), to start with web roles can start life as a website, then easily be added to a web role at a later stage if they require these additional capabilities. Worker roles are a bit like Windows Services, where they are applications with no user interface, which can perform long-running tasks from things such as processing data of a table to hosting a proprietary TCP server. Cloud service roles have the following characteristics:

- They run on their own virtual machine
- They can be scaled as required
- They can be deployed to multideployment environments (staging and live)
- They allow remote desktop onto their virtual machines
- They execute start-up tasks

Data services

Data services are a collection of data-storage-related services including fully relational SQL Server Database, table storage, various **Binary Large Objects (blobs)** and disk-storage options, and storage queues. We'll take a look at each one in more detail now.

SQL Server Database

Microsoft Azure SQL Database is a fully managed, highly scalable relational database with a high availability (99.95 percent SLA). Microsoft Azure SQL Server is very similar to a SQL Server in terms of **Transact-SQL (TSQL)** and **Tabular Data Stream (TDS)** but has a number of features it does not support, such as:

- Backup and restore (this will be supported when the new service tiers are made available)
- Replication
- Extended stored procedures
- SQL Server agent/jobs

A full list of differences can be found here, although it doesn't currently mention SQL Server 2012 or 2014: `http://msdn.microsoft.com/en-us/library/ff394115.aspx`.

Databases are available in three tiers of service:

- **Web**: This is a scalable managed database up to 10 MB
- **Business editions**: These are scalable managed databases up to 150 GB
- **Premium edition**: This is the same as premium editions but with reserved resource capacity for applications that may have a high peak loading, many concurrent requests, or require guaranteed low request latency

Databases benefit from having two data center replicas (for any tier of service) and the option to scale out as required (splitting large databases across multiple servers to improve performance).

Storages

Microsoft Azure storage offers resilient, scalable storage for unstructured text and binary data such as logfiles, images, and videos. There are four types of storages:

- **Block blobs**: This is the simplest way of storing large volumes of nonstructured data. Blobs can be accessed through managed SDKs and from anywhere via REST APIs. Block blobs are made up of a maximum of 50,000 blocks, having a size of up to 4 MB each, with a maximum total size of 200 GB.

- **Page blobs and disks**: Page blobs are optimized for frequent updates and random access and are actually used as the storage media for Microsoft Azure VHD disks. Page blobs are collections of 512 byte pages; pages worth 1 to 4 MB can be written in one go and a maximum of 1 TB is available for a single blob.

- **Tables**: Tables are a NoSQL (a nonrelational database) way of storing data, rather than storing data in a relational way, like in a traditional SQL Server Database, where we have tables, which have relationships with other tables via primary and foreign keys; Microsoft Azure tables allow you to create a container table, and then define classes that belong to it. These classes have a partition key, row key, and timestamp property, which allow them to be queried. Microsoft Azure tables allow us to store large amounts of data in a highly scalable way while still allowing efficient querying.

- **Queues**: Queues are a messaging system that allows processes to exchange data between tiers of a system via a message queue. They are helpful for building scalable worker processes. Queues can be accessed via native SDKs and REST services.

HDInsight

HDInsight is a relatively new addition to the Microsoft Azure service family; it is a service based on Apache Hadoop (`http://hadoop.apache.org/`), which helps us integrate multiple data sources of different types and structures into Microsoft **Business Intelligence (BI)** tools such as Power Pivot and Power View.

Cache

Microsoft Azure Cache is a high-performance, in-memory distributed cache that allows scaled-out applications to share data without having to use a database. This can be useful for adding session state and page caching to ASP.NET applications (although session state is not generally a good practice for modern web applications, it may be useful for legacy applications or if you really can't live without it!) and also doing your own custom caching in worker roles for maintaining the state across instances. Cache is available in three tiers:

- **Basic**: This is a shared cache with a size ranging from 128 MB to 1 GB

- **Standard**: This is a dedicated cache with a size ranging from 1 GB to 10 GB

- **Premium**: This is a dedicated cache with a size ranging from 5 GB to 150 GB

Recovery services

The recovery services allow you to create Hyper-V recovery manager vaults, which allow you to back up your Hyper-V system to the Microsoft Azure cloud and backup vaults, which can be used for backing up files and folders from servers.

App services

App services are a collection of services that help cloud and on-premises applications and services to interact with each other. They can be implemented on systems ranging from media-streaming services to multi-tier enterprise business systems. We'll look at each of these now.

Media services

Media services provide a scalable media processing workflow for digital media systems such as video-streaming services, from ingest through encoding, format conversion, and content protection, to on-demand and live streaming.

Service Bus

Service Bus is a collection of services used for enabling communication between different processes in distributed, multi-tier systems. The various Service Buses are as follows:

- **Queue**: Service Bus queues as with .NET queues are first in, first out (FIFO) collections of messages that allow applications to communicate with each other asynchronously by publishing and consuming messages. This can be very helpful for building scalable systems across multiple tiers especially when part of the system may not always be online. It can also help with load leveling, where a consuming application can process batches of data in a controlled way rather than being driven by the producing application. Messages are processed by a single consumer and can be read in the **ReceiveAndDelete** mode, where the message will immediately be marked as consumed and returned to the provider and the **PeekLock** mode, where a consumer can get a temporary lock while it processes the request; then, if it cannot process the message, it can abandon it, or if it fails completely, the message will time out, allowing another process to consume it.

- **Topic**: In contrast to queues, where we have a one-to-one relationship between a provider and a consumer, topics have a one-to-many relationship, where we create a topic with a number of subscriptions. Then, a provider can send messages to the topic, and subscribing clients can receive messages from subscriptions they are interested in.

- **Relay**: Relays are different from topics and queues in that they don't offer disconnected services; instead, they can securely expose on-premises service endpoints, allowing them to be accessed directly by applications in the cloud.

- **Notification Hub**: The Notification Hub service is a really nice way of handling push notifications to mobile apps from backend services in an efficient, scalable manner. Mobile apps on all major platforms can register to receive push notifications (in the case of Windows Store and Windows Phone applications, these are **Toast**, **Tile**, **Badge**, and **Raw** notifications), and from the backend service, just one request per platform is required to make the request rather than making requests per subscribed channel. The Notifications Hub also has a tagging feature, where users can subscribe to certain tagged topics and also template notifications, which can be used for localization support. The Notifications Hub handles all communications with the native **Push Notification Services (PNS)**.

Visual Studio Online

Visual Studio Online services allow Visual Studio Online accounts to be integrated into Microsoft Azure, enabling us to view, build, and load the testing status in the dashboard and enable continuous deployment so that websites can be deployed to a test environment on build when code is checked in.

BizTalk Services

BizTalk Services allow on-premises applications to interact with each other via the cloud, providing messaging endpoints and transforming messages between services for interoperability.

Scheduler

The scheduler allows scheduled jobs to be created to perform operations such as making HTTP requests and performing actions on storage queues. Jobs can be scheduled to run once on demand, at a specific time, or at various intervals.

Active Directory (AD)

The following are the features of Azure AD:

- Azure AD allows you to manage user credentials and application access in your Microsoft Azure system. It is an Azure-specific, REST-based implementation of Active Directory, which is used with on-premises systems.

- **Access Control Service (ACS)** provide an easy way of authorizing and authenticating users with support for the following authentication mechanisms:
    ○ **Windows Identity Foundation (WIF)**
    ○ Built-in support for Microsoft Account, Google, Yahoo, Facebook, and Twitter
    ○ **Active Directory Federated Services (ADFS)**
    ○ OAuth 2.0
    ○ **JSON Web Token (JWT)**, SAML 1.1, SAML 2.0, and **Simple Web Token (SWT)**

  ACS also offers Home Realm Discovery, allowing users to choose an identity provider, an OData-based management service, and a browser-based management portal.

- Multifactor authentication is an extra layer of security for applications. If you have a Windows Store account, you must have noticed that a PIN is sent to a configured mobile phone or e-mail address, which you must enter before signing in with your Microsoft account. This can be added to on-premises applications using ADFS, and to systems integrated with Windows Azure AD.

Network services

Network services are a collection of services related to networking between services, and allow us to create virtual networks and load balance traffic across services in different Azure locations.

Virtual Network

Virtual Network allows you to create a private IPv4 network space in Azure, securely extend your on-premises networks into Azure, and configure a custom DNS server for services on Virtual Network.

Traffic Manager

Traffic Manager allows user traffic to be distributed to the most appropriate cloud service or website within the same data center or across global data centers depending on the load-balancing method chosen. Traffic management requires one of the following three load-balancing methods:

- **Performance**: This allows users to be redirected to the closest geographic endpoints
- **Round-Robin**: This evenly distributes traffic between services
- **Failover**: If a service fails or goes offline, requests will be rerouted to another service

Summary

We've covered a lot of preliminary subject matter regarding the decision process that will help us choose to build a system using Microsoft Azure, and also explored all the services available to us.

Next, we're going to look at how to go about architecting a system for Microsoft Azure and introduce a case study on which the examples in this book are based. We'll use the knowledge we've gained about the different Microsoft Azure services available to us to help design the system in the case study and choose the right service for each part of the system.

Throughout this book, we'll examine services in detail as we build the system in the case study.

Questions

1. What are the three types of cloud service models?
2. What does PaaS stand for?
3. What is Azure Pack?
4. In which two ways can we pay for Azure subscriptions?
5. What are the three notification types that can appear on the portal toolbar?
6. Name the three website modes.
7. Which two operating systems are available on virtual machines?

8. Name four platforms supported by Azure Mobile Services.

9. What are the two types of cloud services?

10. How many deployment environments does a cloud service have?

11. What is a Notifications Hub?

12. What are the three Traffic Manager load balancing methods?

Answers

1. IaaS, PaaS, and SaaS.

2. Platform as a Service.

3. It allows Azure to be installed in a private data center offering a private cloud deployment model.

4. Credit card or invoice.

5. Error, Warning, and Info.

6. Free, Shared, and Standard.

7. Windows Server or Linux.

8. Any of these: Windows Store, Windows Phone, iOS, Android, HTML, Xamarin, and Sencha.

9. Web role and worker role.

10. Two—staging and production.

11. It is a Service Bus service, which provides a scalable way of handling push notifications from backend services.

12. Failover, Round Robin, and Performance.

2
Designing a System for Microsoft Azure

There are challenges in designing any software system, whether it is a small system with a single website and database backend or a large distributed multi-tier system with multiple applications and storage solutions that span multiple business domains and geographic locations. We face some of the same issues and challenges while designing a system for Microsoft Azure as we would face on an on-premises system, such as how to divide our system into different applications, services, and databases, and we may have some new or different challenges such as making the system scalable (larger organizations often support scalability to some degree with multiple web servers and load balancing, but Microsoft Azure offers advanced scaling options such as scheduled and metric-based scaling) and tackling authentication on a cloud system.

All real-life systems are rarely implemented using the same technology and are likely to incorporate new and legacy subsystems across a number of different platforms, subsystems, and business domains. They are likely to be owned by different business units and may even operate under different IT departments. This is why I wanted a case study with a number of subsystems that belong to different business units. Although we're doing everything in .NET using the latest technologies (because it would take too long to use legacy technologies and different software platforms) we'll design the system to have a flexible, service-oriented architecture allowing it to span multiple business domains and accommodate future developments with minimal disruption to the existing system.

Most of the time, we all use our own experience and judgment to help us design systems, and particularly, on small systems, we don't go through a procedural process. However, I didn't want to just introduce a case study pre-architected without at least explaining the process to come up with a design. This book is not about how to architect a system; that's a topic in its own right; however, it's an important part of systems especially when it comes to working out how to choose the right Microsoft Azure Services.

In this chapter, we'll examine the processes involved to take a system of any size, break it down into subsystems, and select the right Microsoft Azure Services to build it. We'll also cover the environments we may need to support a system during its life cycle.

Designing scalable and resilient systems

One of the main features of the Microsoft Azure technology is scalability. By carefully designing our system, we can build it to manually or automatically scale (elastic scaling) to meet our business requirements as the business grows, or to cope with peaks in system load. Databases and storages can also be designed to be distributed across databases and storage partitions, allowing large volumes of data to scale while maintaining performance.

Scale out means increasing computing capacity by increasing the number of compute instances in a system (for websites and cloud services, this would mean increasing the number of virtual machines). Scale up means increasing the computational resources of a compute instance (for websites and cloud services, this would mean more CPU/memory/disk allocation for a virtual machine instance).

By breaking down large systems into smaller, decoupled subsystems, which interact with each other in an asynchronous fault-tolerant manner, we can make the system, as a whole, more resilient. The following are examples of services we can use to achieve this:

- **Websites**: When we build websites, if we're careful in making them stateless, we can create a website that can be scaled out across multiple shared or dedicated web servers as the demand changes. This increases the number of requests that can be processed and increases the processing capacity. If it's absolutely necessary to use a session state or caching, we can implement an Azure Cache to host the session state in a scalable, resilient manner, without depending on a single web server instance (this is known as persistence, and you may hear the term **sticky session**).

- **Cloud services**: Worker roles can be used to perform long running processing tasks on dedicated VMs, which can be scaled up and down to meet processing requirements. Worker roles can be designed to scale by being careful about how they receive work, so there is no contention between instances, and work is not duplicated; we can use storage queues, Service Bus queues, and Service Bus topics for this.

- **Mobile services**: Mobile services provide a number of great features for integrating mobile applications on all major mobile platforms. Table and custom APIs, a flexible authentication model, and the Notification Hub allow us to easily build new standalone backend services or backend services, which integrate into a larger enterprise system. Mobile services scale in the same way as websites, so the same design principles apply. The Notification Hub allows push notifications to be scaled out effectively using the Azure Service Bus, which would be otherwise difficult to achieve if we write our own push notifications services.

- **Decoupling applications**: Storage queues, Service Bus queues, and Service Bus topics help us pass data between scaled-out system tiers in a robust, reliable way. Using these services, we can decouple services and allow systems that may not be online at the same time, or may not be able to keep up with each other to message each other and process messages in their own time. Message-locking mechanisms within these systems allow multiple applications to safely work in parallel without the need to design complicated custom voting and locking systems on shared data sources.

- **SQL databases**: Scaling up databases to maintain performance over large volumes of data in Microsoft Azure SQL databases can be achieved by implementing a federated database, where data is split horizontally (in rows rather than columns) across multiple databases (this is also known as sharding). Implementing a federated database requires careful design to include a federation-distributed key, which allows data to be split across federation members (individual databases with the federation), with new records being distributed evenly and not just added to one member.

- **Table storage**: As with Azure SQL databases, table storage requires a partition key, which must be carefully designed to allow data to be scaled and load balanced across partitions (depending on the chosen redundancy tier).

- **Azure Active Directory**: Using Azure Active Directory, we can provide a consistent, scalable authentication and authorization mechanism for our systems. Large multi-tier systems that span websites, mobile services, and on-premises client applications can all be integrated into an Azure AD tenant, allowing users to use any of these systems with the same credentials and still have granular authorization via roles and groups.

Systems architecture

IT systems can vary dramatically in their scale, the number of business domains they span, the number of platforms they include, and the number of geographical locations they serve. Some parts of the system may need to communicate with each other; some parts are entirely self-sufficient and need no interaction with other systems. When working on a larger system, we are likely to be integrating existing legacy systems into a new system or integrating new systems into a legacy system.

The complexity and size of many systems can reflect the level of automation versus a manual process within a business. Commonly, larger organizations will have the capital to invest in automated systems, which relieve the requirement for a number of manual processes, but will introduce some more specialized administrative overhead.

A large system may look very complicated as a whole, but we can break down any system into smaller subsystems, making it easier to design and helping to create a scalable architecture.

The following illustration shows the steps we'll take in this chapter to architect a system to run on Microsoft Azure:

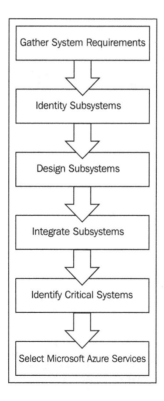

The steps involved in architecting a system to run on Microsoft Azure are as follows:

1. **Gather System Requirements**: Before we do anything, we need to know what the system is supposed to do, who the users are, and what the budget is.

2. **Identify Subsystems**: All systems can be broken down into smaller subsystems, making them easier to design and build, and particularly for Azure systems, making them more scalable.

3. **Design Subsystems**: Once we have identified the subsystems, we need to design them at a high level, thinking about application types, storage requirements, and security.

4. **Integrate Subsystems**: Subsystems need to interact with each other, whether it's through a shared database or messaging across a Service Bus topic. We need to work out the best way to effectively bring the systems together to get them working as an entire system.

5. **Identify Critical Systems**: Before we start selecting services, we need to know which of them are business-critical, so we can choose an appropriate service tier and scale it to meet the required SLA.

6. **Select Microsoft Azure Services**: This step is where we choose services and service tiers to build the system we've designed.

We'll look at a couple of examples of contrasting systems and see how they can be broken down. The first example is a small business system and the second one is a large business multi-tier system, which form the basis of the book's examples.

A case study of a small business system

A small business, for example, an independent stationary shop that consists of a few employees with a shop (bricks and mortar) and an online shop (website) requires a small system, which can allow customers to order stationary online, track orders, manage stock for both shops, and produce monthly reports.

System requirements

If we break down the business requirements, we can understand more about the type of system:

- Customer website
- Administration system
- Manually order stock from suppliers

- Manually arrange delivery
- Low order volume (less than 100 units per day)
- No need for legacy system integration requirement
- No interest in owning IT infrastructure
- Very limited budget for IT

Although it is listed last, the budget requirement will probably be the main factor in designing a system. If service providers have an initial budget of $5,000 to get a system built, and they only want to spend a maximum of $100 a month on running the system, then we're not looking at a multi-tier system with 10 web nodes running on the highest spec server image; we're going to want a small system, which can adequately cope with the volume of orders and cost as little as possible.

Identifying subsystems

From the business requirements, we can see that we need the following IT subsystems:

- **Customer website**: This is needed for allowing customers to order stationary
- **Administration system**: This is needed for managing orders and stock

We can look at each subsystem individually, see how they relate to each other, and start making some choices about which technologies to use.

Customer website design

The website needs to allow customers to provide the following facilities:

- Register and log in
- View products
- Make orders
- View order progress
- View order history

Chapter 2

We know we need a website so that it narrows things down a bit; I'm not going to try and be fancy and call it something like a customer portal, and it's obviously not a sensible idea to think about desktop applications, where customers would have to download an application and install it on their PC.

We need a website with pages to view the stock, make orders, and view the order history and a relational database to store stock, customer details, and order data. An illustration of the desired system is shown in the next diagram:

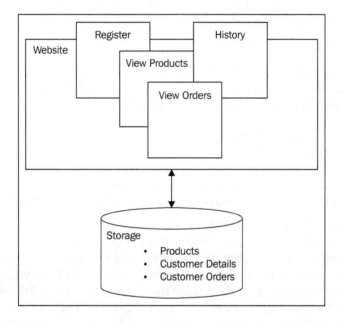

In terms of security, customers should be able to authenticate themselves using existing credentials from a well-known identity provider such as Facebook or Twitter, making it more likely for them to make orders from the website and lowering the user admin overhead in the system.

[43]

Administration system design

The stock and order management system will allow staff to do the following:

- Manage customer orders
- Check stock levels
- Manage product catalogs
- Enter stock into the system when it arrives from suppliers
- Create address labels for orders
- Run financial reports

We have some more choices of the type of platform we use here; we need something that offers us a UI and can easily integrate with the Azure backend services. We could choose the following platforms:

- **Website**: This will provide us with a consistent technology for the customer website, so this would reduce development time and increase code, styling, and markup reusability. It provides us with a simple deployment path that deploys to a single web server rather than distributing executable applications, which will make deploying updates more straightforward.

- **Windows desktop application**: We can use something such as WPF to create a modern UI/UX with good support for Azure integration to interact with the backend services. This will be a different technology to the customer website, so this will require a different developer skill set, which will increase development time and also reduce the amount of reusability on the UI side of the application. Deployment and maintenance will also be more complex as the staff will need to install executable applications on their PCs.

- **Mobile application**: A mobile application may be a good option especially if we build something such as a universal application, where we can target Windows Phone devices, Windows tablets, and PCs, and have an excellent support for Azure integration (we could even use Xamarin, which would give us this in addition to Android and iOS support!). As with the desktop application, we will need another technology skill set, which again will increase development time and reduce code reuse. Mobile applications also either need to be deployed to a store, which is not really appropriate for **line of business (LOB)** systems, or need to implement an enterprise solution, which is probably not viable for small businesses.

From this analysis, the main thing that is apparent is having an application that is consistent with the website, to reduce development and maintenance overheads, so we will choose to create a website, as shown in the following diagram:

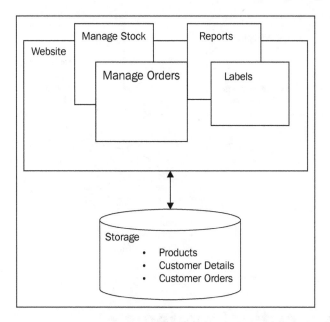

For security, we want users to be centrally managed with the option of having granular control of access to certain areas and functionality within the website.

System integration

From the designs for the two systems, we can see there is a lot of overlap in terms of data storage, and both systems are cloud-hosted websites in the same business domain. This means that it is a sensible choice to share the same storage.

There is no real overlap between the two websites, so there is no strong driver for sharing a website, and for security reasons, it is better to have them separated, as illustrated in the following diagram:

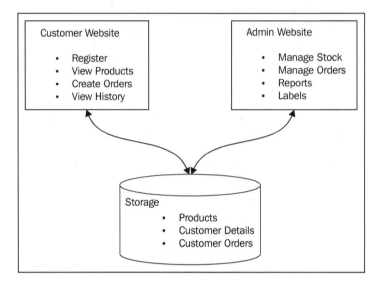

Identifying critical systems

The customer website and storage are probably the most critical subsystems because they support the online customer revenue stream. The admin website is important as it allows the staff to process customer orders; however, if this system fails, customers can still order products while it is fixed.

Selecting services

Now that we have designed the subsystems, worked out how they are integrated, and decided which ones are the most critical, we can start selecting the services we require:

- **Applications**: Both websites are fairly simple and have no special requirements for them to need a web role, so we will use two normal websites. Because we're on a tight budget and we're expecting low traffic through the system, we will go for the lowest service tiers. For the customer's website, we'll choose a pair of shared websites, which will support a custom domain name and high availability with the two instances costing $19.35 per month. For the admin website, we will go for a free website. We can always change the service tiers in future if necessary.

- **Storage**: We have a requirement for a relational data model, so the natural choice is to use an SQL Server over other storage options such as tables, blobs, or disk storage. The database will be shared between both websites. Once we have a more detailed application design, we can try and estimate storage requirements in more detail, but for now, we'll opt for a 1 GB database costing $9.99 per month. For this size of business, it's highly unlikely we'll need a federated database; however, we should still be mindful of this when designing our schema, just in case the database needs scaling out in the future.

- **Messaging**: Because the whole system is small with a low throughput and a shared database, and we don't have any dedicated batch processing applications, there is no need for a messaging system such as storage queues or Service Bus queues.

- **Security**: The customer website will implement OAuth2 security, and the admin website will implement Azure Active Directory authentication.

Conclusion of the small business case study

We've been through a methodical approach for designing this system to be built on Microsoft Azure and have come out with the exact services we require and how much it will cost us monthly. The next step would be to go into the application's design phase. We will not take this particular case study any further in this book as all its subsystems are covered in the following enterprise case study.

A case study of an enterprise system – Azure Bakery

I've tried to come up with a good case study, which will allow us to implement a large number of Microsoft Azure features and services in a realistic way. I wanted to use something that will have long-running processes over distributed systems so that we could incorporate features from websites through Service Bus queues, worker processes, and mobile applications. I came up with an idea of an industrial bakery, which should be a concept that is easy to understand and doesn't need specialist domain knowledge as with many of the systems we work on in our daily jobs!

System requirements

The Azure Bakery makes products such as cakes and pies and deals with large customers such as supermarkets and smaller bakeries that require additional stock (this justifies the supply business unit). To make the bakery more realistic, it's split into three distinct business domains:

- **Sales**: This domain is responsible for selling products to customers
- **Production**: This domain is responsible for manufacturing products
- **Supply**: This domain is responsible for delivering products to customers

An illustration of the three domains is as follows:

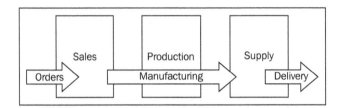

All systems will be self-sufficient and won't rely on data from any other system to function.

Sales requirements

The **Sales** business unit is responsible for the following functions:

- Selling products to customers via a website
- Managing customer orders
- Maintaining product inventory
- Supplying **Production** with product orders automatically
- Keeping customers up-to-date with their orders via a number of channels including a mobile phone application

Customer orders will automatically be sent to production, products will be manually maintained, and customers will be automatically notified of the order's progress.

Production requirements

The **Production** business unit is responsible for the following functions:

- Processing product orders
- Planning batch production
- Maintaining stock levels
- Producing products
- Notifying **Sales** and **Supply** on product status

The system will be automated as far as possible, providing production staff with batch schedules and reports. The system will have the capability to integrate with on-premises systems.

Supply requirements

The **Supply** business unit is responsible for the following:

- Creating and printing tracking barcodes
- Delivering orders to customers
- Notifying **Sales** of the delivery status

Delivery jobs will be sent to a tablet application, which will have the facility to print barcodes and address labels, view customer addresses, and update order status. Jobs must be archived for audit purposes.

Identifying subsystems

Due to the scale of the case study and the requirement to make each business domain autonomous so that it doesn't depend on data from other business domains, we'll examine each system individually.

Sales subsystems

From the business requirements, we can see that we need the following sales subsystems:

- **Sales customer website**: This is required for allowing customers to register, view products, create orders, and view order status
- **Sales administration system**: This is required for the staff to manage orders and product catalog

- **Sales order process system**: This will automatically update the order data and notify customers of the order progress

- **Sales customer phone app**: This is required for allowing customers to view orders and receive notifications on order progress

Production subsystems

The production system can be broken down into the following subsystems:

- **Production order processor**: This will automatically process orders coming from sales, allocate ingredients, create batch schedules, and order ingredients. This system will be fully automated.

- **Production management system**: This is required for the production staff to view batch schedules and update batch progress. This system will also have the capability of interfacing with on-premises systems for displaying plant data.

Supply subsystems

The supply system can be broken down into the following subsystems:

- **Supply processing system**: This will automatically process the delivery requests coming from production, work out how to geographically group orders, allocate them to vehicles and drivers, and create address labels and barcodes for printing. This system will be fully automated.

- **Supply tablet application**: A tablet application is required for the supply staff, allowing them to work easily while performing activities around the warehouse. It will allow them to print address labels and barcodes for deliveries and allocate deliveries to vehicles and drivers.

System design

Now that we've broken down the enterprise system into its subsystems, we've simplified the design process so that we don't have to try and think about how the whole thing works at once. Actually, the two sales websites look nearly identical to the websites of the small business system, with the slight difference that order messages must be sent to the messaging middleware for the production system.

As the websites are very similar and to save time, we'll just look at the system designs for the sales order processing system and the sales customer phone app, and miss out on the production and supply during the design phase, although with a real system, we would apply the process for the entire system.

System design – the sales customer phone app

The phone app needs to allow customers to do the following:

- Register and log in (the same account as the customer website)
- View products
- Make orders
- View order progress
- Receive notifications of new products
- Receive notifications of order progress

The app will interact with data via a secure web service and will receive push notifications for the product updates and order progress, as shown in the following diagram:

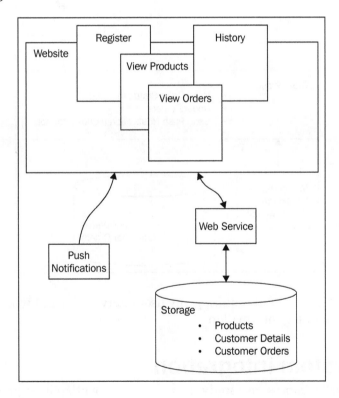

For consistency with the websites, customers should be able to authenticate themselves using existing credentials from a well-known identity provider such as Facebook or Twitter, making it more likely for them to make orders from the website and lowering the user admin overhead in the system.

System design – sales order processor

The order processor system will automatically perform the following tasks:

- Receive order status messages from middleware
- Update order status in the sales system
- Send push notifications to customers for order status change

The working of the order-processing system is shown in the following diagram:

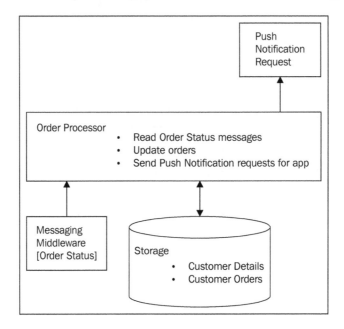

The process will run without requiring any user intervention, but will provide diagnostic and error log information.

Sales system integration

As with the small business case study, there is a lot of overlap in terms of storage, and because we are building a small system with a low order throughput, we can bring our costs down without impacting the performance, by sharing the same storage mechanism.

There is no real overlap between the two websites, so there is no strong driver for sharing a website; for security reasons, it is better to have them separated.

Identifying critical services

There are a number of critical services, which have a direct impact on a company's revenue and need special consideration when selecting service tiers and scalability; these critical services are as follows:

- **Sales customer website**: This is the most critical system; if customers cannot make an order, the business loses revenue, and customers may take their business elsewhere.

- **Production order processor**: This is the point at which orders come into the production system, so it is very important; if it fails or cannot meet the load demands, orders will not automatically come through to the production management app.

- **Production management Web API**: This API allows the production management application to access production data. Production staff need this to see product batch schedules and ingredient stock levels, so they know what to bake, and when and what ingredients need replacing.

- **Production database**: The criticality of the database matches with the processing system and management app API as it links the two together.

- **Supply process**: As with the production order processor, this is the source of work for the supply business domain, so this is very important.

- **Supply mobile API**: This API allows the supply tablet app to access data for order delivery, so this is important for completing the order process.

- **Supply deliveries table**: As with the production database, the criticality of the table matches with the processing system and management app API as it links the two together.

The other systems are still important but a failure or performance degradation will not have a disastrous impact on the whole system. They are as follows:

- Sales admin website
- Sales database
- Sales mobile API
- Sales order processor

These systems can be deployed on more economical service tiers without impacting the performance or availability of the whole system.

Selecting Microsoft Azure Services

Now that we've identified all the services with the system and their criticality, we can start selecting the Microsoft Azure Services and service tiers.

Selecting common services

Because all the domain systems need to integrate together to form the full enterprise system, we need to choose services for the middleware messaging layer, which allow the systems to communicate with each other in a disconnected loosely-coupled way. We also need to look at authentication mechanisms so that we can centralize the user account and access control.

Messaging services

We have a requirement for processes that span the whole system to be able to consume order status messages, so we will use a Service Bus topic, which allows multiple consumers to subscribe to filtered messages. If we want a queue, we will need to decide whether to use a Service Bus queue or storage queue, so this simplifies the decision-making process at this point, but we'll talk about this more later in the book.

Authentication

For the noncustomer systems, we will use Azure Active Directory, which will allow user authentication and application access to be centrally controlled across all three sites and also make it easier for staff to access systems on different business domains if needed.

Selecting sales services

In this section, we are going to select individual services for the sales business domain:

- **The customer website**: As with the small business case study, the website is fairly simple and has no special requirements for it to have a web role, so we will use a normal website. We're expecting a fairly high volume of orders through this system. It's an extremely important system as customer sales are the primary revenue stream for the company, so we will start with two medium-sized instances (two cores, 3.5 GB RAM) on a **STANDARD** tier. We get the following benefits:
    - Redundancy and load balancing with two instances
    - Good performance for generating high volume, data-driven, server-side web content with medium-sized instances

- ° Staging slot support with a **STANDARD** tier to allow the site to be warmed up before swopping to production after deployment
- ° Custom domain and SSL certificate support in a **STANDARD** tier
- ° The system will be evaluated under load testing to see how well it performs, then the base instance count can be adjusted and auto scaling will be applied on **go-live**

- **The admin website**: Again, the website has no special requirements for it to have a web role, so we will use a normal website. This site will have a fairly low volume of traffic and will be used by a small number of users, so we will start with two small instances (one core, 1.75 GB RAM) on a **BASIC** tier to save cost. However, this site still gives us higher availability over one instance. The system will be evaluated under moderate load testing to see how well it performs, and will then be adjusted if required. We will not use auto scaling here as we will have a very consistent usage profile.

- **The order processor**: The order processor needs to automatically update the order status in the sales database and make push notification requests for the customer phone application when the order status messages are received on its Service Bus topic subscription. A worker role is the natural choice for this type of system as it provides a scalable solution for long-running, unattended processes. This service is not business-critical as it is only updating order statuses and notifying customers and not impacting directly on order throughput through the system, so we will start with two small instances (1.6 GHz CPU, 1.75 GB RAM) that give us the following benefits:
  - ° Redundancy and load balancing with two instances
  - ° Reasonable performance for processing order updates with small-sized instances

As with the website, the system will be evaluated under moderate load testing to see how well it performs, and then the base instance count can be adjusted and auto scaling can be applied on go-live.

- **The mobile API**: The mobile API allows the customer phone app to securely interact with system data. We'll use a .NET mobile service, which makes the OAuth2 implementation straightforward and will allow us to reuse the data access layer components from the website. We'll use the free service tier for this as it's not critical and it's not the main customer interface to the system. If we find that we're exceeding the 500K API calls limit, we can change the service tier.

- **Storage**: We have a requirement for a relational data model, so the natural choice is to use an SQL Server over other storage options such as tables, blobs, or disk storage. The database will be shared between both websites. Once we have a more detailed application design, we can try and estimate storage requirements in more detail, but for now, we'll opt for a single (no partitioning) 30 GB database. There will be an additional storage overhead for diagnostic data for which we will use the lowest tier of table storage.

- **Security**: The customer website and phone application will implement OAuth2 security, and the admin website will implement Azure Active Directory authentication.

Selecting production services

Now, we are going to select individual services for the production business domain:

- **The order processor**: The order processor needs to automatically add the order into the batch schedule and allocate ingredients in the production database when order status messages are received on its Service Bus topic subscription. As with the sales order processor, a worker role is the natural choice for this type of system. This service is business-critical as it controls the batch schedule, which governs when the products are baked, so we will start with two medium instances (2 x 1.6 GHz CPU, 3.5 GB RAM) giving us the following benefits:

  ○ Redundancy and load-balancing with two instances

  ○ Good performance for processing orders with medium-sized instances

  The system will be evaluated under high-volume load testing to see how well it performs; then, the base instance count can be adjusted and auto scaling can be applied on go-live.

- **The Web API**: The Web API allows the production management app (this will be an on-premises desktop application, which can interact with plant on-site) to securely interact with system data. We'll create an MVC Web API website deployed to a Microsoft Azure website. This site will have a fairly low volume of traffic and will be used by a small number of users, so we will start with two small instances (one core, 1.75 GB RAM) on a **BASIC** tier. The system will be evaluated under moderate load testing to see how well it performs, and then adjusted if required. We will not use auto scaling here as we will have a very consistent usage profile.

- **Storage**: Again, we have a requirement for a relational data model, so the natural choice is to use an SQL Server. The database will be shared between the order processor and the Web API. Once we have a more detailed application design, we can try and estimate storage requirements in more detail, but for now, we'll opt for a 30 GB database. There will be an additional storage overhead for diagnostic data, for which we will use the lowest tier of table storage.

Selecting supply services

Finally, we are going to select individual services for the sales business domain:

- **Order processor**: The order processor needs to automatically allocate orders to vehicles and drivers to create delivery jobs when the **ready for dispatch** order status messages are received on its Service Bus topic subscription. As with the sales order processor, a worker role is the natural choice for this type of system. This service is business-critical as it controls the dispatch jobs for delivering orders to customers so we will start with two medium instances (2 x 1.6 GHz CPU, 3.5 GB RAM), giving us the following benefits:

    ○ Redundancy and load balancing with two instances

    ○ Good performance for processing orders with medium-sized instances

    The system will be evaluated under high-volume load testing to see how well it performs, then the base instance count can be adjusted, and auto scaling can be applied on go-live.

- **The mobile API**: The mobile API allows the supply tablet app to securely interact with system data. We'll use a .NET mobile service, which can now provide Azure Active Directory authentication support.

- **Storage**: We don't have a requirement for a relational data model here, so we will use table storage for our data. We will use 200 GB locally redundant storage as we are operating in a single location.

Conclusion of an enterprise system case study – Azure Bakery

We've been through a methodical approach in designing our system to be built on Microsoft Azure, and come out with the exact service we require and how much it will cost us monthly. The next step would be to go into the application design phase; however, we will stop at this point with the small case study and move on to the main enterprise case study.

The following diagram shows us how all the selected services fit together:

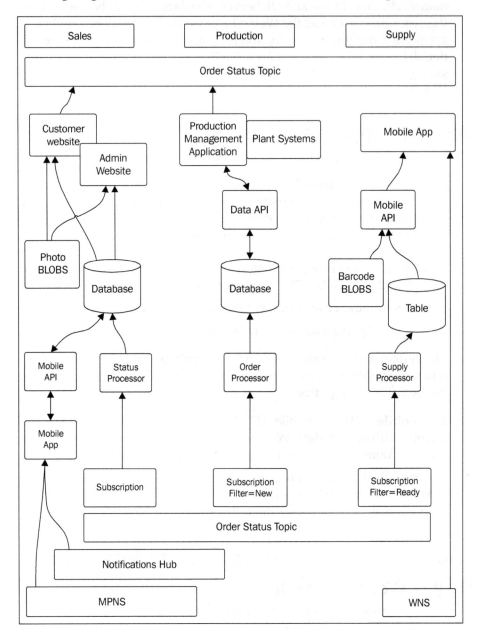

As we draw diagrams of the business and think about how its systems fit together using Microsoft Azure, it's easy to see how it can be extended and scaled up. In our case study, we're not going to worry about where the product designs come from, but it's quite easy to imagine that we have a product development department with their own systems; they have an experimental kitchen, where they come up with new product designs and work out recipes for production; then, when they are ready, they can send the product description to the sales system and the recipes to the production systems.

Designing platform environments

While we're preparing our development environment, it's a good time to talk about planning our platform environments (in an on-premises or IaaS system, we may say server environments). These environments are used to host our system during the different phases of their life cycle between development and production (or live).

The scales of a business and budget are the major factors in this decision process; if we have a large business and a large system, it might take a number of testers to test the changes made to a system and do full regression tests when needed. If the budget for a system is tight, it may not be possible to have a perfect set of environments, so compromises may have to be made. We also need to remember that we're not just talking about a single website; we need to include databases, table storage, worker roles, Service Bus queues and topics, and so on. We'll look at different types of environments and examples of environment sets for different types of businesses, and then have a look at a couple of Microsoft Azure features that are relevant to this.

Common environment roles

We're going to take a look at four common environments you may find in IT systems in any business and their role in the application's life cycle:

- **Production environment**: The production environment is where the system is published once it has passed all testing phases and is ready to be used by the end user, which could be the general public or staff within an organization. This environment will be allocated the most compute resources and scalability of all the environments; however, some businesses (where financially allowable) like to have a test or QA environment matching production exactly so that the system performs the same as in production to help gather realistic load testing and performance statistics.

- **QA environment**: Typically, before a system goes into production, the end user will want to test it to make sure that it meets their requirements (commonly against a specification) and doesn't have any bugs, which will affect the running of the business. QA environments can also be used for training as they often closely match the production environment.

- **Test environment**: After a system is developed, it is always tested by a dedicated test team or by the developers themselves, if a business does not have a test team. In a small business, as a minimum, there should be a test environment before production to not only allow independent testing but also to prove that the system can be taken from a developer machine, where a system was created, and published on another environment without problems, a bit like a dress rehearsal!

- **Development/Integration**: The development environment is where developers can do pretty much what they need to develop the system, prototype new things, and work out how to put a system together without going anywhere near a production system. If the environment is on-premises, these are not ideal environments for testing as there are often developer tools such as Visual Studio and developer SDKs to help debug applications and elevated privileges, which can be an unrealistic representation of the production system. In Azure, this is not the case as we are often deploying a PaaS solution to develop against and not installing tools or altering permissions on the infrastructure. When we're talking about the development environment, we're talking about a development sandboxed server environment and not about the local machine that the developer writes code on. If we implement continuous integration, this is an ideal environment to deploy to.

Example environment sets

To put these environments into a context, we'll have a look at how these different environmental requirements can be sensibly implemented in businesses of different sizes and requirements:

- **Small business**: In a small business or for personal projects where there isn't the budget or time to build, manage, and use more than a few environments, it's probably sensible to have a multipurpose development/test/integration and a production environment, as shown in the following diagram:

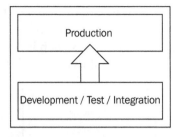

Systems can be developed locally and then published to the test environment for all phases of testing. If an end user needs to perform a QA test, it's important that the developers don't publish changes during testing cycles to avoid disrupting a test. If a continuous deployment strategy is deployed, where a system is published as code is checked in and built, it is extremely important to make sure this is disabled during testing if active development is underway.

- **Medium business**: In a medium business, which has a testing team or more stringent requirements for QA testing, it's good to separate the test and development environments so that QA and system tests can be performed in complete isolation from the development environment, as shown in the following diagram:

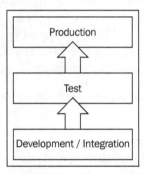

This means that the development team doesn't disrupt the test environment and their normal work activities aren't impacted during test cycles. Another advantage of having the extra environment is that the development team can work on a different version of code to the one being tested, which is helpful for productive release management.

- **Large business**: Large businesses that have a testing team and require a permanent QA environment for end user testing and training may require another dedicated QA environment, which is only used by end users and not system testers, as shown in the following diagram:

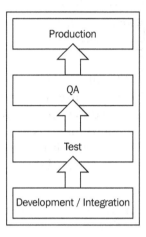

Using website deployment slots

Website deployment slots are a new feature (currently in preview), which allow a staging slot to be added to a website, allowing changes to be tested in a mirror of the production environment, and then swapped with a live environment when ready. There is also a nice feature, where the site is warmed up before it's put into production, so there is not an initial performance hit caused by a cold website start.

We need to be careful about how we use website deployment slots as there are a few things that may catch us out:

- Some configurations including general settings, connection strings, handler mappings, and monitoring and diagnostic settings are copied across on swap, so we will end up using the same database and diagnostics storage in staging, as with production, if we don't manually change them before swapping

- Deployment slots currently run on the same VM as production, so anything you do on a staging slot, whether it's UI testing or load testing, will have an impact on the performance of the production system

For medium and large businesses, I would recommend that you use a deployment slot in the production environment, purely to get the benefit of doing a final touch test (checking site runs, looking at read-only data, or working on data for a special test account) and doing a warm swap into live. I would not use it for a QA environment due to limitations of website configuration and VM resources, as mentioned in the preceding bullet list.

For a small business or personal projects, it might be a good option to use a deployment slot as a test environment; however, you may prefer two separate websites on a **FREE** service tier to save the cost of having one on a **STANDARD** tier.

Using cloud service staging environments

Web roles and worker roles have staging slots by default, which in contrast to website deployment slots, have separate configurations that aren't swopped and run on separate instances. When a swap occurs, the virtual IP address of the production and staging VM is swopped, so staging becomes production and production becomes staging.

A staging slot can be used as a QA or test environment to streamline the deployment process; however, you will still need to update the staging environment to the production version after a swap.

If the staging slot is only used in the production environment, it can be deleted once it is successfully swopped with the live environment, to save on compute cost.

For large businesses that require a full set of application environments, I recommend that you use the staging slot as part of the production environment to expedite the deployment process and also have a regression plan available (swapping back again to the previous live deployment), in case any problems are found after go-live.

For medium and small businesses, I recommend that you consider using the staging slot as a QA or test environment.

Summary

We've been through quite a lot of theory around how to design a system for Microsoft Azure and also introduced the Azure Bakery case study, which we will build on throughout the book. From this point on, we'll be diving deeper into building a number of systems for the case study.

In this book, we'll concentrate on code examples to cover as many different Microsoft Azure services as possible without duplicating things too much; for example, we'll be building two websites for the sales system, we'll look at the customer website in detail, but only look at the Azure AD integration for the admin website. There will be three worker roles across the system, and again, we'll only look at the sales one in detail, and then look at relevant features of the others. In the code samples, everything will be included, so we can run orders end to end.

In the next chapter, we'll start laying the foundations for building the Azure Bakery system, starting with preparing the development environment and looking at creating a basic website.

Questions

1. Why must websites be stateless in order to be scalable?
2. Which Azure services can be used to implement decoupled messaging between system tiers?
3. What does the term sharding mean in storage?
4. If we were building a small business system on a limited budget, which needs a customer website and administration system, why should we choose to build a website for the administration system?
5. What is the cheapest web tier for hosting a site with a custom domain?
6. Why is it important to identify the most critical parts of a system?
7. If we need to store large volumes of structured but nonrelational data, what will be a suitable storage option?
8. What purpose does a QA environment serve for a system?
9. Why do we need to be careful when using deployment slots on websites?
10. If we use a cloud service staging slot as a QA environment, what should we remember to do after we swap it with live?

11. Think about a small system you have worked on in the past and try to design it to run on Azure. Break down the system into logical subsystems and choose suitable Azure services for each system. Factor in scalability and cost in your design.

12. Do the same as question 11, but this time, for a larger system you've worked on. If it spans multiple business domains and needs to include legacy platforms and applications, it's even better!

Answers

1. Websites that use technology such as session state and server-side caching cannot be scaled out easily since the stored data is not synchronized across multiple server instances.

2. Service Bus queues and topics and storage queues.

3. This is horizontal scaling of a database or storage, where data is split across multiple databases or storage providers with the same structure. Data is stored with a partition key, which is used to help you split the data across storage containers.

4. We already have a customer website, so it makes sense to create another website using the same technology as we will need the same development skills and deployment path.

5. Shared.

6. It helps us choose the appropriate service tiers and scalability options for the most critical systems and save cost on less critical or noncritical systems.

7. Table storage as it is a low cost, no SQL alternative to an SQL Server but it still provides structured storage.

8. QA environments are commonly used for user acceptance testing on a system, which closely replicate the production environment. Because of the similarities to the production environment, they are often used for training purposes too.

9. When a slot is swopped from staging to live, the settings are all copied across so if the staging slot has different settings to live, they must be manually updated, and also, they run on the same machine, which may impact performance.

10. Update the staging slot again so that it matches production.

11. NA.

12. NA.

3
Starting to Develop with Microsoft Azure

So far, we've got everything ready in the Microsoft Azure portal with an account setup, and designed the architecture of our system. Next, we're going to start preparing ourselves to build the case study services by covering the following topics:

- Preparing our development environment
- Signing up for Visual Studio Online for source version control
- Creating the initial sales customer website
- Publishing the website to Azure
- Setting up continuous deployment

Preparing our development environment

There's a fair chance you've got all the tools you need, and if you're already doing some Microsoft Azure development, you can probably skip most of this. If you want to look at phone development in, it's worth reading the *Mobile development* section.

Setting up software

Throughout this book, I will be using Visual Studio Professional 2013 as it allows me to work on various project types in one solution. Don't worry if you don't have a premium version such as Professional or Ultimate as you can use multiple versions of Visual Studio Express instead, which are as follows:

- **Visual Studio Express 2013 for Web**: You'll mostly need this, and when I talk about Visual Studio without being specific, this is the one to use if you're sticking to Express versions

- **Visual Studio Express 2013 for Windows Desktop**: If you want to build the WPF apps for the production management system and the Service Bus messaging simulator, you'll need this

- **Visual Studio Express 2013 for Windows**: If you want to build a store app during *Chapter 11, Integrating a Mobile Application Using Mobile Services*, you'll need this

Of course, you can use Professional and Ultimate versions of Visual Studio, and it'll be easier for you as you can develop different project types in the same solution.

We'll use **SQL Server Management Studio (SSMS)** for connecting to Azure Databases, so it's worth installing that now too. I'm using SSMS, which comes bundled with SQL Server Express 2012, but 2014 will be fine too. Here's the download link, which allows you to pick the parts of an SQL Server to download: `http://www.microsoft.com/en-gb/download/details.aspx?id=29062`. I chose to download the Express with tools version (`ENU\x64\SQLEXPRWT_x64_ENU.exe`), which contains the database engine and tools including SSMS, so we can run websites locally against a local database and use SSMS to connect to local and Azure Databases.

Mobile development

For Windows Store app development, there is no special hardware requirement; however, to develop apps for Windows Phone 8, you need a machine that has specific requirements in order to run the Hyper-V phone emulators. The Windows Phone 8 SDK will perform a prerequisite check before installation; however, you can read the exact requirements at `http://msdn.microsoft.com/en-us/library/windowsphone/develop/ff626524(v=vs.105).aspx`.

For phone development, it is always helpful to have a handset to test on, and I would advise testing any app on a real device before publishing, to make sure everything works. The same goes for Windows 8, although Surface Pros and other tablets that run full Windows 8 have exactly the same OS as PCs and laptops; it's helpful to test the touch gestures as well, since keyboard and Surfaces (formerly, Surface RTs) run on a different OS designed for ARM devices so that it is useful to have access to a tablet or machine with a touch screen.

To publish your apps, you need a Store account and you'll also need an account to implement push notifications in Windows Store apps. Unlike Microsoft Azure, you actually need to pay for these, and there is no free option. Previously, you needed separate accounts for Store and Phone apps; however, these have now been merged and only cost $19 for an individual. You can sign up at `https://appdev.microsoft.com/StorePortals/en-us/Account/Signup/Start`.

The Microsoft Azure SDK

The Microsoft Azure SDK for Visual Studio provides us with excellent tooling for Azure development from Visual Studio. It also includes the following:

- Integration into the Server Explorer, allowing us to interact with services and view data
- Automatic provisioning of Azure Services during publishing and project creation
- Compute and storage emulators for cloud services
- Special project types for cloud services
- Remote debugging

We need to install the Azure SDK, which can be downloaded from `http://www.windowsazure.com/en-us/downloads/;` currently, there are versions for Visual Studio 2012 and 2013; as I've mentioned, I'm going to use 2013; go ahead and use 2012 if you like, but I can't guarantee everything will look the same as in screenshots and examples.

Checking for Visual Studio updates

It's worth checking for updates periodically because the toolset is constantly changing to match updates and new features in Azure. We can see notifications in the notifications hub (`http://blogs.msdn.com/b/visualstudio/archive/2013/09/16/notifications-in-visual-studio-2013.aspx`) and also by going to **TOOLS | Extensions and Updates...**, as shown in the following screenshot:

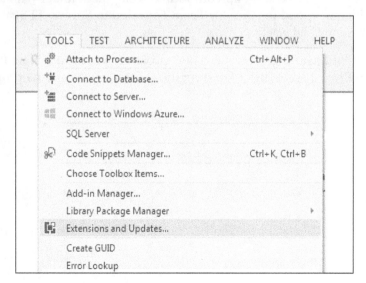

Then, update all the extensions and updates you need. There are two important ones for us here, **Visual Studio 2013 Update 1** and **Windows Azure SDK 2.3**:

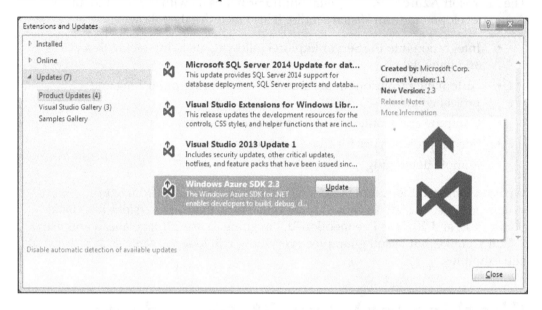

Creating a website

We're going to create a basic MVC 5 website, which will become our sales customer website for the case study.

Before you create the project, set up your local development folder with a main subfolder, which is a good practice for **Team Foundation Server (TFS)** allowing solutions to be branched easily.

Launch Visual Studio and go to create a new project (go to **Start | New Project** or press *Ctrl + Shift + N*) and select **Web** from the categories and enter a project name:

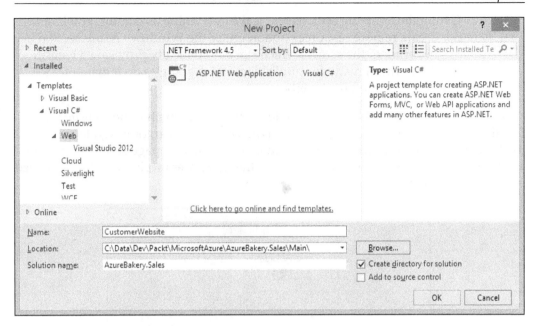

Click on **OK** and we will see the **Web** template options dialog; in the previous versions of Visual Studio, templates will be in the **Project** dialog:

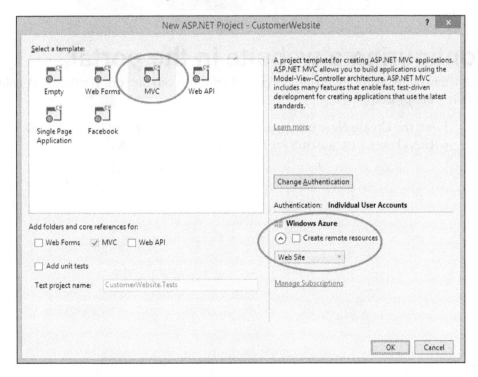

Select **MVC** from the template options and leave everything as default. You'll notice that there is a **Create remote resources** option under the **Windows Azure** section in the bottom-right corner of the screen, which can automatically provision a website (and database, if required) ready for publishing. We're going to do it manually to help explain how everything fits together.

Click on **OK** and wait for the solution to load. Next, test whether the website works locally by clicking on the **Debug** button on the **Debug** toolbar, or navigate to **DEBUG | Start Debugging** from the main menu. Your web page should appear in the browser, and you should also notice that the IIS Express web server has launched and is available in the system's tray:

Configuring a website in the portal

Next, we need to create a website in Azure to publish our site on. We'll do this using the following procedure:

1. From the **Create New** menu, go to **COMPUTE | WEB SITE | QUICK CREATE** and pick a name for the website:

2. Click on **CREATE WEBSITE** and you should see your new website listed in the portal:

3. Click on the newly listed website to go to the website's workspace:

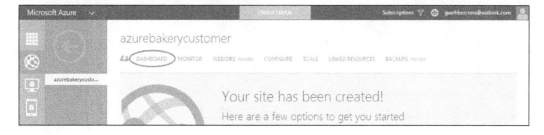

4. We're going to enable staged deployments, so we can deploy to a staged environment for testing, and then swap later for production (in *Chapter 2, Designing a System for Microsoft Azure*, we covered a section on environments and we're going to use a staging slot for testing). First, we need to put the website in a **STANDARD** service mode; so click on the **SCALE** tab and click on **STANDARD** under the **WEB HOSTING PLAN MODE** section:

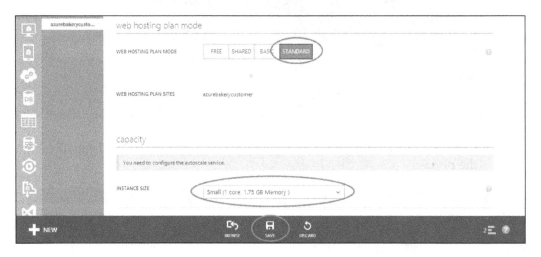

5. Watch the **INSTANCE SIZE** field as it may default to a large value incurring the highest cost; I dropped mine down to the smallest instance.

6. Click on **SAVE** on the bottom toolbar, and then click on **DASHBOARD** so that we can enable staging:

7. Click on the **Add a new deployment slot** link, enter a name for the deployment slot (staging is a sensible choice), and then click on the tick button. We'll see that the new staging site appears under the main site by clicking on the arrow:

8. To publish the website, go to **BUILD | Publish CustomerWebsite** (you
    should select the name of your project):

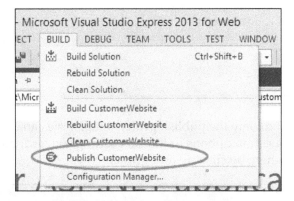

9. Select **Windows Azure Web Sites** as the publish target (this is probably the
    quickest way to publish for the first time; the **Import** option allows you to
    import a publish profile you've downloaded from the website dashboard,
    and **Custom** allows you to manually enter the publish details):

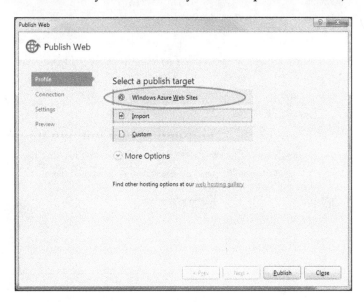

10. Sign in with the Microsoft account you are using in the Azure portal, and then select the site you want to publish to from the drop-down list:

11. Next, we will review the publish profile details. We can change the build and database connection options in the next settings wizard, but we can publish straight from here by clicking on **Publish**:

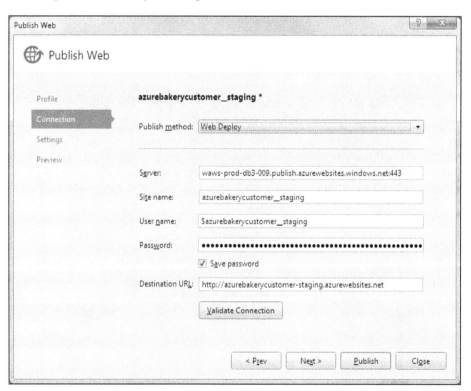

12. Once we do this, we will see the publish profile included in the solution, which will speed up the process on the subsequent publish:

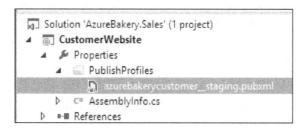

13. We can watch the deployment process in the output window in Visual Studio; then, the default browser should launch, displaying our website in the Azure!

Creating a Visual Studio Online project

Visual Studio Online is a fairly new product, which offers us online application development tools and **Application Lifecycle Management** (**ALM**) tools such as team projects, code repositories, bug tracking, task management, and others, depending on your user plan; if you've used **Team Foundation Server** (**TFS**), you'll find that Visual Studio Online is pretty much the same.

There are a number of user plans available, which depend on the size of the development team and the specific requirements you may have. You can check out the different options in detail at `http://www.visualstudio.com/products/visual-studio-online-overview-vs`.

Azure also has good support for Git version control too, allowing Node.js backend mobile services and websites to be pushed to the cloud. It's also possible to set up continuous deployment from a web repository such as GitHub or Bitbucket to an Azure website. The **Kudu** service built in all Azure websites compiles the website when it's pushed from source control before publishing.

We're going to use Visual Studio Online for source control and also to create a build agent, which will allow us to continually build and deploy our website to the website-staging slot on code check-in and build. Later in this book, we'll also create a website and cloud service deployment packages using the Visual Studio Online Team Foundation Build server, which is something we couldn't easily do with Git and a web repository.

There's a bit of a gotcha with Visual Studio Online website continuous deployment as it only supports solutions with a single website, or it picks the first website in a solution if there is more than one website.

Creating a Visual Studio Online account

Before we create a project, we need to create a Visual Studio Online account. From the Microsoft Azure portal, you can either link to an existing account or create a new one against one of your subscriptions. I'm going to create a new one on my **Pay-As-You-Go** subscription:

1. From the **New Service** button, select **APP SERVICES | VISUAL STUDIO ONLINE | QUICK CREATE**, enter a URL, choose a subscription, and click on **CREATE ACCOUNT**:

2. Once the account is created, it should appear as an option in the **VISUAL STUDIO ONLINE** portal:

3. Clicking on **BROWSE** will take us to the **Visual Studio Online** portal, where we will have to enter a few more details before logging into our account.

   If we go back to the Microsoft Azure portal and click on our listed linked account, we can see a nice **DASHBOARD** page that displays a **BUILD** and **LOAD TESTING** usage graph and other metrics; then, on the **SCALE** tab, we have the option to add extra licenses and change the **BUILD** and **LOAD TESTING** tariffs, which will be charged to your subscription when they go over the free allowance.

Creating a Visual Studio Online project

Go to the **Visual Studio Online** portal, where we can create our first project:

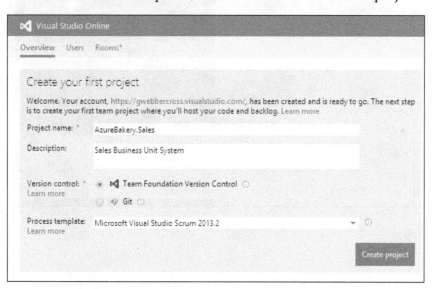

Enter **Project name** and **Description** and select the **Team Foundation Version Control** option (this is the default option), and then click on **Create project**. Now, we can check out our solution.

Setting up continuous deployment

We're now going to check our website into TFS and set up continuous deployment so that our website is built and published to the staging slot whenever we check in code changes.

Adding a solution to source control

To add a solution to source control, perform the following steps:

1. First of all, we need to add our solution to TFS in our Visual Studio Online account. From the **FILE** menu, go to **Source Control | Add Solution to Source Control...**:

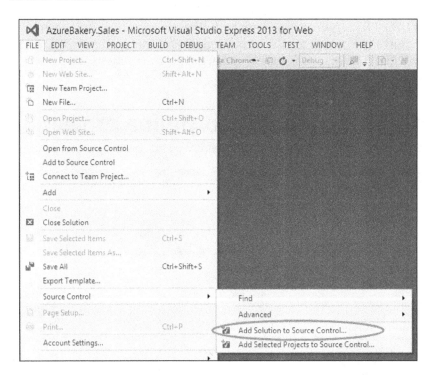

2. Select **Team Foundation Version Control** (default) from the next dialog and click on **OK**. In the **Connect to Team Foundation Server** dialog, click on the **Servers...** button; then, on the **Add/Remove Team Foundation Server** dialog, click on **Add....** After that, enter the URL of our Visual Studio Online account from the Azure portal:

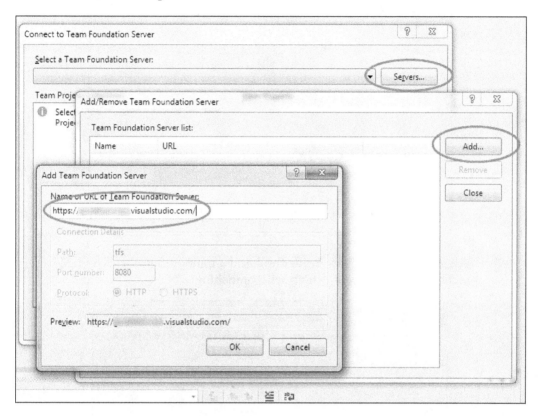

3. Sign in when prompted, and then click on **Close** on the **Add/Remove Team Foundation Server** dialog.

4. Select the team project in the **Connect to Team Foundation Server** dialog and click on **Connect**:

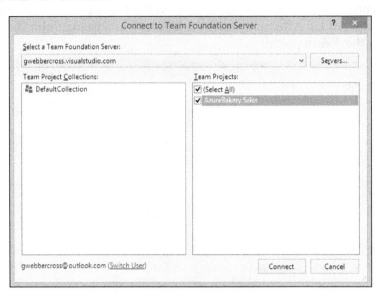

5. Next, click on **Make New Folder** and add a main folder; this is a good practice for TFS projects to help with branching:

6. Once we've done this, we'll see a lot of little **+** symbols next to each file in the solution; this means the files are added to source control but not checked in. Next, we need to check in the code to see if it's safely stored on the TFS server, so right-click on the solution and select **Check In...**:

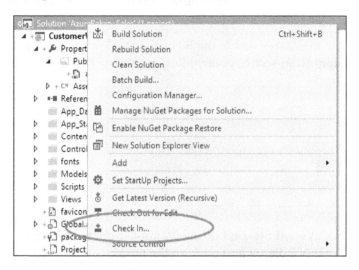

7. Enter a comment (it's always important to enter a comment as it shows up in the version control history, helping you if you need to revert the code or create a branch at a certain point) and click on **Check In**:

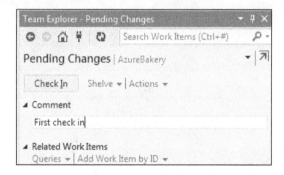

8. Now, all the files in our solution should have blue padlocks next to them, showing that they are all checked in and there are no pending modifications.

Configuring continuous deployment

Continuous deployment is performed by a TFS build agent, which can build code triggered by a number of different events. We're going to use the wizard in the Azure portal to set up our build agent for us, and then we'll have a look at what is done:

1. First, go to the dashboard of the website's staging slot and click on the **Set up deployment from source control** link:

2. Next, select **Visual Studio Online** (default) from the **SET UP DEPLOYMENT** dialog and click on the next arrow.

3. Now, enter the name of the Visual Studio Online account and click on **Authorize Now**:

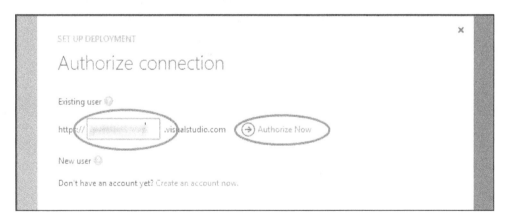

4. Accept the connection request, choose the repository, and accept it; then, the project will be linked and will appear under the **DEPLOYMENTS** tab:

We can now test continual deployment's working by changing something in the website, checking it in, and then browsing the Azure website to see the changes:

1. In the website project, open the `Views/Home/Index.cshtml` file and make some changes to the markup; I changed the `ViewBag.Title` property, which will change the title. Then, I changed the first `div` element and deleted the rest of the markup like this:

```
@{
    ViewBag.Title = "Azure Bakery";
}

<div class="jumbotron">
    <h1>Azure Bakery</h1>
    <p class="lead">Welcome to Azure Bakery!</p>
</div>
```

Downloading the example code

You can download the example code files for all Packt books you have purchased from your account at `http://www.packtpub.com`. If you purchased this book elsewhere, you can visit `http://www.packtpub.com/support` and register to have the files e-mailed directly to you.

2. Now, if we save this and check it in (using the same process as when we first checked in the code), a build should trigger, and then our website will be published. While we wait for this to happen, we'll go and take a closer look at what's going on, so in the **Team Explorer** window, click the drop-down menu and select **Builds** (you can also get to this via the menu on the home tab):

3. We should then see a build listed under the **My Builds** heading; if we double-click on it, a window will open, showing us the current status of the build (if you miss the build and it's completed already, you can right-click on the build definition and select **Queue New Build** to rebuild manually; I did this while I was trying to type everything, so this is why you can see two builds):

4. Once it's complete, you will see it update with a **Build succeeded** status and a green tick:

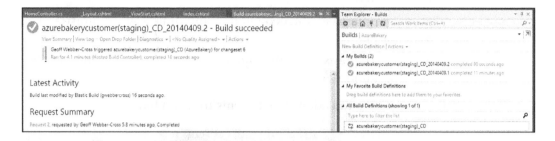

5. If we have any problems during the build, we can view the build log from here (as shown in the previous screenshot), which will show us any errors and warnings to help us diagnose the problem.

6. Finally, if we refresh our staging website, we should see that the code changes have been deployed!

Examining the build definition

To complete this section, we'll take a look at the build definition that the Azure wizard has created for us:

1. In the **Team Explorer** window, right-click on the build definition and select **Edit Build Definition**:

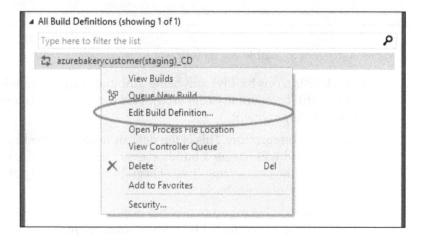

2. In the **General** tab, we have options to control how the build is queued:

   ○ **Enabled**: This allows requests to be queued and built in priority order.

   ○ **Paused**: Requests are queued but not built (unless an administrator forces them).

   ○ **Disabled**: Requests are neither queued nor built. This can be used to stop continuous deployment.

3. In the **Trigger** tab, we can adjust what events trigger a build:

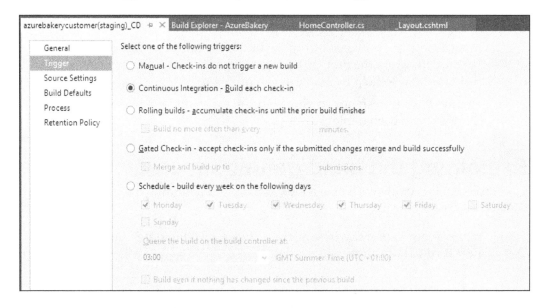

The various triggers available are as follows:

   ○ **Manual**: This stops builds from being automatically triggered (they can still be manually triggered). This can be used to stop continuous deployment.

   ○ **Continuous Integration**: This is the default setting created by the wizard and will trigger a build on every single check-in, which might not be the best setting if you check in code regularly as you will find build requests backing up.

   ○ **Rolling builds**: This might be a better option for continuous deployment as you could set it to build not more than every 30 minutes, for example, so you don't get a backlog of requests queuing.

- ° **Gated Check-in**: In this configuration, changes that the developer makes are placed in shelve sets (like a staged check in) and are only checked in once the build server has successfully built the changes. This can stop developers from breaking code in source control.

- ° **Schedule**: It can be quite common to have a scheduled build to check the integrity of the code at regular intervals if continuous integration is not used.

4. The **Source Settings** tab shows us how **Source Control Folder** maps to **Build Agent Folder**. Don't change this unless you need to.

5. The **Build Defaults** tab allows us to change the location of where the build output is deployed. Don't change this unless you need to.

6. The **Process** tab is where the build process template is defined and configured. Don't change this unless you need to.

7. The **Retention Policy** tab allows you to change how builds are retained by the server.

Setting up alerts

It can be useful to set up alerts in Visual Studio Online especially if you are working in a team. The following alert types are available:

- **Work Item Alerts**: These are triggered when any work item related to you changes

- **Checkin Alerts**: These occur when various checks on criteria are met

- **Build Alerts**: These are triggered under various build events

- **Code review Alerts**: These occur when a code review you are working on or a code review in the project changes

Setting up alerts allows us to view and edit our alert settings:

1. In the **Visual Studio Online** portal, go to the dashboard for your project and click on the settings button in the top-right corner of the screen:

2. In the admin window that opens, click on the **Alerts** tab and notice that there are some quick links down on the left-hand side under the **CREATE NEW ALERT WHEN** title, which we will use to quickly create some alerts:

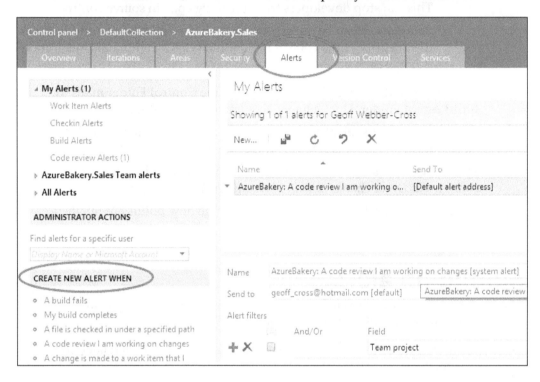

3. We want to know when a build fails, so click on the **A build fails** link, have a quick look at the alert rules, change the **Send to** field if required (if you do change it, you will be sent an e-mail to verify the change), and accept it:

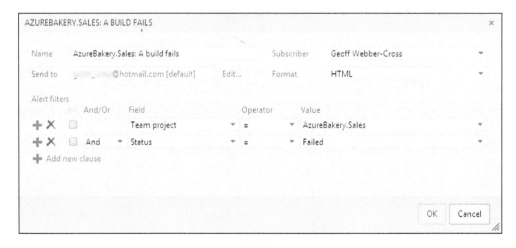

4. Do the same for the **My build completes** link.

5. We'll now see our new alerts listed (and one demo alert automatically created for us); click on the **Save all modified alerts** button:

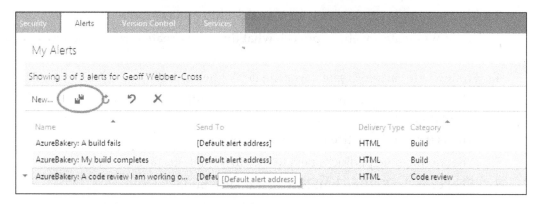

6. Now, manually trigger a build from Visual Studio by right-clicking on the build definition and selecting **Queue New Build**.

7. Once the build has completed, we should receive an e-mail alert. If it happened to fail, which it certainly shouldn't at this stage, we would get an e-mail alert that tells us it had failed.

Summary

We've covered quite a lot in this chapter, preparing peripheral things such as setting up version control, continuous deployment, and alerts. This might seem like a lot to do initially, but we will benefit from doing these things now before we get deeper into the development process. Even if you don't want to implement continuous deployment, it's still a good practice to set up a build process to validate the integrity of your code during development, especially if you are working in a team.

Next, we're going to start looking at the data layer of our customer website for the Azure Bakery case study.

Questions

1. Which version of Visual Studio Express allows us to develop web applications for Azure and what SDK do we need to install?

2. Why is it important to check for Visual Studio updates?

3. When we create a website project, what does the **Create remote resources** setting do?

4. From where can we create a website deployment slot?

5. What benefits do we get from using Visual Studio Online with Azure projects?

6. Why is it a good practice to put a `Main` folder under the TFS project root?

7. What do the blue padlocks next to files in Visual Studio indicate?

8. What does the **Rolling builds** trigger do in a build definition?

9. Try creating a new website project in Visual Studio and publish it to the cloud. This time, don't configure the website in the portal; instead, let Visual Studio provision it for you when you create the project.

10. Create a daily build for the new project to test the integrity of the code. Set up alerts, so if the build fails, you get an e-mail.

Answers

1. Visual Studio 2013 Express for Web and Microsoft Azure SDK.

2. Because the Azure SDKs and Visual Studio tooling are constantly changing to provide support for new and improved Azure features.

3. If it's (**Create remote resources**) enabled, it will automatically provision a website for us in Azure without having to manually create one.

4. From the **quick glance** section in the website's dashboard.

5. Source control, website continuous deployment, and deployment package builds, not to mention the extra ALM project tools.

6. To make it easier to branch the project.

7. It shows that they are checked into Visual Studio Online with no pending changes.

8. Allows a number of check-ins to accumulate before building.

9. NA.

10. NA.

4

Creating and Managing a Windows Azure SQL Server Database

We're going to start building the database for our sales business domain, which will serve the customer website, administrator website, phone application, and order processor worker role. We'll cover the following topics:

- Creating a database in the portal
- Building the database using Entity Framework Code First Migrations
- Different tools for managing Azure SQL Servers and databases
- Backing up and restoring a database

Once we've covered these topics, we'll have complete local and Azure SQL databases and understand how to manage these databases using a number of different tools.

Microsoft Azure services are continually expanding, improving, and changing, and Azure SQL Databases are no different. The Web and Business editions are due to be retired in April 2015, where they will be replaced with Basic, Standard, and Premium tiers, which will be available as a preview before then. These new tiers offer six levels of services for different performance requirements and offer self-service restore and active geo-replication.

Creating a database using the Azure management portal

We're going to start by creating a database called `AzureBakerySales` for the sales websites in the Azure management portal:

1. From the **NEW** service menu, go to **DATA SERVICES | SQL DATABASE | QUICK CREATE**, and we will see this wizard that can be used to quickly create a basic database:

2. By default, this creates a **WEB EDITION** database with the lowest **MAX SIZE** allocation (1 GB) and the default collation (`SQL_Latin1_General_CP1_CI_AS`). It's possible to change the **EDITION** and **MAX SIZE** settings in the **SCALE** tab of the portal.

3. Instead of **QUICK CREATE**, we'll use the **CUSTOM CREATE** option, which gives us more control over the database options:

   1. From the **NEW** service menu, go to **DATA SERVICES | SQL DATABASE | CUSTOM CREATE**.

   2. Enter the details for the database in the **NEW SQL DATABASE** dialog. I've chosen to use **BUSINESS** as **EDITION** with **20 GB** of **MAX SIZE** (this can be changed) the default **COLLATION** (`http://msdn.microsoft.com/en-us/library/ms143726.aspx`), and **New SQL database server** from the **SERVER** options (if you, like me, have no database server configured yet, you must select this option):

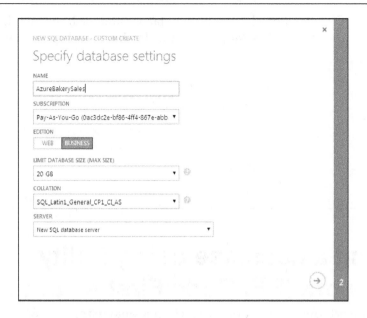

3. Click on the next arrow, and then fill in the **LOGIN NAME** and **LOGIN PASSWORD** fields (make a note of these as they are the SA credentials for the database, and you will need them later). Select a **REGION** nearest to your end user's geographic location and leave **ALLOW WINDOWS AZURE SERVICES TO ACCESS THE SERVER** checked; otherwise, the firewall will need to manually configure the service host IP addresses of services that require access to the database:

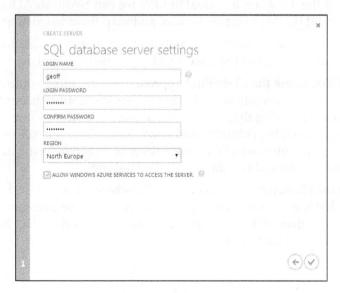

4. Click on the tick to create a database and we'll see that the newly created database appears in the database workspace in the portal:

Building a database using Entity Framework (EF) Code First Migrations

Entity Framework (EF) is Microsoft's **object-relational mapper (ORM)** for .NET, which allows developers to easily work with relational data inside their applications using domain objects. Instead of manually writing data access layers to read/write and parse data, as you would by using native ADO.NET, using an ORM saves time and effort. When we use EF in our projects, we have a number of different options to create our database and entities:

- **Database-First**: With this technique, we can create our database (or use an existing database) in a tool such as SQL Management Studio using SQL scripts or the designer. In Visual Studio, we can create an ADO.NET **Entity Data Model (EDM)** to create entities and map them to existing tables.

- **Model-First**: This is similar to Database-First, where we use an EDM to design our entities, but then, we let EF to create our database from it.

- **Code First**: Using the Code First approach, we get more control over our code, and we can create an entity model, which represents our business domain easily rather than worrying too much about how our entities will translate into tables, columns, and rows. Using Code First, we can use migrations to automatically manage schema changes during development and seed default and test data into our database.

- **Code First (Reverse engineered)**: This is where we can use a tool such as EF Power Tools to take an existing database and reverse engineer a set of **Plain Old CLR Object (POCO)** entities and mappings as if we had built them ourselves using Code First.

We're going to build our data model using the Code First approach in this book as we don't have an existing database. We'll let EF do all the mapping for us throughout the book, but it's worth reading up on the EF fluent API at `http://msdn.microsoft.com/en-gb/data/jj591617.aspx`, which gives you more power over entity mapping.

 If you are using continuous deployment as discussed in *Chapter 3, Starting to Develop with Microsoft Azure*, don't check in any changes until you get to the **Publishing with Migrations** section because we need to modify the publish settings in order to build the database.

Creating the data model

The following entity relationship diagram shows us the different entities in the sales domain and how they relate to each other:

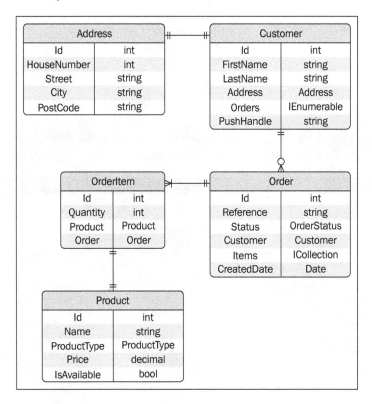

We'll create our model in a new assembly, which will allow us to easily share it between the sales customer website, administrator website, mobile application, and order processor. In Visual Studio, right-click on the solution, go to **Add | New Project**, select **Class Library** from the template types, and give it a name:

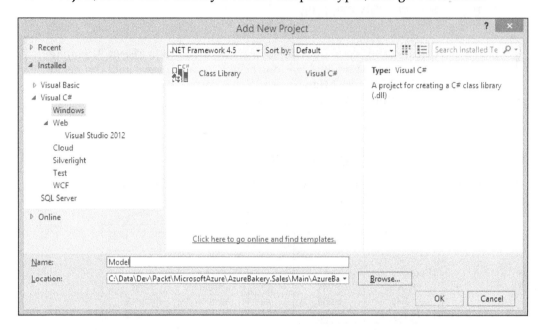

I have changed the **Assembly name** and **Default namespace** fields in the properties of the project (to do this, right-click on the project and select **Properties**):

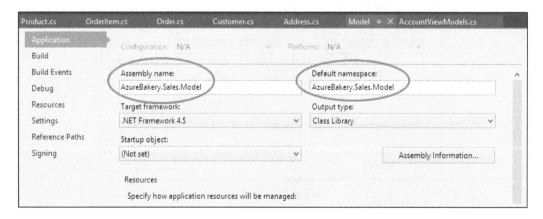

Next, we can start adding our entity classes. Add a class for each entity in the model using the following code. This is the `Address` model, which has no relational dependencies.

```
namespace AzureBakery.Sales.Model
{
    public class Address
    {
        public int Id { get; set; }

        public int HouseNumber { get; set; }

        public string Street { get; set; }

        public string City { get; set; }

        public string PostCode { get; set; }
    }
}
```

When we have entities that have a relational dependency on another entity, we create what is known as a `Navigation` property, which must be marked as `virtual`, and which allows us to navigate through an entity to the related entities. This is the `Customer` model:

```
using System.Collections.Generic;

namespace AzureBakery.Sales.Model
{
    public class Customer
    {
        public int Id { get; set; }

        public string FirstName { get; set; }

        public string LastName { get; set; }

        public virtual Address Address { get; set; }

        public virtual IEnumerable<Order> Orders { get; set; }

        public string PushHandle { get; set; }
    }
}
```

We won't look at the code for each model here as they pretty much have the same features, so refer to them in the code samples.

In order to use the new model project in our website, we need to right-click on the References folder and select **Add Reference...**:

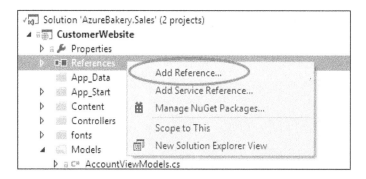

Click on the **Solution** tab and then select the new **Model** project from the list:

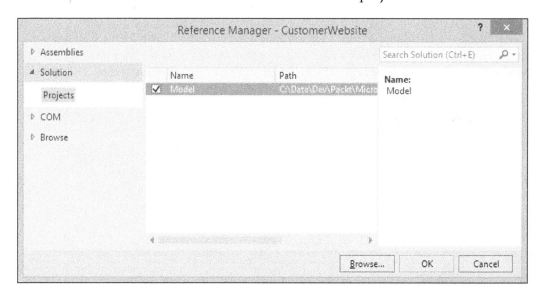

Configuring a database context

Now, we have a model and we need to add it to an EF `DbContext` so that we can start interacting with the database. In our sales customer website, we have a class called `ApplicationDbContext`, which is tucked away inside the `Models/IdentityModels` file:

```
public class ApplicationDbContext :
  IdentityDbContext<ApplicationUser>
{
    public ApplicationDbContext()
            : base("DefaultConnection")
    {
       }
}
```

This is a special implementation of `DbContext`, which implements `IdentityDbContext`, which looks like this:

```
public class IdentityDbContext<TUser> : DbContext where TUser :
  Microsoft.AspNet.Identity.EntityFramework.IdentityUser
{
    public IdentityDbContext();
    public IdentityDbContext(string nameOrConnectionString);

    public virtual IDbSet<IdentityRole> Roles { get; set; }
    public virtual IDbSet<TUser> Users { get; set; }

    protected override void OnModelCreating(DbModelBuilder
      modelBuilder);
    protected override DbEntityValidationResult
      ValidateEntity(DbEntityEntry entityEntry,
        IDictionary<object, object> items);
}
```

We can see that we have the `IDbSet<T>` properties, which allow us to access ASP.NET authentication's `Role` and `User` data.

We can add new `DbSet<T>` properties to the `ApplicationDbContext` class so that EF can add our models to the schema and allow us to interact with the data:

```
public class ApplicationDbContext : IdentityDbContext<ApplicationUser>
{
    public ApplicationDbContext()
            : base("DefaultConnection")
    {
    }

    public DbSet<Customer> Customers { get; set; }

    public DbSet<Order> Orders { get; set; }

    public DbSet<Product> Products { get; set; }

    public DbSet<OrderItem> OrderItems { get; set; }
}
```

Linking an authenticated user to the model

Our data model has a `Customer` entity, which needs to be related to the authenticated user who has logged in to the application. To do this, we simply add a `navigation` property to the `ApplicationUser` entity, and this allows us to relate the authenticated user to a `Customer` entity:

```
public class ApplicationUser : IdentityUser
{
    public virtual Customer Customer  { get; set; }
}
```

In a controller, we can now do something like this to find the customer:

```
private readonly ApplicationDbContext _ctx =
  new ApplicationDbContext();

public ActionResult Index()
{
    // Get customer details
    var uid = User.Identity.GetUserId();
```

```
var customer = this._ctx.Users
    .Include(u => u.Customer)
    .Single(u => u.Id == uid).Customer;
}
```

Configuring the connection string

Our default MVC project will have a connection string like this in the `Web.config` file, which tells EF how to connect to our database:

```
Data Source=(LocalDb)\v11.0;AttachDbFilename=|DataDirectory|\
aspnet-ABPoC-20140417010730.mdf;Initial Catalog=aspnet-AzureBakery-
20140417010730;Integrated Security=True
```

This is using the `LocalDb` database server, which is the lightweight developer version of an SQL Server, and is loading the database from the `mdf` file in the website's directory structure. `LocalDb` is not a full server and runs under a single process under the context of the executing user, which means it's not suitable for use by multiple users and applications. We are going to be sharing our database across two websites, a worker role and mobile API, so we will use a local SQL Express instance for local development purposes and an Azure SQL Database for our published applications.

Our local connection string looks like this:

```
Data Source=localhost;Initial Catalog=AzureBakerySales;Integrated
Security=True"
        providerName="System.Data.SqlClient
```

We can replace the default connection string in the `Web.config` file like this:

```
<connectionStrings>
    <add name="DefaultConnection" connectionString="Data
Source=localhost;Initial Catalog= AzureBakerySales;Integrated
Security=True" providerName="System.Data.SqlClient" />

</connectionStrings>
```

Enabling migrations and updating the database

First, we need to open the **Package Manager Console** so that we can use EF PowerShell cmdlets (`http://msdn.microsoft.com/en-us/library/ms714395(v=vs.85).aspx`) to set up migrations. To do this, go to **VIEW | Other Windows | Package Manager Console,** and the console should load into the bottom panel:

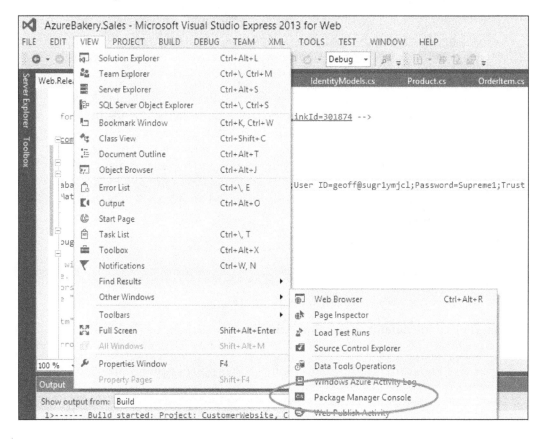

In the console, check that the website is selected in the **Default project** picker and enter the following command to enable migrations:

```
enable-migrations
```

This creates a `Migrations` folder, which contains a `Configuration.cs` file that allows us to control how migrations are configured. We should see the console output like this:

```
PM> enable-migrations
Checking if the context targets an existing database...
Code First Migrations enabled for project CustomerWebsite.
```

Now, type the following command to add an initial migration:

```
add-migration Inititial
```

We should see an output like this in the console:

```
PM> add-migration Initial
Scaffolding migration 'Initial'.
```

The designer code for this migration file includes a snapshot of your current Code First model. This snapshot is used to calculate the changes to your model when you scaffold the next migration.

We'll now see our `Migrations` folder populated with our `Configuration.cs` and initial migration files, shown as follows:

```
▷    fonts
▲    Migrations
     ▲ + C# 201404282005117_Initial.cs
       ▷ + 201404282005117_Initial.Designer.cs
         + 201404282005117_Initial.resx
     ▷ + C# Configuration.cs
▷    Models
```

The initial migration file (with a timestamp prefix to help keep them in order) is the benchmark for the schema versioning. If we look at the file created, we have the up and down methods, which create our tables with primary keys, foreign keys, and indexes, when the migration is applied, and remove them when it's rolled back:

```
public partial class initialcreate : DbMigration
{
public override void Up()
{
  CreateTable(
          "dbo.Customers",
          c => new
              {
```

```
                                Id = c.Int(nullable: false, identity: true),
                                FirstName = c.String(),
                                LastName = c.String(),
                                PushHandle = c.String(),
                                Address_Id = c.Int(),
                            })
                    .PrimaryKey(t => t.Id)
                    .ForeignKey("dbo.Addresses", t => t.Address_Id)
                    .Index(t => t.Address_Id);

        // Other create methods removed for brevity
    }

    public override void Down()
    {
            DropForeignKey("dbo.Orders", "Customer_Id", "dbo.Customers");
            DropForeignKey("dbo.Customers", "Address_Id", "dbo.
            Addresses");
            DropIndex("dbo.Orders", new[] { "Customer_Id" });
            DropIndex("dbo.Customers", new[] { "Address_Id" });
            DropTable("dbo.Customers");

        // Other drop methods removed for brevity
    }
}
```

When we make subsequent changes to our model/schema, we can use the `add-migration` command again to scaffold another migration, shown as follows:

add-migration pushhandle

After running the preceding command, we will see that the model changes like this:

```
    public partial class pushhandle : DbMigration
    {
    public override void Up()
    {
        AddColumn("dbo.Customers", "PushHandle", c => c.String());
    }

    public override void Down()
    {
        DropColumn("dbo.Customers", "PushHandle");
    }
    }
```

Once we have done this, we can customize our `Configuration.cs` file to initially seed the database with default or test data:

```
internal sealed class Configuration : DbMigrationsConfiguration<
  CustomerWebsite.Models.ApplicationDbContext>
{
    public Configuration()
    {
        AutomaticMigrationsEnabled = true;
        ContextKey = "ABPoC.Models.ApplicationDbContext";
    }

    protected override void
      Seed(CustomerWebsite.Models.ApplicationDbContext context)
    {
        //  This method will be called after migrating to the
        latest version.
        context.Products.AddOrUpdate(
            p => p.Name,
            new Product("Cheese Pasty", ProductType.Pastries,
                0.75m),
            new Product("Cornish Pasty", ProductType.Pastries,
                0.83m),
            new Product("Steak Pasty", ProductType.Pastries,
                0.88m),
            new Product("Chicken & Mushroom Pasty",
                ProductType.Pastries, 0.76m),
            new Product("Donut", ProductType.Cakes, 0.23m),
            new Product("Jam Donut", ProductType.Cakes, 0.25m),
            new Product("Cup Cake", ProductType.Cakes, 0.63m),
            new Product("Fruit Cake", ProductType.Cakes, 0.84m),
            new Product("Fairy Cake", ProductType.Cakes, 0.56m),
            new Product("Chocolate Crispie", ProductType.Cakes,
                0.24m)
            );
            // Etc
    }
}

public class ApplicationDbContext :
  IdentityDbContext<ApplicationUser>
    {
        public ApplicationDbContext()
            : base("DefaultConnection")
        {
            base.Configuration.ProxyCreationEnabled = false;
        }
```

I've added some extra bits to the constructor to change the `DbContext` behavior:

- `ProxyCreationEnabled` is disabled to stop EF from creating proxies for POCO entities

We can now build the database using our initial migration and seed method by typing the following command:

```
update-database
```

We should see the console output, shown as follows:

```
PM> update-database
Specify the '-Verbose' flag to view the SQL statements being applied to the target database.
Applying explicit migrations: [201404282005117_Initial].
Applying explicit migration: 201404282005117_Initial.
Running Seed method.
```

If we now connect to our local database using SSMS, we should see that our database has been built and our product table has been seeded:

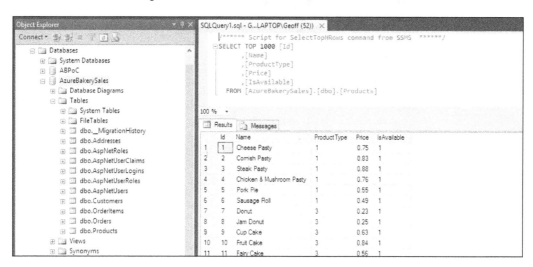

Publishing with migrations

In the previous step, we used the `update-database` cmdlet to update our database using migrations. When we publish the website, we're using a slightly different mechanism where the publish process changes the `Web.config` file to use the `MigrateDatabaseToLatestVersion` initializer, which will create the database when the `DbContext` is first touched, which will not currently happen in our application, so we'll put in some temporary code to list the sales products on the `Home/Index` page. To do this, we need to perform the following steps:

1. Change the `HomeController.cs` index action to read a list of products from the data context and pass it to `View`, like this:

```
using System;
using System.Collections.Generic;
using System.Linq;
using System.Web;
using System.Web.Mvc;
using AzureBakery.Sales.CustomerWebsite.Models;

namespace AzureBakery.Sales.CustomerWebsite.Controllers
{
    public class HomeController : Controller
    {
        public ActionResult Index()
        {
            var ctx = new ApplicationDbContext();
            var products = ctx.Products.ToList();

            return View(products);
        }
}
```

2. Modify the `Home/Index.cshtml` file to have a model of type `IEnumerable<Product>` (passed from the controller) and add some Razor scaffolding to create a table of products, as shown in the following code:

```
@using AzureBakery.Sales.Model;

@model IEnumerable<Product>

@{
    ViewBag.Title = "Azure Bakery";
}

<div class="jumbotron">
    <h1>Azure Bakery</h1>
```

```
        <p class="lead">Welcome to Azure Bakery!</p>
    </div>

    <table class="table">
        <tr>
            <th>Name</th>
            <th>Price</th>
        </tr>

        @foreach (var item in Model)
        {
            <tr>
                <td>
                    @Html.DisplayFor(modelItem => item.Name)
                </td>
                <td>
                    @Html.DisplayFor(modelItem => item.Price)
                </td>
            </tr>
        }

    </table>
```

3. Before we check in our code and trigger a build, we need to change the publish settings, so go to **BUILD | Publish CustomerWebsite**:

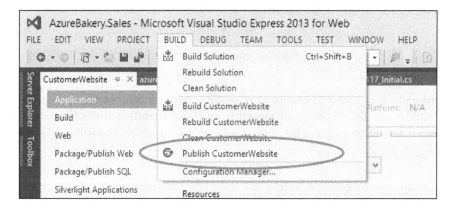

4. Next, in the **Settings** tab, check **Execute Code First Migrations (runs on application start)**:

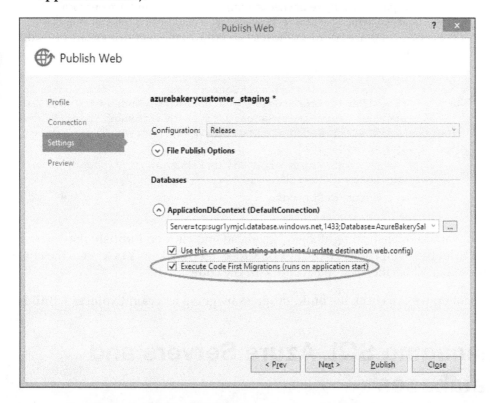

5. Leave the **Use this connection string at runtime (update destination web. config)** option checked and check whether the string is correct. To get the connection string for our Azure Database, go to the dashboard and click on the **Show connection strings** link and copy the ADO.NET string, shown as follows:

```
Server=tcp:sugr1ymjcl.database.windows.net,1433;Database=Azure
BakerySales;User ID=geoff@sugr1ymjcl;Password={your_password_
here};Trusted_Connection=False;Encrypt=True;Connection Timeout=30;
```

> You need to remember to swap the {your_password_here} bit for your password! If we unchecked this, it would try and use our local database, which isn't there; however, you could put a transform in the web.Release.config file to change the connection string there instead, shown as follows:

```
<connectionStrings>
    <add name="DefaultConnection"            connectionSt
ring="Server=tcp:sugr1ymjcl.database.windows.net,1433;D
atabase=AzureBakerySales;User ID=geoff@sugr1ymjcl;Passw
ord=XXXXX;Trusted_Connection=False;Encrypt=True;Connect
ion Timeout=30;"
        xdt:Transform="SetAttributes"
xdt:Locator="Match(name)"/>
</connectionStrings>
```

If you want to publish straight away, go ahead and click on **Publish**; however, if you want to let the build agent do it, click on **Close**, then click on **Yes** to save the changes to the pubxml file, and then select **check-in the code**.

Remember, we can check the build progress by going to **Team Explorer** | **Builds**.

Managing SQL Azure Servers and databases

Although we've just built our database using EF Code First Migrations, we still need to be able to view and sometimes modify our data and also perform activities such as adding users or creating federations.

To do this, we have a number of tools available:

- The SQL management portal
- **SQL Server Management Studio (SSMS)**
- Visual Studio SQL Server Object Explorer
- The PowerShell console

Managing a database through the portal

We're going to take a look at managing a database through the management portal:

1. In the database workspace, select the database we just created and click on **MANAGE** on the bottom toolbar:

2. We should see an alert appear, asking if we want to add our machine's public IP address to the firewall list:

3. Click on **YES** and **YES** again when it asks if you want to manage the database:

4. If nothing happens, check that the popup is not blocked.

5. We should now see a login screen for the database, so enter the SA details we noted earlier and click on **Log on**:

6. Once we're logged in, we will see the **Administration** page in the management portal.

Features of the management portal

The management portal has a number of common features for its different views:

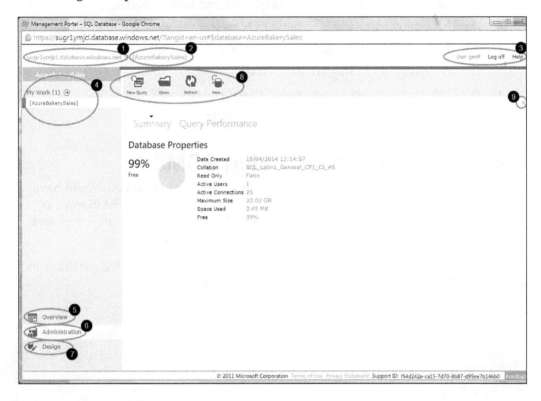

The various features of the management portal are as follows:

- **(1)**: This is the Azure SQL Server Database shortcut, which navigates to the server's summary page.
- **(2)**: This is the current database name; clicking on it navigates you to the database summary view. The top crumb trail (**1** and **2**) is hierarchal and additional nodes are added when we go down further into tables, views, and so on.

- **(3)**: This is the user menu that allows us to see the current user log off and launch the (no longer working!) help page.

- **(4)**: This shows work items such as queries and table designs.

- **(5)**: This navigates to the SQL Server **Overview** view.

- **(6)**: This navigates to the database **Administration** view.

- **(7)**: This navigates to the database **Design** view.

- **(8)**: This is where view-context-sensitive menus appear.

- **(9)**: This allows us to close the current work item.

Managing a database using SSMS

If you've worked with an SQL Server before, it's highly likely that you would have used SSMS to build databases and work with data. We can still use SSMS to work with Microsoft Azure SQL Servers, although there are a number of differences and limitations, which we shall now see.

First, we need to add our machine's IP address to the allowed IP addresses list in the server workspace's **CONFIGURE** tab, and click on **SAVE**:

Next, open SSMS, enter the SQL Azure Server name, select **SQL Server Authentication**, then enter your credentials, and click on **Connect**:

When SSMS opens, the first thing we notice in the **Object Explorer** window is that the Azure server has a different symbol, so we can easily differentiate between that and normal SQL Servers; if we expand all the folders, we can see that we have a lot less features in the Azure SQL Server:

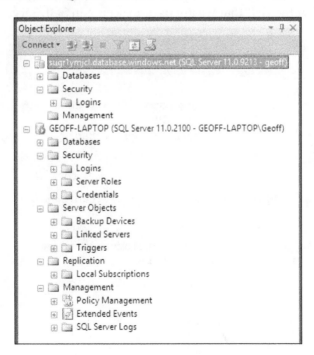

Basically, we only have **Databases** and **Security** options in Azure SQL Server; the missing features are mostly replaced with services in the Azure SQL Server platform.

Another big difference between Azure SQL Server and SQL Server in SSMS is we don't get GUIs for different operations; instead, we get template SQL scripts. If we right-click on a table, we can see the different scripting options:

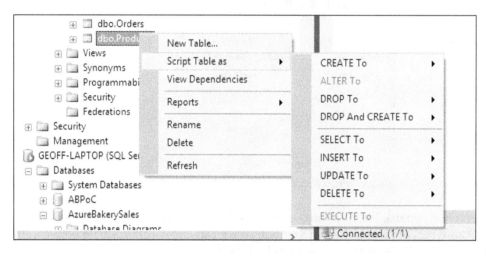

If we right-click on **Tables** and select **New Table...**, we get the following script template instead of the GUI that we are used to seeing in SQL Server Databases:

```
-- =========================================
-- Create table template SQL Azure Database
-- =========================================

IF OBJECT_ID('<schema_name, sysname, dbo>.<table_name, sysname,
    sample_table>', 'U') IS NOT NULL
    DROP TABLE <schema_name, sysname, dbo>.<table_name, sysname,
    sample_table>
GO

CREATE TABLE <schema_name, sysname, dbo>.<table_name, sysname,
    sample_table>
(
    <columns_in_primary_key, , c1> <column1_datatype, , int>
        <column1_nullability,, NOT NULL>,
```

```
    <column2_name, sysname, c2> <column2_datatype, , char(10)>
      <column2_nullability,, NULL>,
    <column3_name, sysname, c3> <column3_datatype, , datetime>
      <column3_nullability,, NULL>,
      CONSTRAINT <contraint_name, sysname, PK_sample_table> PRIMARY
        KEY (<columns_in_primary_key, , c1>)
)
GO
```

Federations are an extra thing we see in our Azure Database; the Federations folder allows us to manage federations, and if we right-click and select **New Federation**, we get a template script:

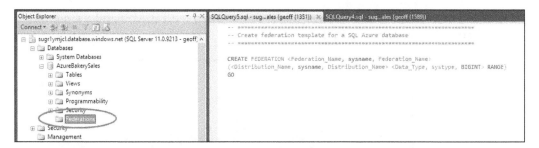

Federations allow us to scale out our databases by horizontally partitioning our database across multiple federation members.

Managing a database through Visual Studio

We can work with Azure SQL Server Databases from the SQL Server **Object Explorer** window in Visual Studio:

1. To open this, go to **VIEW | SQL Server Object Explorer**:

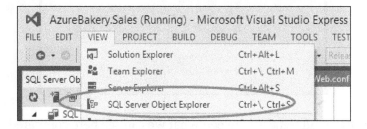

2. In the **SQL Server Object Explorer** window, click on the add button to add our Azure SQL Server:

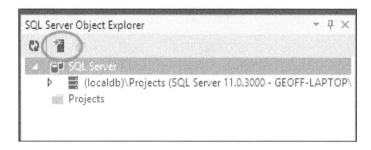

3. Fill in the connection details (this is the same as with SSMS) and we should see our server appear in the window:

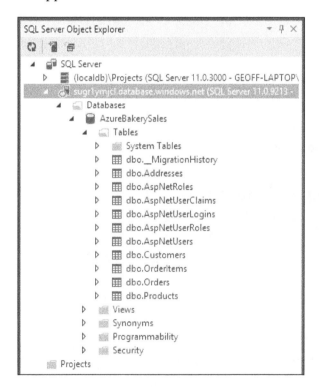

We notice we have differences between what we can see here compared to SSMS; we neither have any server security options (we do have database security options though) nor the **Federations** option. This makes sense, as we are in a software development environment, where we shouldn't be worrying about database administration.

For working with tables, we actually have a lot more flexibility over SSMS; we can use scripts and a GUI to perform actions. If we right-click on a table, we see all the different options:

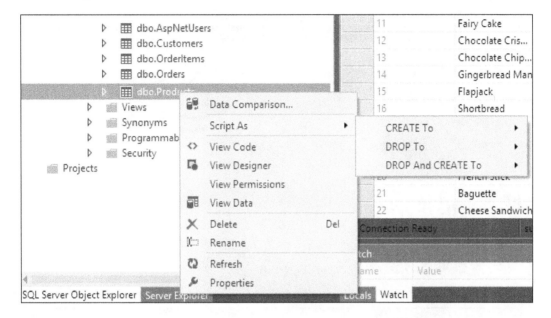

The various options available when you right-click on a table are as follows:

- **Data Comparison…**: This allows us to compare data with another database, so we could compare an Azure SQL Server Database table with an on-premises database or another Azure Database
- **Script As**: This allows us to create or drop tables using SQL script templates
- **View Code**: This shows us the SQL code for creating the table
- **View Designer**: This shows us the table in a designer
- **View Permissions**: This shows us the explicit permissions available on the table
- **View Data**: This is a nice feature, which displays a tabular view of the data

The preceding functionality is the same for SQL Server Databases and is more powerful than SSMS for working with databases.

Using the table designer

When we choose the **View Designer** option for a table, we get a nice GUI for editing a table:

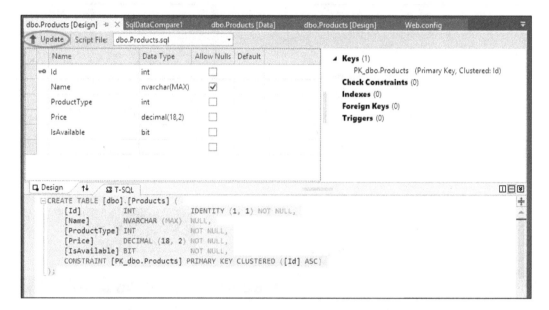

We can design the table using the **Design** grid or use **T-SQL**. We can also use the panel on the right-hand side to work with advanced table features such as **Indexes** and **Triggers**.

When we've finished designing a table, we click on the **Update** button in the top-left corner of the screen. We will be shown the changes and have the **Generate Script** (to manually perform an update or save for reference) and **Update Database** options directly:

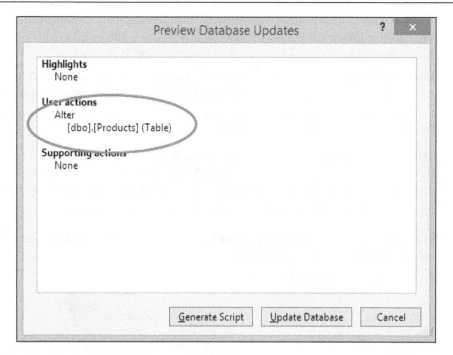

Using Azure PowerShell

To get started using PowerShell in order to manage the database, we need to perform the following steps:

1. Install the Azure PowerShell module using the Web Platform Installer from
    `http://go.microsoft.com/fwlink/p/?linkid=320376&clcid=0x409`.

2. Next, run the Azure PowerShell console (it'll be named Windows Azure PowerShell).

3. On the first run, you'll see a warning like this; enter A to trust the publisher and always run:

    ```
    Do you want to run software from this untrusted publisher?
    File C:\Program Files (x86)\Microsoft SDKs\Windows Azure\
    PowerShell\Azure\ShortcutStartup.ps1 is published by
    CN=Microsoft Corporation, OU=MOPR, O=Microsoft Corporation,
    L=Redmond, S=Washington, C=US and is not trusted on your
    system. Only run scripts from trusted publishers.
    [V] Never run  [D] Do not run  [R] Run once  [A] Always run  [?]
    Help (default is "D"):
    ```

4. Next, we need to set our Azure subscription to establish a connection. We can use the one we already downloaded or use the `get-AzurePublishSettingsFile` cmdlet to download it for us.

5. Once we have a `.publishsettings` file, we can import it with the `Import-AzurePublishSettingsFile` command and the file path argument like this:

   ```
   PS C:\> Import-AzurePublishSettingsFile C:\Users\Geoff\Downloads\
   Pay-As-You-Go-4-30-2014-credentials.publishsettings
   ```

6. This will set a default subscription; you can view other subscriptions using the `Get-AzureSubscription` command and then change it using the `Select-AzureSubscription` cmdlet (arguments are case-sensitive), like this:

   ```
   PS C:\> select-azuresubscription -current Pay-As-You-Go
   ```

7. We can now test it with a cmdlet such as `get-SqlAzureDatabaseServer`, which lists all our servers like this:

   ```
   PS C:\> get-azuresqldatabaseserver


   ServerName                               Location
   AdministratorLogin

   ----------                               --------
   ------------------
   sugrlymjcl                               North Europe
   Geoff
   ```

8. To get a full list of commands, type the following command:

   ```
   help sql.
   ```

Choosing a management tool

The Azure SQL Server management portal is a good option because it lets you do everything that is possible with Azure SQL Servers and databases; however, the GUI isn't particularly intuitive and is quite outdated compared to the rest of the portal.

If you want to do SQL Server specific management, then SSMS is a good option; conversely, if you want to do database development work, Visual Studio **SQL Server Object Explorer** is a good option.

If you're a DBA or PowerShell script-nut, you might choose to use PowerShell to do everything, but this is probably not the most accessible option for everybody!

Backing up and restoring databases

Although Microsoft Azure SQL Databases are replicated to different servers and data centers for disaster recovery, currently, they are not backed up to allow users to restore databases after accidental data loss. There are a number of ways of achieving backup and restore; we'll look at using automated exports to create backups on schedule and then restore them to a new database.

Automated exports

Automated exports allow us to back up databases to bacpac files stored in Azure blob storage (a blob storage is used to store unstructured binary and text data, you can learn more about blobs at http://msdn.microsoft.com/en-us/library/azure/ee691964.aspx) on a schedule. We can control how often backups are made and how long they are kept.

First, we need to create a storage account for the exports to be stored in. From the **NEW** service button, go to **DATA SERVICES | STORAGE | QUICK CREATE**, enter a URL, and choose the **LOCATION/AFFINITY GROUP**, **SUBSCRIPTION**, and **REPLICATION** options:

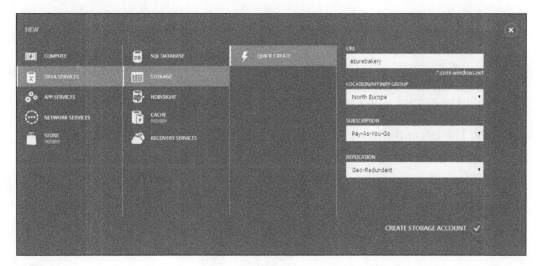

Now, we can go to the **CONFIGURE** tab for our database in the portal and configure an automated export to the new storage account:

We need to be careful with this feature as there is a cost involved in generating the temporary database copy, network usage transferring data and blob storage to hold the copy. The larger the database, the bigger the cost involved, so we need to be careful so as to not automate backups too frequently.

Backup files will appear under **CONTAINERS** in our **STORAGE** account:

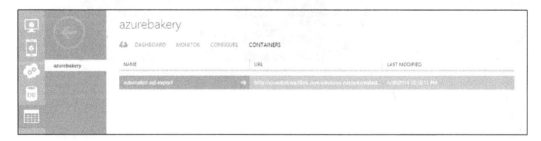

If we select the container, we can see the individual timestamped `.bacpac` files with their full URLs:

We can download these locally, edit the metadata and delete the backups from here.

If we go back to the database's **CONFIGURE** tab, we can do a database restore by clicking on the **NEW DATABASE** button in the **CREATE FROM EXPORT** section:

Next, select the BACPAC file to import, give it a name (unfortunately, you can't restore to the same database with this technique), and choose **SUBSCRIPTION**, **EDITION**, **SIZE**, and **SERVER**:

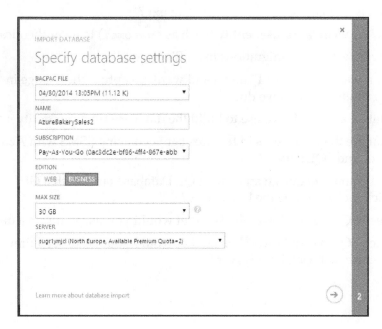

On the next tab, enter the server's login credentials to complete the import.

Summary

We've now got the foundations for our sales business domain, so we can start building our applications. The production business domain will also have a database built using EF Code First Migrations, and this will not be covered in the book, but all the code will be available in the samples.

Next, we're going to build the sales customer website. This will allow customers to make and manage orders, which will implement an OAuth authentication provider and the administrator website. This will allow administrators to manage customers and orders and will implement Azure Active Directory authentication.

Questions

1. What impact would unchecking the **ALLOW WINDOWS AZURE SERVICES TO ACCESS THE SERVER** checkbox have, when creating a database from the portal?

2. Describe the Database-First approach to creating an Entity Framework data model

3. In an EF entity, what is a `navigation` property, and which property modifier must be used?

4. What is special about `IdentityDbContext`?

5. How do we relate a user entity (such as `Customer`) to an authenticated user?

6. How do we enable migrations in an EF project?

7. When we change our EF model and want to capture the change in migrations, what do we do?

8. What EF cmdlet do we use to build the database from our entity model?

9. What are the differences in features between using SSMS with Azure SQL Server and SQL Server?

10. If we wanted to design an Azure SQL Database table with a GUI editor, which tool would be the best choice?

11. Which SQL Azure PowerShell cmdlet would you use to delete a database?

12. Which SQL Azure PowerShell cmdlet would you use to set a firewall rule on an Azure SQL Database Server?

Answers

1. We'd have to manually configure the database server firewall to allow our services to access the database.

2. With this technique, we can create our database (or use an existing database) in a tool such as SQL Management Studio using SQL scripts or the designer, then in Visual Studio, we can create an ADO.NET EDM to create entities and map them to existing tables.

3. The `Navigation` properties allow us to access related entities through a given entity. We use the virtual modifier on `navigation` properties.

4. It extends a normal `DbContext` with access to the ASP.NET authentication users and roles tables.

5. Add a `navigation` property to our user entity in the `ApplicationUser` entity.

6. Enter the `enable-migrations` cmdlet in the NuGet package manager console.

7. Use the `add-migration` command with a label to indicate the model change, which will create a new migration with the differences from the previous migration.

8. `update-database`.

9. Azure SQL Server only has **Database** and **Security** options, which are a limited subset of SQL Server's options. There is no GUI for Azure SQL Server operations, which can be implemented with template scripts instead. Azure SQL Server has the option to create federations for scaling out a database.

10. Visual Studio table designer (available from the SQL Server **Object Explorer** window), which provides us with a powerful GUI for editing tables and creating table scripts.

11. `Remove-AzureSqlDatabase`.

12. `Set-AzureSqlDatabaseServerFirewallRule`.

5
Building Azure MVC Websites

In this chapter, we're going to build up the customer and administrator websites for the sales business domain, which will share the data model we created in the previous chapter. We'll cover the following topics:

- Implementing Twitter authentication in the customer website
- Completing the customer sales website
- Adding a custom domain name to a website
- Implementing an SSL certificate
- Adding Azure AD single sign-on to a website
- Implementing Azure AD group authorization
- Completing the admin sales website

We're going to look at subjects specific to Azure and touch on relevant parts of website development. We will not go into great detail about how to write MVC applications; however, the code samples have fully working websites to take away.

Implementing OAuth authentication

The customer sales website is required to implement OAuth authentication where users can use their existing accounts with well-known authentication providers such as Microsoft, Twitter, Facebook, and Google. There is a good overview of OAuth at http://en.wikipedia.org/wiki/OAuth. All the providers are very similar to use; you need to create an app in the respective developer portal, which will give you an ID and a secret key.

The following are links of the developer portals for some popular authentication providers:

- `http://msdn.microsoft.com/en-us/live`

- `https://dev.twitter.com/`

- `https://developers.facebook.com/`

- `https://console.developers.google.com`

Creating a Twitter application

Now, we will look at implementing Twitter authentication with the following procedure:

1. Go to `https://dev.twitter.com/` and click on **Sign in** at the top-right corner of the screen.

2. Once signed in, select **My applications** from the dropdown in the top-right corner:

3. Click on the **Create New App** button.

4. Fill in the **Name**, **Description**, **Website**, and **Callback URL** fields (you can use the URL of your website although it can be changed):

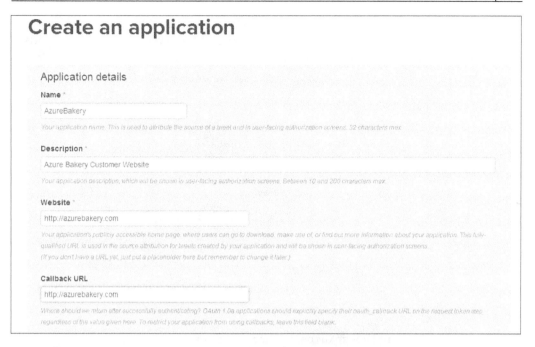

5. Agree to the **Developer Rules of the Road** option and click on **Create your Twitter application**.

6. Go to the **API Keys** tab and notice the **API Key** and **API Secret** (leave the web page open and we can copy these into our code) values.

Modifying the external login

We need to modify the external login code to use our Twitter application and collect the extra customer address details needed for our data model. We'll do this in the following procedure:

1. In our web project, open `App_Start/Startup.Auth.cs`, uncomment the `app.UseTwitterAuthentication` block, and fill in the keys like this:

```
app.UseTwitterAuthentication(
            consumerKey: "XXXXxxxx",
            consumerSecret: "ZZZZZZZZZZZZZzzzzzzzzzzzzzzzzzz
            zz");
```

2. Next, we need to modify the `ExternalLoginConfirmationViewModel` (inside the `Models/AccountViewModels.cs` file) to retrieve our extra fields for the customer entity like this:

```
public class ExternalLoginConfirmationViewModel
{
    [Required]
    [Display(Name = "User name")]
    public string UserName { get; set; }

    [Required]
    [Display(Name = "First Name")]
    public string FirstName { get; set; }

    [Required]
    [Display(Name = "Last Name")]
    public string LastName { get; set; }

    [Required]
    [Display(Name = "HouseNumber")]
    public int HouseNumber { get; set; }

    [Required]
    [Display(Name = "Street")]
    public string Street { get; set; }

    [Required]
    [Display(Name = "City")]
    public string City { get; set; }

    [Required]
    [Display(Name = "PostCode")]
    public string PostCode { get; set; }
}
```

3. Now, we will modify the `ExtrenalLoginConfirmation.cshtml` view to include new fields. Add the following scaffolding code after the `UserName` scaffolding code:

```
<!-- Customer -->
@Html.LabelFor(m => m.FirstName, new { @class = "col-md-2
  control-label" })
<div class="col-md-10">
    @Html.TextBoxFor(m => m.FirstName, new { @class =
      "form-control" })
    @Html.ValidationMessageFor(m => m.FirstName)
```

```
    </div>
    @Html.LabelFor(m => m.LastName, new { @class = "col-md-2
      control-label" })
    <div class="col-md-10">
        @Html.TextBoxFor(m => m.LastName, new { @class =
          "form-control" })
        @Html.ValidationMessageFor(m => m.LastName)
    </div>

    <!-- Address -->
    @Html.LabelFor(m => m.HouseNumber, new { @class = "col-md-2
      control-label" })
    <div class="col-md-10">
        @Html.TextBoxFor(m => m.HouseNumber, new { @class =
          "form-control" })
        @Html.ValidationMessageFor(m => m.HouseNumber)
    </div>
    @Html.LabelFor(m => m.Street, new { @class = "col-md-2
      control-label" })
    <div class="col-md-10">
        @Html.TextBoxFor(m => m.Street, new { @class =
          "form-control" })
        @Html.ValidationMessageFor(m => m.Street)
    </div>
    @Html.LabelFor(m => m.City, new { @class = "col-md-2
      control-label" })
        <div class="col-md-10">
    @Html.TextBoxFor(m => m.City, new { @class =
      "form-control" })
    @Html.ValidationMessageFor(m => m.City)
    </div>
    @Html.LabelFor(m => m.PostCode, new { @class = "col-md-2
      control-label" })
    <div class="col-md-10">
        @Html.TextBoxFor(m => m.PostCode, new { @class =
          "form-control" })
        @Html.ValidationMessageFor(m => m.PostCode)
    </div>
```

4. Next, we need to modify the `ExternalLoginConfirmation` action in `AccountController`. The following line of code creates a user:

```
var user = new ApplicationUser() { UserName =
  model.UserName };
```

Replace this with the following code, which creates our new user with the `Person` and `Address` entities associated (you'll need to add a `using` statement for the `Model` project):

```
var user = new ApplicationUser()
{
    UserName = model.UserName,
    Customer = new Customer()
    {
        FirstName = model.FirstName,
        LastName = model.LastName,
        Address = new Address()
        {
            HouseNumber = model.HouseNumber ,
            Street = model.Street,
            City = model.City,
            PostCode = model.PostCode
        }
    }
};
```

Testing the Twitter login

We're ready to test the Twitter authentication login now, so run the website locally and follow this login procedure:

1. Click on the **Log in** link in the top-right corner.

2. On the login page, click on the **Twitter** button:

3. We'll now be redirected to the Twitter authorization page, where you can log in with your Twitter account and authorize the app to use your credentials:

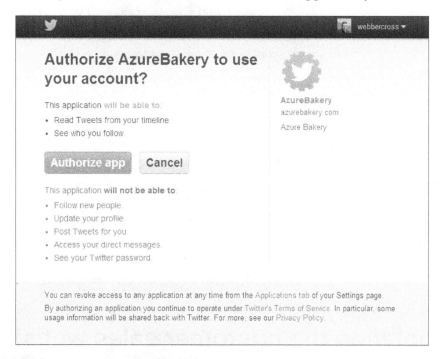

4. We should now be redirected back to our website and see our **Register** page. Fill in some details and click on **Register**:

5. We should now see the home page with a welcome message at the top.

If we go and look at our database now (use SSMS or Visual Studio **SQL Server Object Explorer**), we can see that we have related entries in dbo.AspNetUsers, dbo.AspNetUserLogins, dbo.Customers, and dbo.Addresses. I've used a SQL query to display all the data at once, as shown in the following screenshot:

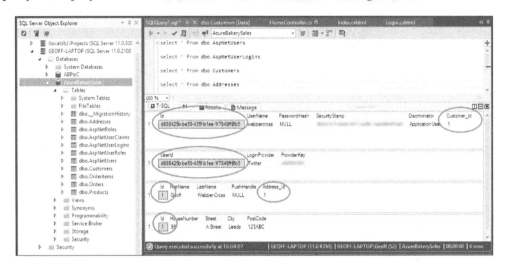

Completing the customer sales website

We've got all the tricky bits done, so we need to sit down and finish writing our website. We're not learning MVC in this book and unfortunately, there isn't space to go through everything in detail, so we'll look at a few bits, and you can get the finished website in the code samples. I've simplified the website, so we can quickly get a working user interface, where we can view products and create orders; I've not implemented any **dependency injection (DI)**, **inversion-of-control (IoC)**, repository, or **unit of work (UoW)** patterns, so as to not distract from the subject in hand too much, but I would strongly advise you to use these techniques in your own applications.

Modifying the user account panel

In this website, we're only using Twitter authentication, so we can remove the **Register** link and add links to **Orders** and **Basket**, which show the current order. To modify the user account panel, complete the following steps:

1. Add a new class called BasketHelper with a method to return the customer's basket count:

    ```
    using System.Linq;
    using System.Data.Entity;
    ```

```
using AzureBakery.Sales.CustomerWebsite.Models;
using AzureBakery.Sales.Model;

namespace AzureBakery.Sales.CustomerWebsite.Helpers
{
    public class BasketHelper
    {
        public static int GetCount(string uid)
        {
            var ctx = new ApplicationDbContext();

            // Find customer
            var customer = ctx.Users
                .Include(u => u.Customer)
                .Single(u => u.Id == uid).Customer;

            // Count order items
            var items = ctx.OrderItems
                .Include(oi => oi.Order.Customer)
                .Where(oi => oi.Order.Customer.Id ==
                    customer.Id && oi.Order.Status ==
                        OrderStatus.Open);

            int count = items.Count() > 0 ? items.Sum(oi =>
              oi.Quantity) : 0;

            return count;
        }
    }
}
```

2. Now, modify the `_LoginPartial.cshtml` view to implement these changes:

```
@using Microsoft.AspNet.Identity;
@using AzureBakery.Sales.CustomerWebsite.Helpers;
@if (Request.IsAuthenticated)
{
    using (Html.BeginForm("LogOff", "Account",
      FormMethod.Post, new { id = "logoutForm", @class =
        "navbar-right" }))
    {
    @Html.AntiForgeryToken()

    <ul class="nav navbar-nav navbar-right">
        <li>
```

```
            @Html.ActionLink("Hello " +
              User.Identity.GetUserName() + "!", "Manage",
                "Account", routeValues: null,
                  htmlAttributes: new { title = "Manage" })
        </li>

        @*Orders Action Link*@
        <li>
            @Html.ActionLink("Orders", "Index", "Order")
        </li>

        @*Basket Action Link*@
        <li>
            @Html.ActionLink("Basket (" +
              BasketHelper.GetCount(User.Identity.GetUserId()) +
              ")",
                "Basket", "Order")
        </li>

        <li><a
          href="javascript:document.getElementById('logoutForm').
          submit()">Log off</a></li>
    </ul>
    }
}
else
{
    <ul class="nav navbar-nav navbar-right">
        <li>@Html.ActionLink("Log in", "Login", "Account",
          routeValues: null, htmlAttributes: new { id =
          "loginLink" })</li>
    </ul>
}
```

Temporary PayConfirm action

The order controller has a number of actions for the ordering process and the final
one is the PayConfirm action:

```
public ActionResult PayConfirm()
{
    var order = this.GetOpenOrder();

    // At this point we would need to take a card payment or setup
      an invoice
```

```
    // But this isn't real so we'll order the item!

    // Update status
    order.Status = OrderStatus.New;
    this._ctx.SaveChanges();

    // Todo: Send to messaging middleware

    return View();
}
```

The comments say that this is the point where we would handle the payment; however, as this is a mock website, we will not do this. When we start looking at implementing Service Bus messaging, we'll revisit this action to send an order message, which will be picked up by the production systems to continue the order process.

Final activities

As mentioned before, there's no space in the book to cover all the steps needed to finish the sales customer website; therefore, I've listed the remaining activities here. You can see the full website in the code samples:

- Change application's name
- Remove temporary code for listing products from the Home Index.cshtml view
- Remove the local account option from the Login.cshtml view
- Add ProductController.cs and OrderController.cs controllers
- Add the ProductsViewModel.cs view models
- Add the OrdersViewModel.cs and OrderViewModel.cs view models
- Add the BasketViewModel.cs and OrderItemViewModel.cs view models
- Add links on the home page for each product type
- Create the product Index.cshtml view
- Create the order Index.cshtml, Basket.cshtml, Pay.cshtml, and PayConfirm.cshtml views
- Remove local login from the Manage.cshtml view

Adding a custom domain name to a website

It's highly likely that you will want a custom domain name of your own to use for customer websites rather than using the default `mywebsite.azurewebsites.net` subdomain. If you want to do this, buy a custom domain and make sure you give yourself plenty of time before you need it live (a few days) for the domain host DNS records to update.

We're going to add a custom domain to our sales customer website with the following procedure:

1. First, we'll swop the staging website to the production website by clicking on the **SWOP** button on the bottom toolbar.

2. In the **CONFIGURE** tab of the production website, click on **manage domains**:

3. We need to use the information from the **Manage custom domains** dialog to configure our domain host:

    We need the IP address to configure the DNS A records and the subdomain name for the CNAME records.

4. In your domain host control panel (this is not in the Azure portal), edit the DNS A records to point to this IP address, and add two CNAME records to point to our Azure subdomain:

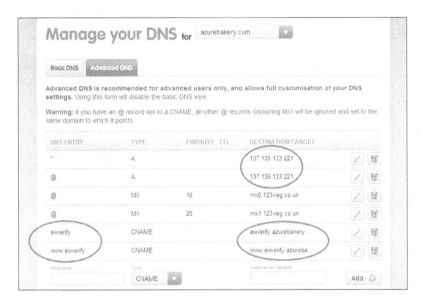

To be extra clear, here are the changes in a table:

DNS ENTRY	TYPE	DESTINATION TARGET	Note
*	A	137.135.133.221	This is the updated destination target of the Azure IP address
@	A	137.135.133.221	This is the updated destination target of the Azure IP address
@	MX	mx0.123-reg.co.uk	No change
@	MX	mx1.123-reg.co.uk	No change
awverify	CNAME	awverify. azurebakerycustomer. azurewebsites.net	We added a CNAME record, and awverify points to our Azure subdomain
www. awverify	CNAME	www. awverify. azurebakerycustomer. azurewebsites.net	We added a CNAME record, and www. awverify points to our www Azure subdomain

5. Once you've done this, you will need to leave it for the DNS records to become active; my provider suggests 24 to 48 hours.

6. You can test it any time by typing your custom domain name into the **Manage custom domains** dialog. If the DNS records are not ready, you will get a warning like this:

7. Once the DNS records are ready, you should see a green tick like this:

8. Now, if you type your custom domain name into the browser, you should see your Azure website!

Implementing an SSL certificate

HTTP web traffic sent between the server and browser is sent unencrypted *in the clear text*, which is a security risk since a third party can potentially hijack the traffic and read the data, which may contain sensitive information such as names, addresses, and bank details.

When we implement a **Secure Socket Layer** (**SSL**) certificate and use an **HTTP Secure** (**HTTPS**) endpoint, the traffic is encrypted, making it difficult to steal by a third party (although not impossible—look up the man-in-the-middle attack and brute force attack; the former is associated with hackers and the latter with government agencies that have super computers!).

Using HTTPS has a performance impact as every connection made has an initial handshake between the browser and server to set up the encryption (using an SSL certificate) before data is sent, so it's important to decide where to use it.

Azure websites have SSL endpoints by default, provided by the `.azurewebsites.net` wildcard SSL certificate, which covers all the subdomains, so if you are not implementing a custom domain, you can simply type `https://` at the start of your Azure domain. The sales administrator website does not have a custom domain and uses this.

Purchase an SSL certificate (I bought mine from the same place as the custom domain name). Follow their procedure to make a **Certificate Signing Request** (**CSR**); you can either use their tool (I did this) or use IIS. The tool I used generated the `.pem`, `.key`, and `.password` files; then, I received an approval e-mail from GlobalSign, which I accepted, and later received an e-mail that contained an intermediary certificate and an SSL certificate, which you need to copy and paste into a text editor such as Notepad and save as `.crt` files. Note that you need to include the `-----BEGIN CERTIFICATE-----` and `-----END CERTIFICATE-----` text. Once you have all these files, copy them to the same directory and you should have something like this:

▷ Local Disk (C:) ▷ SSL			
Name ▵	Date modified	Type	Size
azurebakery.com.crt	12/05/2014 19:01	Security Certificate	2 KB
azurebakery.com_csr.pem	05/05/2014 18:57	PEM File	1 KB
gs_intermediate_ca.crt	12/05/2014 19:00	Security Certificate	2 KB
private-key.key	05/05/2014 18:57	KEY File	2 KB
private-key.password	05/05/2014 18:57	PASSWORD File	1 KB
README	05/05/2014 18:57	File	2 KB

Creating CER files

Next, we need to export the .crt files to the .cer files. You need to do this for both .crt files:

1. In Windows Explorer, double-click on the file and click on the **Details** tab, and then click on the **Copy to File...** button:

2. Click on **Next**, select **Base-64 encode X.509 (.CER)**, and click on **Next** again:

3. In the next dialog, enter the name (the same name as that of the `.crt` file makes sense—I chose `azurebakery.com`), and click on **Next** and then on **Finish** to complete.

4. We should now have a set of files including the new `.cer` files, as shown in the following screenshot:

Using OpenSSL to create a PFX certificate

We need to use OpenSSL.exe to create a .pfx certificate from our .cer files to load data into the website's workspace in the portal:

1. Download and install the prerequisites of the OpenSSL VC++ 2008 Redistributables from the following links:

   ○ **32 bit**: http://www.microsoft.com/en-us/download/ confirmation.aspx?id=29

   ○ **64 bit**: http://www.microsoft.com/en-us/download/ confirmation.aspx?id=15336

2. Download and install the OpenSSL installer from http://slproweb.com/ products/Win32OpenSSL.html. The 32-bit and 64-bit links will look like this but the versions may change:

   ○ **32-bit full**: http://slproweb.com/download/Win32OpenSSL-1_0_1i.exe

   ○ **64-bit full**: http://slproweb.com/download/Win64OpenSSL-1_0_1i.exe

3. Open a command prompt as administrator and navigate to the c:\OpenSSL\ Win64\bin directory (or 32-bit equivalent) and type the following command to set the OPENSSL_CONF environmental variable (otherwise, we'll get errors):

   ```
   set OPENSSL_CONF=c:\OpenSSL-Win64\bin\openssl.cfg
   ```

4. Now, enter the following command to generate our .pfx file:

   ```
   openssl pkcs12 -export -out c:\ssl\azurebakery.com.pfx
   -inkey c:\ssl\private-key.key -in c:\ssl\AzureBakery.com.cer
   -certfile c:\ssl\gs_intermediate_ca.cer
   ```

5. Enter the pass phrase when prompted, then password (and the confirmation for the .pfx file):

Uploading the certificate

We should now have our .pfx file ready to assign to the website:

1. Go to the **CONFIGURE** tab of the website workspace in the portal and click on **upload a certificate**:

2. Select the .pfx file we just created, enter the **PASSWORD**, and click on the tick button:

3. Now, associate the custom domain with the uploaded certificate under the **ssl bindings** section:

4. Click on **SAVE** on the toolbar to apply the changes.

5. You may see a warning about the pricing impact for SSL bindings; however, since April 2014, you should get one free SSL certificate allowance.

6. Now, when we open our website with `https://azurebakery.com`, we can see the page load without any warnings, and our data is encrypted between the browser and web server.

Redirecting all HTTP traffic to HTTPS

Now that we have an SSL certificate implemented, we want to make sure that the HTTP endpoints are not available for some controllers, actions, or the entire website.

To force a controller or action to use HTTPS, we can use the `RequireHttps` attribute like this:

```
[RequireHttps]
public class HomeController : Controller
{
    public ActionResult Index()
    {
        return View();
    }
}
```

To redirect HTTP traffic to HTTPS endpoints for the whole website (I've done this in the customer website), we can put a rewrite rule transform in our `web.Release.config` file, which will run on publish:

```
<system.webServer xdt:Transform="Replace">
    <modules>
      <remove name="FormsAuthenticationModule" />
    </modules>
    <!-- Add redirect rule to redirect all HTTP requests to HTTPS
      -->
    <rewrite>
      <rules>
        <clear />
        <rule name="HTTP to HTTPS redirect" stopProcessing="true">
          <match url="(.*)" />
          <conditions>
            <add input="{HTTPS}" pattern="off" ignoreCase="true"
            />
          </conditions>
          <action type="Redirect" redirectType="Found"
            url="https://{HTTP_HOST}/{R:1}" />
```

```
            </rule>
        </rules>
    </rewrite>
    </system.webServer>
```

This replaces the whole `system.webServer` block, so be careful to include everything from the base `Web.config` file.

Adding Azure AD single sign-on to a website

Our sales administrator website requires Azure AD authentication so that users for the whole company can be centrally managed. In this section, we're going to create an Azure AD for the company, then add a user and configure a new administrator website to implement Azure AD single sign-on

Configuring AD

First, we need to create an AD and an initial user account to sign in with. To do this, perform the following steps:

1. From the **NEW** services menu, go to **ACTIVE DIRECTORY | DIRECTORY | CUSTOM CREATE**:

2. Fill out the **NAME** of the directory, its **DOMAIN NAME**, and the **COUNTRY OR REGION**.

3. Now, from the AD **USERS** workspace, click on **ADD USER** from the bottom toolbar to add a user:

4. Fill in the **USER NAME** field. I've left **TYPE OF USER** as **New user in your organization**, although you can add an existing Microsoft account or Windows Azure AD.

5. Next, fill in the user details, select **Global Administrator** for the **ROLE** field, and click on the next arrow.

6. Click on **create** on the next tab to get the temporary password for the user. Make a note of it and also enter an e-mail ID to send it to, and then click on the tick button to finish.

Configuring an MVC website for AD single sign-on

Next, we'll create a new MVC website and use the wizard to help us set up AD single sign-on. In Visual Studio 2012, this was quite tricky to do with a fair amount of manual configuration in the portal and the website's Web.config, but it's quite straightforward in Visual Studio 2013:

1. In Visual Studio, add a new ASP.NET web application. From the template dialog, select the **MVC** template, check **Create remote resources** under the **Windows Azure** section, and then click on **Change Authentication**:

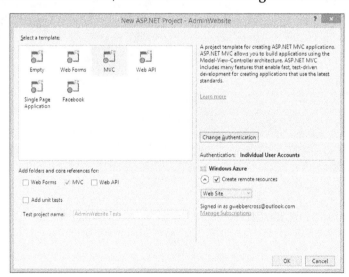

2. Select **Organizational Accounts** and enter the AD domain name for the AD we just created, and click on **OK**:

3. Sign in using the new AD user, and then click on **OK** in the previous dialog (be careful to change the user to your Azure portal account when prompted to sign into Azure).

4. Enter **Site name**, and choose **Subscription**, **Region**, and **Database Server** (select **No database** because we're using the existing one).

5. Click on **OK**; this will now provision the website, set up an AD application, and create our MVC project for us.

6. We can test this locally by simply running the website from Visual Studio. You will get a security warning due to the implementation of a temporary SSL certificate on your local web server.

7. Accept the warning (**Continue to this website (not recommended)**), and you will then see the AD **Sign in** page:

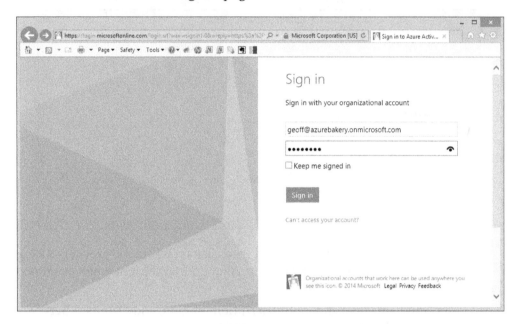

8. Log in with your new user, and the website should load.

Publishing the website with AD single sign-on

When Visual Studio provisioned our website for us, it created an application entry in the AD **APPLICATIONS** tab for our local debug configuration:

Rather than changing the **APPLICATION CONFIGURATION** settings for our production website, when we publish the application, there is an option, **Enable Organizational Authentication**, which will add a new application entry in AD and rewrite the `federation` section of the `Web.config` file for us on publish:

```
<system.identityModel.services>
    <federationConfiguration>
      <cookieHandler requireSsl="true" />
      <wsFederation passiveRedirectEnabled="true"
        issuer="https://login.windows.net/azurebakery.onmicrosoft.com/
        wsfed"
         realm="https://azurebakery.onmicrosoft.com/AdminWebsite"
         requireHttps="true" />
    </federationConfiguration>
  </system.identityModel.services>
```

In the **Publish Web** dialog, check **Enable Organizational Authentication** and enter the AD **Domain** name. You will need to include a connection string for your database as the website will update the database with entries in the new `IssuingAuthorityKeys` and `Tenants` tables:

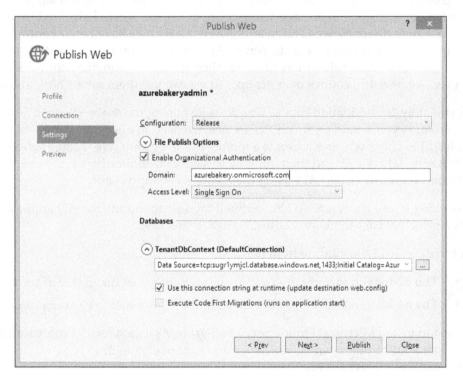

Once the application is published, we will see a new entry in the AD
APPLICATIONS workspace:

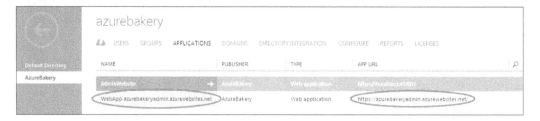

This is great as we don't need to reconfigure the applications between running locally
in the Debug configuration and publishing to Azure in the Release configuration.

Implementing Azure AD group authorization

We talked about implementing AD single sign-on authentication to our sales
administrator website, but because we're going to use the Azure Bakery AD across
all the business domains, we need to add groups so that we have better control over
users in the different business units. Azure AD doesn't currently allow addition
of new roles or custom roles; there are a number of built-in administrator roles;
however, we have full control over groups, so we can use them for authorization.

Unfortunately, authorization isn't as simple as just using the Authorize attribute
with a role, as you would with ASP.NET roles; we need to query the Azure AD
Graph API to check whether a user is a member of the group. We'll add a sales group
to the Azure Bakery AD, and then implement a custom AuthorizeAttribute to
query the Azure AD Graph API using the Azure AD Graph client.

We're going to use the Azure AD PowerShell module to modify the AD application
service principal later in the procedure, so install this first.

You can download the module from here:

- **The 32-bit version**: http://go.microsoft.com/fwlink/p/?linkid=236298
- **The 64-bit version**: http://go.microsoft.com/fwlink/p/?linkid=236297

I needed to install Microsoft Online Services Sign-In Assistant for IT Professionals
BETA (not RTW) from http://www.microsoft.com/en-us/download/
confirmation.aspx?id=39267.

Creating an AD group

We'll create an AD group for the sales business domain and add our new user to it now:

1. First, go to the AD **GROUP** workspace in the portal for our AD and click on **ADD GROUP** in the toolbar:

2. Enter **NAME** and **DESCRIPTION** of the group and click on the tick button to create it.

3. Next, click on the newly created group and then click on **ADD MEMBERS** on the toolbar:

4. In the **Add members** dialog, click on the AD user we created to add it to the **SELECTED** list, and click on the tick button to confirm:

5. Now, go to the **GROUP CONFIGURE** tab and make a note of **OBJECT ID**, as we'll need this later.

6. Now, we need to create a key for our application that will allow us to access the Graph API, so create a new key in the **APPLICATION** workspace's **CONFIGURE** tab:

7. Make a note of this and the **CLIENT ID**.

8. We need to create keys for the local and Azure AD applications.

Modifying the application service principal

We need to modify our application's service principal so that it has the permission to access the Graph API; in theory, this should be done by adjusting the permissions in the **other applications** section of the **APPLICATION CONFIGURATION** tab, but at the time of writing this, it doesn't work. Please try it yourself, and if it doesn't work for you (you will get an unauthorized exception in the AD Graph API client), use the following procedure to manually add the service principal to an administrator role:

1. Launch the Azure AD PowerShell console (from the desktop shortcut, if you choose to use it).

2. First, we need to obtain our AD credentials, so type the following command and enter your AD user credentials when prompted:

   ```
   $msolcred = get-credential
   ```

   This stores the credentials in a variable called $msolcred.

3. Next, we need to connect to the console by typing the following command:

   ```
   connect-msolservice -credential $msolcred
   ```

   For a quick test, we can use the get-msoluser command to list the AD users. We should see something like this:

   ```
   PS C:\WINDOWS\system32> get-msoluser

   UserPrincipalName          DisplayName              isLicensed
   -----------------          -----------              ----------
   ```

| gwebbercross_outlook.co... | Geoff Webber-Cross | False |
| geoff@azurebakery.onmic... | Geoff | False |

4. Now, we need to get the service principal for our application using the following command:

```
$msolServicePrincipal = Get-MsolServicePrincipal -AppPrincipalId
YourClientId
```

You can get **CLIENT ID** from the **CONFIGURE** tab of the AD **APPLICATION** workspace for the application associated with the website:

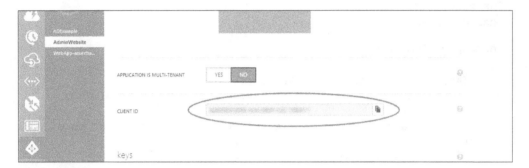

5. We can see the properties of the service principal object by outputting it like this:

```
write-output $msolServicePrincipal
```

6. Next, we need to add the service principal to an administrator role like this:

```
Add-MsolRoleMember -RoleName "Company Administrator"
   -RoleMemberObjectId $msolServicePrincipal.ObjectId
      -RoleMemberType ServicePrincipal
```

Implementing AzureAdAuthorizeAttribute

We're going to create a class called AzureAdAuthorizeAttribute, which can be added to a controller with either a group name or the group ObjectId specified. The ObjectId implementation is more efficient as it doesn't require an additional query to look up the ID from the name.

We need to install the Microsoft.Azure.ActiveDirectory.GraphClient and Microsoft.IdentityModel.Clients.ActiveDirectory NuGet packages by entering the following commands:

```
Install-Package Microsoft.Azure.ActiveDirectory.GraphClient
Install-Package Microsoft.IdentityModel.Clients.ActiveDirectory
```

The following is the complete code for the attribute; the comments in the code explain what's going on:

```
using Microsoft.Azure.ActiveDirectory.GraphClient;
using Microsoft.IdentityModel.Clients.ActiveDirectory;
using System;
using System.Collections.Generic;
using System.Configuration;
using System.Linq;
using System.Security.Claims;
using System.Web;
using System.Web.Mvc;

namespace AdminWebsite.Auth
{
    [AttributeUsageAttribute(AttributeTargets.Class |
      AttributeTargets.Method, Inherited = true, AllowMultiple =
        true)]
    public class AzureAdAuthorizeAttribute : AuthorizeAttribute
    {
        private readonly string _clientId = null;
        private readonly string _appKey = null;
        private readonly string _graphResourceID =
          "https://graph.windows.net";

        public string AdGroup { get; set; }
        public string AdGroupObjectId { get; set; }

        public AzureAdAuthorizeAttribute()
        {
            this._clientId =
              ConfigurationManager.AppSettings["ida:ClientID"];
            this._appKey =
              ConfigurationManager.AppSettings["ida:Password"];
        }

        protected override bool AuthorizeCore(HttpContextBase
          httpContext)
        {
            // First check if user is authenticated
            if (!ClaimsPrincipal.Current.Identity.IsAuthenticated)
                return false;
            else if (this.AdGroup == null && this.AdGroupObjectId
              == null) // If there are no groups return here
                return base.AuthorizeCore(httpContext);
```

```
// Now check if user is in group by querying Azure AD
Graph API using client
bool inGroup = false;

try
{
    // Get information from user claim
    string signedInUserId =
      ClaimsPrincipal.Current.FindFirst(ClaimTypes.
        NameIdentifier).Value;
    string tenantId =
      ClaimsPrincipal.Current.FindFirst("http://schemas.
        microsoft.com/id
     entity/claims/tenantid").Value;
    string userObjectId =
      ClaimsPrincipal.Current.FindFirst("http://schemas.
        microsoft.com/id
        entity/claims/objectidentifier").Value;


    // Get AuthenticationResult for access token
    var clientCred = new ClientCredential(_clientId, _
      appKey);
    var authContext = new
     AuthenticationContext(string.Format
     ("https://login.windows.net/{0}", tenantId));
    var authResult =
    authContext.AcquireToken(_graphResourceID,
      clientCred);

    // Create graph connection with our access token
    and API version
    var currentCallContext = new
    CallContext(authResult.AccessToken,
     Guid.NewGuid(), "2013-11-08");
    var graphConnection = new
    GraphConnection(currentCallContext);

    // If we don't have a group id, we can query the
    graph API to find it
    if (this.AdGroupObjectId == null)
    {
        // Get all groups
        var groups = graphConnection.List<Group>(null,
          null);

        if (groups != null && groups.Results != null)
        {
```

```
            // Find group object
            var group =
             groups.Results.SingleOrDefault(r =>
                (r as Group).DisplayName == this.AdGroup);

            // check if user is in group
            if (group != null)
                this.AdGroupObjectId = group.ObjectId;
        }
    }

    if (this.AdGroupObjectId != null)
        inGroup =
            graphConnection.IsMemberOf(this.
                AdGroupObjectId, userObjectId);
}
catch(Exception ex)
{
    string message = string.Format("Unable to
     authorize AD user: {0} against group: {1}",
      ClaimsPrincipal.Current.Identity.Name, this.
        AdGroup);

    throw new Exception(message, ex);
}

return inGroup;
        }
    }
}
```

Once we've created this class, we need to add the `ida:ClientID` and `ida:Password` settings to the `Web.config` file like this:

```
<appSettings>
  <add key="ida:ClientID" value="d30553b1-21f3-4ee5-bda5-
    63cf9b2d9861" />
  <add key="ida:Password" value="60VVjSMWB5IHNtfIBym9eIv7XXXXXXXXXX
    XXXXXXXXXXXXXX=" />
</appSettings>
```

Once we've done this, we can simply add the attribute to our controllers to implement the Azure AD group authorization like this:

```
namespace AdminWebsite.Controllers
{
    [AzureAdAuthorize(AdGroup = "Sales", AdGroupObjectId = "f8a96bf1-
      c152-41a8-9878-200db968ca95")]
    public class HomeController : Controller
    {
        public ActionResult Index()
        {
            return View();
        }
```

This code will automatically switch the Web.config settings for the Azure web application; we can simply add the following transform to web.Release.config, which will be run during publishing:

```
<appSettings>
    <add key="ida:ClientID" value="123456-58a2-4549-95fc-
      AABBCCDDee"
      xdt:Transform="SetAttributes" xdt:Locator="Match(key)" />
    <add key="ida:Password"
     value="dXqblNwqly//
       qOsgI3mD69KfxIFNfXXXXXXXXXXXXXXXXXXXXXXXXXXXXXXXXX="
      xdt:Transform="SetAttributes" xdt:Locator="Match(key)" />
    </appSettings>
  <system.web>
```

Completing the admin sales website

The administrator website isn't getting as much attention as the customer website as we don't need it to drive the case study. I'm going to use the Visual Studio scaffold view and controllers for each entity in our data model to save time, using the following procedure for each entity:

1. Add a reference to our Model project as we did for the customer website.

2. Right-click on the Controllers folder and go to **Add** | **Controller**.

3. Select **MVC 5 Controller with views, using Entity Framework** from the options and click on **Add**:

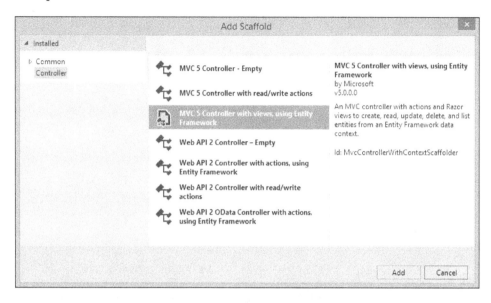

4. Enter **Controller name** and select the related entity from the **Model class** list:

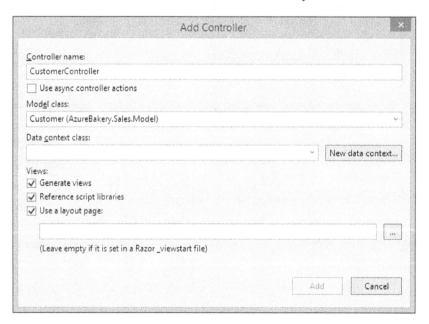

5. For the first one, I'm going to click on **New data context....** I'm not going to modify the `TenantDbContext` class as it's unrelated to our sales data model (I changed the name from the default to `AdminWebsite.Models.SalesContext`).

6. Next, click on **Add**, and Visual Studio will build a controller for you with a full set of views for performing basic CRUD operations.

7. Do the same for the other entities and use the data context class we just created.

8. In the `Web.config` file, I deleted the new `SalesContext` database connection string that was created:

```
<add name="SalesContext" connectionString="Data
    Source=(localdb)\v11.0;
    Initial Catalog=SalesContext-20140514071433;
    Integrated Security=True;
    MultipleActiveResultSets=True;
    AttachDbFilename=|DataDirectory|SalesContext-20140514071433.mdf"
        providerName="System.Data.SqlClient" />
```

9. Then, change the `SalesContext` constructor to use the `DefaultContext` connection string like this:

```
public SalesContext()
            : base("name=DefaultConnection")
        {
        }
```

I'm not putting links on the home page; we can manually type the controller name into the browser to see the different views.

Summary

We've now done most of the work on our sales websites in order to get them working functionally, with data access and security implemented locally and on Azure. To make the websites manageable in a live system, we need to start instrumenting them so that we can easily diagnose and fix any problems.

In the next chapter, we'll look at the options available to us for tracing and logging in to Azure websites using Azure storage in order to store the diagnostic data. We'll also look at remote debugging to help us step through the live code that runs on Azure web servers.

Questions

1. In an MVC project, where do we configure the details of OAuth providers?

2. If we wanted to make these OAuth settings configurable so that we can have different settings for different application environments without changing the code, what can we do?

3. When is it important to use an SSL certificate in a website and why?

4. Why would we not implement an SSL encryption everywhere?

5. What type of SSL certificates are all Azure websites protected by?

6. What can we do to make sure our HTTPS endpoint is used instead of the HTTPS endpoint in a website?

7. When we configure a website to use Azure AD authentication, which option do we pick from the following:

   - **No Authentication**
   - **Individual User Accounts**
   - **Organizational Accounts**
   - **Windows Authentication**

8. During publishing, which option can we set to create a new Azure AD application for the website so that we don't have to manually configure one?

9. Which API do we use to query Azure AD?

10. Which Azure AD PowerShell cmdlet is used to obtain Azure AD credentials?

Answers

1. In the `App_Start/Startup.Auth.cs` class.

2. Put the setting in `Web.config` and use `ConfigurationManager` to retrieve the settings at runtime.

3. If we are working with sensitive information such as names, addresses, and bank account details, we should use an SSL encryption to protect the user and ourselves from malicious third parties interested in stealing our data.

4. There is a performance overhead using SSL, so if our content is not sensitive, then we get no benefit from encrypting it, and we degrade the performance.

5. A wildcard certificate.

6. Add a redirect to the `Web.config` file. Doing this in a transform allows us to apply this to release configs, so we can debug against the HTTP endpoint too.

7. **Organizational Accounts**.

8. **Enable Organizational Authentication**.

9. Azure Active Directory Graph API.

·10. `get-credential`.

6
Azure Website Diagnostics and Debugging

Diagnostics is an extremely important feature of any server application, and we have some great tools available in Microsoft Azure to effectively implement various types of diagnostics for our websites.

We need diagnostics on websites to help us track down and fix bugs and performance issues during all phases of the website's life cycle.

If we instrument our applications properly with tracing and error handling, we can determine where and why errors occur, and work out which parts of an application are taking too long to complete, causing performance issues, using tracing.

Using server logging, we can log all HTTP traffic, detailed error messages for HTTP response codes greater than or equal to 400 (which can help us diagnose why an error response is being returned), and failed request logging, which will help us detect server performance issues (possibly from under-resourcing) causing requests to fail.

In this chapter, we're going to look at the following topics:

- Enabling diagnostics in Azure websites
- Working with logfiles
- Application logging
- Site diagnostics
- Kudu
- Remote debugging

Using code, we'll implement the standard diagnostics instrumentation on various listeners for the sales customer website.

Enabling diagnostics

We can configure basic website diagnostic settings through the **Server Explorer** window in Visual Studio by right-clicking on the website and selecting **View Settings**:

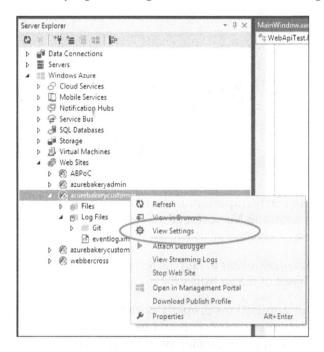

We can configure **Web Server Logging, Detailed Error Messages, Failed Request Tracing, Application Logging (File System only, not storage)**, and **Remote Debugging**. This example shows **Web Server Logging enabled**; to apply changes, click on **Save**:

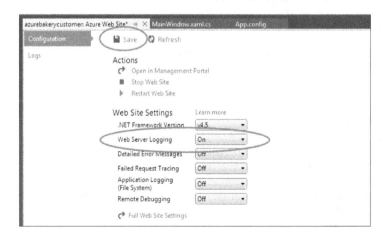

The same settings with some more advanced options (which we will cover in more detail in this section) are available in the **CONFIGURATION** tab in the website's workspace.

> When you swop a staging website for a production website, the configuration (including logging) settings are swopped too, so make sure the staging configuration is correct before swopping.

Working with logfiles

Filesystem logging is the lowest common denominator for all the logging types in an Azure website, whether it's application logging or server diagnostics. We'll look at how we can access and work with the logfiles before we look at the individual options first.

Viewing logfiles in Visual Studio

We can view logfiles in the Visual Studio **Server Explorer** by going to **Web Sites | [website] | Log Files**:

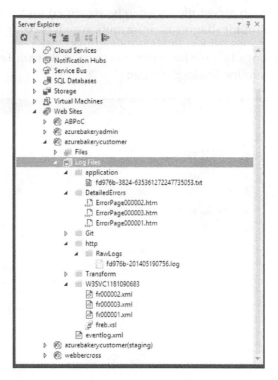

The following table shows the relationship between configuration settings and file path; the naming convention of the logging files provides us with extra information about the server instance ID, which is important for separating different instances in a scaled system, and the process ID, which is the IIS application pool ID that will separate different app pools:

Setting	Path or file-naming convention
WEB SERVER LOGGING	`Log Files/http/RawLogs/[Instance Id]-[TimeStamp].log`
DETAILED ERROR MESSAGES	`Log Files/DetailedErrors/ErrorPage[Id].html`
FAILED REQUEST TRACING	`Log Files/W3SVC0000/[Id].xml`
APPLICATION LOGGING (FILE SYSTEM)	`Log Files/application/[Instance Id]-[PID]-[EventTickCount].txt`

Double-clicking on a file will download it and open it for viewing inside Visual Studio.

Streaming logs

Application logs and web server file logs can be streamed into Visual Studio real-time, so we can monitor diagnostic information as it is being logged.

Then, if we go to the **Logs** tab, we have options such as **Stream Logs** or **Download Logs** in a ZIP file to examine the logs offline:

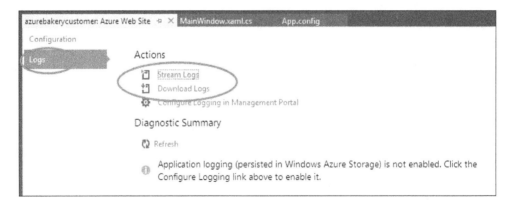

If we click on **Stream Logs**, we will see the **Output** window switch to **Show output from** in our website. To choose which logs to view, we need to click on the setting button in the **Output** window:

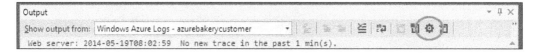

We can select the logs we're interested in, to prevent multiple logs from being written to writing to the output simultaneously, making the output confusing:

Now, if we open our website and start navigating around it, we'll see the logs appear like this:

```
Output                                                             ▾ ⊓ ×
Show output from: Windows Azure Logs - azurebakerycustomer    ▾
Web server: 2014-05-19T08:02:59  No new trace in the past 1 min(s).
Web server: 2014-05-19 08:02:05 AZUREBAKERYCUSTOMER__030A GET /Product productType=Pastries&X-ARR-LOG-ID
Web server: 2014-05-19 08:02:16 AZUREBAKERYCUSTOMER__030A GET /Product productType=Bread&X-ARR-LOG-ID=6e
Web server: 2014-05-19 08:02:31 ~1AZUREBAKERYCUSTOMER__030A GET /dump/ X-ARR-LOG-ID=2649ba1a-6996-4206-8
Web server: 2014-05-19 08:02:36 AZUREBAKERYCUSTOMER__030A GET /Product productType=Bread&X-ARR-LOG-ID=1b
Web server: 2014-05-19 08:02:38 AZUREBAKERYCUSTOMER__030A GET /Product productType=Pastries&X-ARR-LOG-ID
Web server: 2014-05-19 08:02:38 AZUREBAKERYCUSTOMER__030A GET /Product productType=Cakes&X-ARR-LOG-ID=d2
Web server: 2014-05-19 08:02:40 AZUREBAKERYCUSTOMER__030A GET / X-ARR-LOG-ID=368911c0-add5-4246-82e7-99c
Web server: 2014-05-19 08:03:15 AZUREBAKERYCUSTOMER__030A GET /Account/Login X-ARR-LOG-ID=323d5d2e-ad34-
Web server: 2014-05-19 08:03:15 AZUREBAKERYCUSTOMER__030A GET /bundles/jqueryval v=CscDCYKiyigBhIQTJsxhI
Web server: 2014-05-19 08:03:18 AZUREBAKERYCUSTOMER__030A POST /Account/ExternalLogin X-ARR-LOG-ID=e91ff
Web server: 2014-05-19 08:03:22 AZUREBAKERYCUSTOMER__030A GET /signin-twitter oauth_token=Rit5agqwCgLbAZ
Web server: 2014-05-19 08:03:22 AZUREBAKERYCUSTOMER__030A GET /Account/ExternalLoginCallback X-ARR-LOG-I
Web server: 2014-05-19 08:03:23 AZUREBAKERYCUSTOMER__030A GET / X-ARR-LOG-ID=dd92194c-6ff7-47f6-891d-bbc
Web server: 2014-05-19 08:03:24 AZUREBAKERYCUSTOMER__030A GET /Product productType=Sandwiches&X-ARR-LOG-
Web server: 2014-05-19 08:03:26 AZUREBAKERYCUSTOMER__030A GET /Product/AddToOrder/26 X-ARR-LOG-ID=d133a7
Web server: 2014-05-19 08:03:26 AZUREBAKERYCUSTOMER__030A GET /Product productType=Sandwiches&X-ARR-LOG-
Web server: 2014-05-19 08:03:29 AZUREBAKERYCUSTOMER__030A GET /Product/AddToOrder/28 X-ARR-LOG-ID=f44cf7
Web server: 2014-05-19 08:03:29 AZUREBAKERYCUSTOMER__030A GET /Product productType=Sandwiches&X-ARR-LOG-
Web server: 2014-05-19 08:03:32 AZUREBAKERYCUSTOMER__030A GET /Order/Basket X-ARR-LOG-ID=6548600f-82ec-4
Web server: 2014-05-19 08:03:34 AZUREBAKERYCUSTOMER__030A GET /Order/Pay X-ARR-LOG-ID=5ad19b9e-96f1-4862
Web server: 2014-05-19 08:03:36 AZUREBAKERYCUSTOMER__030A GET /Order/PayConfirm X-ARR-LOG-ID=e1ed8bdb-c1
Web server: 2014-05-19 08:03:39 AZUREBAKERYCUSTOMER__030A GET /Order X-ARR-LOG-ID=dc6cf847-08ab-4945-89b
```

Filtering stream logs

There's a filter option, which is tucked away in the **Output** window, which we can use to filter the log, making it easier to monitor particular items.

Click on the double chevrons on the right-hand side of the toolbar to reveal the filter options:

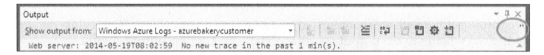

Enter a **Filter** string in the box and press *Enter* (you can use regular expressions if you like, by clicking on the asterisk button):

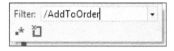

We'll immediately see the filter apply to our output; however, the filter view doesn't seem to filter live streaming logs, which is a shame.

Downloading logs

To download logs, we can click on **Download Logs** from the **Logs** tab in the website's **Settings** window or from the **Download Streaming Logs** button in the **Output** window:

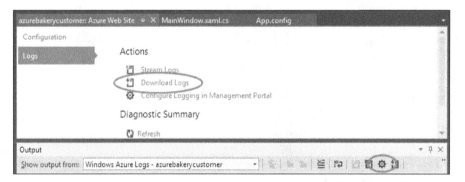

Both these options will download logs in a ZIP file to your profile's downloads folder.

Accessing files using FTP

Logfiles can be accessed using FTP without having to use Visual Studio. To do this, set up deployment credentials in the website's **DASHBOARD** workspace, note the **DEPLOYMENT / FTP USER** setting, and navigate to either **FTP DIAGNOSTIC LOGS** or **FTPS DIAGNOSTIC LOGS** (the latter is secure):

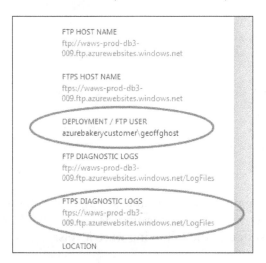

You can use an FTP client such as FileZilla (`https://filezilla-project.org/`) to manage logfiles using FTP.

Application logging

Within our websites, we can use the `System.Diagnostics.Trace` object to help write trace information to the Azure website trace listeners, which write data to the file, table storage, and blob storage. If implemented properly, tracing is useful to help diagnose problems with errors and performance. In normal operations, we can log errors at the **Error** trace level to minimize storage and performance impact; however, if we experience difficulties, we can raise the **LOGGING LEVEL** value to show us more detailed information.

Visual Studio's **Server Explorer** only allows us to configure file logging, but we have full control of the trace listener options in the portal:

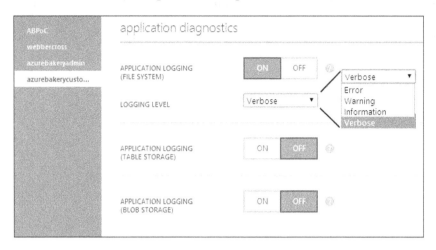

Here, we can enable logging to the file, table storage, and blob storage, and control the **LOGGING LEVEL** value for each option. There are five **LOGGING LEVEL** options, which correspond to the following trace levels:

- **Off**: This indicates that nothing is logged
- **Error**: This indicates 1 or lower logged
- **Warning**: This indicates 2 or lower logged
- **Information**: This indicates 3 or lower logged
- **Verbose**: This indicates 4 or lower logged (everything is logged)

The following System.Diagnostics.Trace methods are particularly useful for tracing in our applications:

Method	Level	Description
TraceError(string)	**Error**	This traces an error with a message text
TraceError(string, object[])	**Error**	This traces an error with a format string and an array of objects to format
TraceInformation(string)	**Information**	This traces information with a message text

Method	Level	Description
`TraceInformation (string, object[])`	**Information**	This traces information with a format string and an array of objects to format
`TraceWarning(string)`	**Warning**	This traces a warning with a message text
`TraceWarning (string, object[])`	**Warning**	This traces a warning with a format string and an array of objects to format
`WriteLine(string)`	**Verbose**	This traces a verbose message

Changing the **LOGGING LEVEL** value does not affect the `Web.config` file, so it doesn't recycle the website's application pool (which would cause the website to become slow to respond while it warms up).

The full list of `Trace` object methods can be found at `http://msdn.microsoft.com/en-us/library/system.diagnostics.trace(v=vs.110).aspx`.

Implementing tracing in the application

I said we weren't going to go into great detail about IoC, DI, repository, and UoW patterns, but I've implemented a cut-down repository and a UoW pattern to access our data to help us illustrate tracing through multiple application layers.

The sales customer website has tracing implemented in the controllers, UoWs, and repository. This is an example of a controller action, which logs the start and end of the action and logs an exception, if thrown:

```
public class ProductController : Controller
{
private readonly ProductUoW _uow = new ProductUoW();

// Other actions removed for brevity

    [Authorize]
    public ActionResult AddToOrder(int id)
    {
        Trace.TraceInformation("ProductController AddToOrder -
            Start");

        OrderItem item = null;
```

```
        try
        {
            // Get customer details
            var uid = User.Identity.GetUserId();

            // Add to order
            item = this._uow.AddToOrder(id, uid);

            // Save
            this._uow.SaveChanges();
        }
        catch (Exception ex)
        {
            Trace.TraceError("ProductController AddToOrder Error:
                {0}", ex);

            throw;
        }

        Trace.TraceInformation("ProductController AddToOrder -
            End");

        return RedirectToAction("Index", new { productType =
            item.Product.ProductType });
    }
```

We're catching and rethrowing the exceptions in the controller, so they can be logged but handled globally (the default configuration in `FilterConfig`) and not swallowed by the controller.

The `ProductUoW.AddToOrder` method has a similar tracing implementation, with a start and end information log and a `catch` block, which logs the exception but rethrows it to the calling method up the stack:

```
public OrderItem AddToOrder(int id, string uid)
{
    Trace.TraceInformation("ProductUoW AddToOrder Start");

    OrderItem item = null;

    try
    {
        var customer = this._users.GetAll()
            .Include(u => u.Customer)
            .Single(u => u.Id == uid).Customer;

        // Try and find order
        Order order = this._orders.GetAll()
```

```
                .Include(o => o.Items.Select(i => i.Product))
                .SingleOrDefault(o => o.Customer.Id == customer.Id &&
                    o.Status == OrderStatus.Open);

            if (order == null)
            {
                order = new Order();
                order.Customer = customer;
                this._orders.Add(order);
            }

            // Look for OrderItem
            item = order.Items.SingleOrDefault(i => i.Product.Id ==
                id);
            if (item == null)
            {
                item = new OrderItem();
                item.Product = this._ctx.Products.Single(p => p.Id ==
                    id);
                order.Items.Add(item);
            }
            else
            {
                item.Quantity++;
            }
        }
        catch (Exception ex)
        {
            Trace.TraceError("ProductUoW AddToOrder Exception: {0}",
                ex);
            throw;
        }

        Trace.TraceInformation("ProductUoW AddToOrder End");

        return item;
    }
```

Although the repository is generic for any entity type T, it has the same tracing implementation and uses the trace formatter overload methods to get the entity type into the message:

```
public IQueryable<T> GetAll()
{
    Trace.TraceInformation("{0} Repository GetAll Start",
        typeof(T));
```

```
        IQueryable<T> entities = null;

        try
        {
            entities = this._dbSet;
        }
        catch(Exception ex)
        {
            Trace.TraceError("{0} Repository GetAll Exception: {1}",
                typeof(T), ex);

            throw;
        }

        Trace.TraceInformation("{0} Repository GetAll End",
            typeof(T));

        return entities;
    }
```

Once the changes to our website are published, if we enable **APPLICATION LOGGING (FILE SYSTEM)** and set **LOGGING LEVEL** to at least **INFORMATION** and then click on **SAVE** to save the changes, we will start gathering the tracing data for our website (notice that the portal warns us that this will only be enabled for **12 hours** as it's not a permanent method for tracing an application):

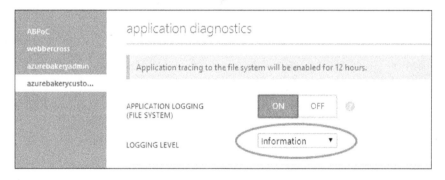

Now, if we go and exercise the action on the website, when we take a look at the log that is generated, we can see the full timestamped trace for the Product AddToOrder action:

```
2014-05-20T20:35:49  PID[1224] Information ProductController
    AddToOrder - Start
2014-05-20T20:35:49  PID[1224] Information ProductUoW AddToOrder
    Start
```

```
2014-05-20T20:35:49  PID[1224] Information
  AzureBakery.Sales.CustomerWebsite.Models.ApplicationUser
    Repository GetAll Start
2014-05-20T20:35:49  PID[1224] Information
  AzureBakery.Sales.CustomerWebsite.Models.ApplicationUser
    Repository GetAll End
2014-05-20T20:35:53  PID[1224] Information
  AzureBakery.Sales.Model.Order Repository GetAll Start
2014-05-20T20:35:53  PID[1224] Information
  AzureBakery.Sales.Model.Order Repository GetAll End
2014-05-20T20:35:53  PID[1224] Information ProductUoW AddToOrder
  End
2014-05-20T20:35:53  PID[1224] Information ProductUoW Save Start
2014-05-20T20:35:54  PID[1224] Information ProductUoW Save End
2014-05-20T20:35:54  PID[1224] Information ProductController
  AddToOrder- End
```

Application logging to table storage

As we saw in the previous section, application file logging is not a permanent logging solution, so we will need to set up an alternative. Table storage is useful as we can interact directly with a table without having to download a log and examine it offline. Once we start using storage, however, we incur additional charges for holding the data; this is why it's sensible to normally only log errors and then enable higher tracing levels when we are fault finding, which we could even temporarily direct to file storage.

We cannot enable table storage through Visual Studio, so in the console, go to the website's workspace **CONFIGURATION** tab and follow this procedure to set it up:

1. Enable **APPLICATION LOGGING (TABLE STORAGE)**. Notice I've set **LOGGING LEVEL** to **Information**, so we can see something in the table; you may want to do the same for testing; you can change it later:

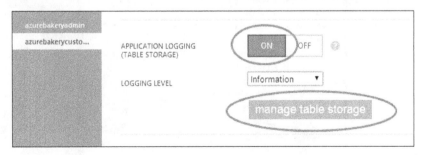

2. Click on **manage table storage** and choose a **STORAGE ACCOUNT** (if you've been following along, we created a storage account for SQL database backups, but create one if you haven't got one). Select **Create new table** (default) from the **WINDOWS AZURE TABLE** picker and change **TABLE NAME** if you like, and then click on the tick to accept:

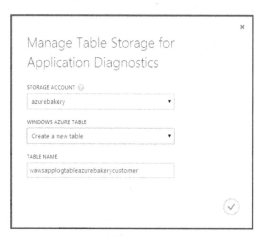

3. Click on **SAVE** on the toolbar to finish.

4. Once this is configured, browse around the website again, then look at the `Tables` folder in the Visual Studio **Server Explorer** window, and we will see our new log table:

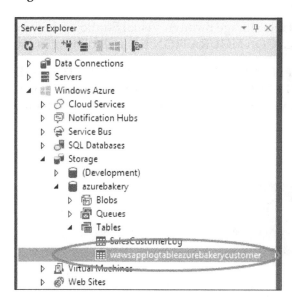

5. If we double-click on it, we will see a paged view of the data:

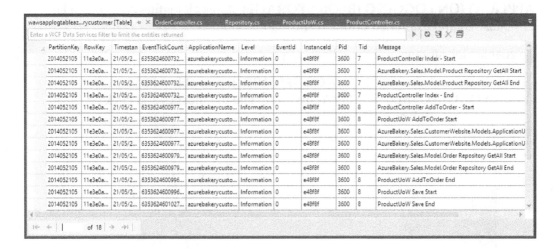

6. There are a number of extra fields (**PartitionKey**, **RowKey**, and **Timestamp**) which are integral to table storage, but the rest of the information is pretty much the same as with file storage, except we don't need to take information such as the server's **InstanceId** or **Pid** from the file name, so it's easier to read and query.

Querying table data

We can use WCF Data Service filters (this gives us a clue to the mechanics of how Visual Studio accesses the data) to help us filter table data; there is a query builder, but it's not very helpful as it only lets us query table key fields.

We can write a filter similar to the one shown in the following code to filter all entries for a particular **InstanceId** and **Message**:

```
InstanceId eq 'e48f8f' and Message eq 'ProductUoW Save End'
```

We'll see the results as shown in the following screenshot:

There is a good reference to create filter strings at http://msdn.microsoft.com/en-us/library/ff683669.aspx.

Application logging to blob storage

APPLICATION LOGGING (BLOB STORAGE) stores all logfiles, which can be downloaded and examined offline from a blob container.

To enable blob storage, use the following procedure:

1. In the website's workspace **CONFIGURE** tab, enable **APPLICATION LOGGING (BLOB STORAGE)** under site diagnostics and click on **manage blob storage**:

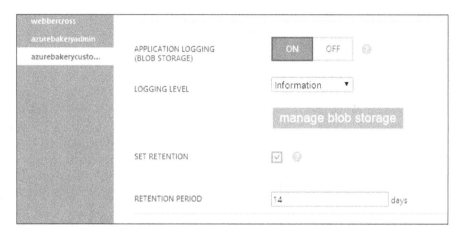

I've enabled **SET RETENTION** with the default **RETENTION PERIOD** of **14 days**, so logs are only kept for 2 weeks.

2. Next, choose a **STORAGE ACCOUNT**, select **Create a new blob container** (default), and change the **BLOB CONTAINER NAME** if you like:

3. Click on the tick button and then on **SAVE** on the toolbar.

4. Go and browse around the website to generate some traffic, then go back to Visual Studio and navigate to the **Storage | Blobs** folder in the **Server Explorer** window, and then double-click on the blob container we just created to see the logfiles:

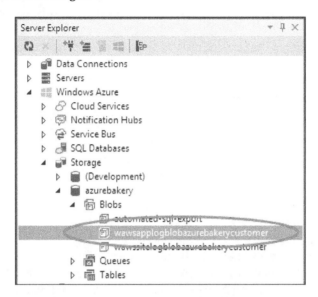

5. To view a log, we can click on the **Open Blob** button, which will download it and launch it in your default CSV editor (probably, Excel), or click on the **Save As** button to save the file:

Diagnosing a real bug

We're going to artificially introduce a bug into our website and deploy it to Azure in the **Release** mode, so the error page doesn't give the bug away (which it would in the **Debug** mode). Then, track it down using diagnostics in table storage.

Setting up the website

To get started, get the chapter's code from the samples, and then follow this procedure:

1. Replace the `OrderUoW.GetCustomerOrders` part with this code:

```
public IQueryable<Order> GetCustomerOrders(string uid)
{
    Trace.TraceInformation("OrderUoW GetCustomerOrders
        Start");

    IQueryable<Order> orders = null;

    try
    {
        var customer = this._ctx.Users
            .Include(u => u.Customer)
            .Single(u => u.UserName == uid).Customer;

        // Try and find orders
        orders = this._ctx.Orders
            .Include(o => o.Customer)
            .Where(o => o.Customer.Id == customer.Id)
            .OrderByDescending(o => o.CreatedDate);
    }
    catch (Exception ex)
    {
        Trace.TraceError("OrderUoW GetCustomerOrders
            Exception: {0}", ex);

        throw;
    }

    Trace.TraceInformation("OrderUoW GetCustomerOrders
        End");

    return orders;
}
```

2. Publish the website in the **Release** mode.

3. Enable **APPLICATION LOGGING (TABLE STORAGE)** in the **CONFIGURE** tab in the portal.

4. Check that **LOGGING LEVEL** is set to **Information** or higher.

Producing an error

Now that the website is ready, log in, navigate around the site, and select **Orders** from the navigation bar. An exception should be thrown by the bug we've introduced, and we should see the custom error page (`Error.cshtml`) telling us that **An error occurred while processing your request**.

We'll now go and look for the error in the following procedure:

1. Open the **wawsapplog** table for the published website in the **Server Explorer** window in Visual Studio.

2. If there are only a few items in the log, the error will be easy to find; however, if there are more than a few pages, we can construct a query to quickly find any recent errors.

3. Enter the following query in the filter box and click on **Execute** to run it:

    ```
    Level eq 'Error' and Timestamp gt datetime'2014-08-18T12:30:00'
    ```

4. Even though we've artificially introduced the bug, we're not going to assume anything about the error at this point, so we've used a general query to filter the log's **Level** to **Error** and the **Timestamp** value around the time we saw the error occur.

5. The results should return two error records, one for the UoW method and one for the controller, where the exception was rethrown. Now that we know more about the error, we can requery the data without the **Level** filter to find more about the sequence of events up to the error, which could potentially help us recreate the bug if we weren't sure what it is.

6. If we double-click on the error for the `OrderUoW` error row, we can see the error:

    ```
    OrderUoW GetCustomerOrders Exception:
      System.InvalidOperationException: Sequence
        contains no elements
       at System.Linq.Enumerable.Single[TSource](IEnumerable`1
    source)
       at …[Middle removed for brevity]
      AzureBakery.Sales.CustomerWebsite.DataAccess.OrderUoW.
    GetCustomerOrders(String uid)
    ```

7. This shows us our formatted error message including the class and method names at the start to help us quickly identify the source of the error and the stack trace, which shows us that the exception was caused by trying to call the `Single` method on an empty enumerable. The full stack trace shows the full name of the method, which called it at the end of the trace.

Site diagnostics

Websites give us a number of site-diagnostic capabilities, which provide us insight into what our website is doing above the application layer (performing **REMOTE DEBUGGING** falls more into the application layer, but the configuration controls whether a debugger can be attached to a web server, which is a site layer). I think of this category of diagnostics in the same way as IIS logging on an on-premises web server.

Site diagnostics offers us the following diagnostic facilities:

- **WEB SERVER LOGGING**: This logs all HTTP transactions for a website, which can be helpful for monitoring transactional throughput of a site and gathering metrics. Logs can be stored to the **FILE SYSTEM** and are limited to a configurable **QUOTA** that ranges between 25 MB and 100 MB, or to a blob storage, which allows greater flexibility for storage size but will incur costs.

- **DETAILED ERROR MESSAGES**: This logs extra detailed error information for HTTP status codes that are 400 or higher and are returned by the web server. Detailed error logs are HTML files linked from a normal web server log with a URI and are located in the Logfiles/DetailedErrors folder. **Detailed Error Messages** can be enabled via the website's workspace **CONFIGURATION** tab in the portal, or through the settings in the Visual Studio **Server Explorer** window, which are the same as the other site's diagnostics settings. We can easily generate a 404 error by typing an invalid site's URL into a browser, for example https://azurebakery.com/nopage.

- **FAILED REQUEST TRACING**: This logs failed HTTP requests to the filesystem, allowing you to diagnose performance issues on websites.

Extra filesystem settings

If we take a look at the **CONFIGURATION** tab of our website's workspace in the portal, we can see there are some extra settings for **WEB SERVER LOGGING** under the **site diagnostics** section:

We can adjust the storage **QUOTA** from 25 MB to 100 MB, which will come out of our website's storage allowance, so there's no additional cost. By default, the logs will be stored indefinitely unless we enable **SET RETENTION** and choose a **RETENTION PERIOD**.

Site diagnostics using blob storage

As well as saving web server logs to a file, we can also save them to Azure blob storage, which can be configured through the portal.

To enable blob storage, use the following procedure:

1. In the website's workspace **CONFIGURE** tab, click on **STORAGE** under **site diagnostics** and click on **manage storage**:

2. Next, choose a **STORAGE ACCOUNT**, select **Create a new blob container** (default), and change the **BLOB CONTAINER NAME** if you like. It's a good idea to use a separate container for each site and application / server diagnostics to make managing logs more straightforward:

3. As with the **FILE SYSTEM** storage, we can enable **SET RETENTION** to automatically remove logs older than a certain age.

4. Click on the tick button and then click on **SAVE** on the toolbar.

5. Go and browse around the website to generate some traffic, then go back to Visual Studio and expand the **Storage | Blobs** folder in **Server Explorer**, and then, double-click on the blob container we just created to see the logfiles:

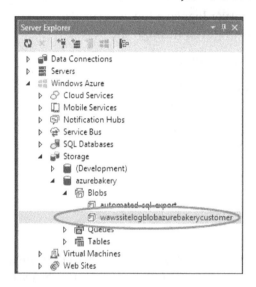

6. To view a log, we can click on the **Open Blob** button, which will launch in your default text editor (probably Notepad) or click on the **Save As** button to save to the file:

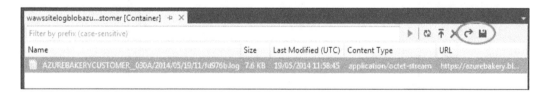

Kudu

Kudu is an open source (https://github.com/projectkudu/kudu) engine, which powers Azure website Git deployments and continuous deployments on all Azure websites. There is a Kudu service in every website, which can be accessed via the following URL https://mysite.scm.azurewebsites.net. If you have a custom domain name implemented, you will need to use the azurewebsites.net endpoint unless you do extra DNS configuration for this endpoint.

The Kudu service website looks like this:

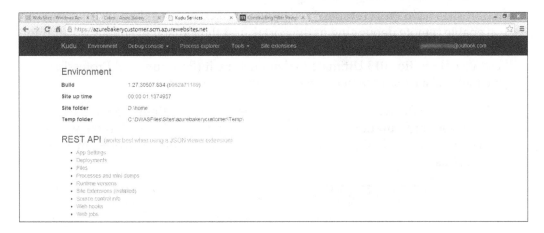

There are some useful tools in here for working with logs; the **Diagnostic Console** (under **Debug Console**) has a CMD and PowerShell console in the browser along with a directory explorer, which allows you to work with logfiles:

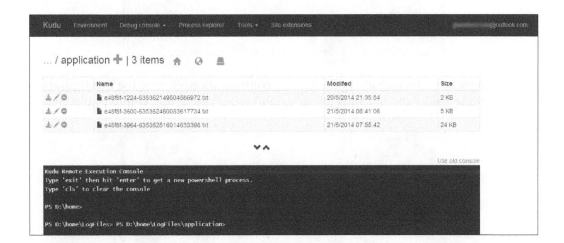

You can get more information on the Kudu service at `https://github.com/projectkudu/kudu/wiki/Accessing-the-kudu-service`.

Remote debugging

Azure websites have great remote debugging support integrated into Visual Studio; we can enable remote debugging in the portal, and then attach the debugger through **Server Explorer**. Unfortunately, this is not supported in Visual Studio Express, so I will use Visual Studio 2013 Ultimate to demonstrate it (Premium and Professional are fine too). To start remote debugging, use the following procedure:

1. Make sure the website is deployed in the **Debug** configuration because the **Release** configuration is optimized and cannot be debugged. If the website is not deployed in the **Debug** configuration, you will see an error message like this:

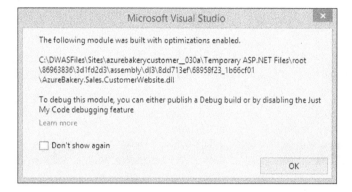

2. To publish the website in the **Debug** configuration, change the **Configuration** setting under the **Settings** tab in the **Publish Web** dialog before publishing:

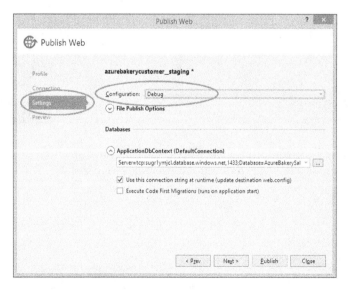

3. In the Azure portal, go to the **CONFIGURATION** tab in our website workspace, scroll down to the **site diagnostics** section, enable **REMOTE DEBUGGING**, and set **REMOTE DEBUGGING VISUAL STUDIO VERSION** to **2013**:

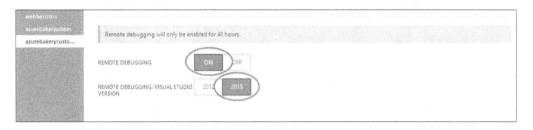

4. Notice that the warning about debugging is only enabled for 48 hours, so if you leave it for a few days and try to connect the debugger and it fails, this is why! Click on **SAVE** on the toolbar.

5. As a test, put a breakpoint in the **HomeController Index** action like this:

```
HomeController.cs + ×
CustomerWebsite                    AzureBakery.Sales.CustomerW
using System;
using System.Collections.Generic;
using System.Linq;
using System.Web;
using System.Web.Mvc;
using AzureBakery.Sales.CustomerWebsite.Models;

namespace AzureBakery.Sales.CustomerWebsite.Controllers
{
    [RequireHttps]
    0 references
    public class HomeController : Controller
    {
        0 references
        public ActionResult Index()
        {
            return View();
        }
    }
```

6. In the Visual Studio **Server Explorer** window, right-click on the website you want to debug and select **Attach Debugger**:

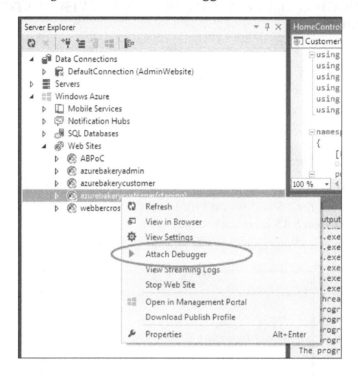

7. The website will open in a new browser window and the remote debugger will attach and break at our breakpoint. We can see the **Call Stack** window too (we don't get IntelliTrace though):

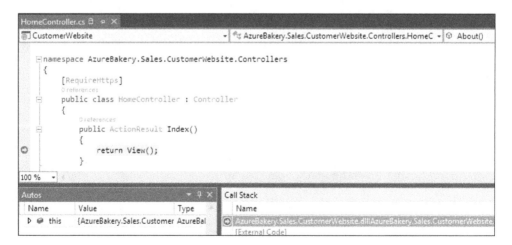

When to use remote debugging

Remote debugging is a really cool bit of functionality, but you need to think carefully about when and if you can actually use it.

If you are working on a development system, remote debugging might be quite helpful; although most of the time, you should be able to satisfactorily debug the application locally.

If you have a serious problem with a production website, remote debugging might not be a viable option to help you determine what the problem is due to the following reasons:

- Your website will be deployed in the **Release** configuration build, so you cannot remotely debug it.

- Deploying the website in the default **Debug** configuration may expose the inner working details in the default error pages, which can reveal potential exploits within the application; in addition to this, there may be some performance degradation from running non-optimized code.

- If your organization doesn't allow developers to administer production systems, you may not be allowed anywhere near the website unless it's an emergency!

For production systems, sufficient diagnostic instrumentation should be implemented to enable administrators and developers to determine a point of failure and possibly catch an exception. This would hopefully help a developer reproduce and fix the problem, or highlight areas of the application that require further diagnostics implementing to help further diagnose the problem.

Summary

We've learned some really useful diagnostic techniques in this chapter to help us find problems in our Azure websites. I was planning on finishing this chapter by covering how to use Entlib SLAB (which is a more advanced logging block from the Microsoft patterns and practices team) with Azure table storage, but ran out of space, so you can read about it on my blog here:

http://webbercross.azurewebsites.net/entlib-slab-with-mvc5-website-and-azure-trace-listener/

In the next chapter, we're going to start configuring our Service Bus topic and integrate the sales customer website so that order messages will be sent to the other business domain systems when orders are created by the customers.

Questions

1. In terms of logging configuration, why is it important to be careful when swopping a staging table to live?

2. What type of logging is available to application logging and server diagnostics?

3. What information does the **APPLICATION LOGGING (FILE SYSTEM)** file-naming convention give us?

4. How do we filter streaming logs in Visual Studio?

5. Which .NET object helps us write trace information in our website?

6. What is a sensible normal logging level for an application and why?

7. What method can we use to trace a formatted message at the **Information** level?

8. In the controller example, why are we catching and rethrowing the exception?

9. How long is application logging to a file enabled for?

10. What types of application logging storage are not configurable through Visual Studio?

11. What type of filter query do we use with table storage?

12. What information do site diagnostics **DETAILED ERROR MESSAGES** give us?

13. What is the URL for a website's Kudu service?

14. Does Visual Studio Express support remote debugging?

15. Why must we publish a website in the **Debug** configuration to allow remote debugging?

16. How long is a remote debugging session enabled for?

17. The `BasketHelper.GetCount` method doesn't have any diagnostics implemented; add some tracing and some error trapping to catch and log any errors.

18. Introduce a bug into the `BasketHelper.GetCount` method, publish the site in the **Release** mode, and examine the logs to check whether the diagnostics are working.

Answers

1. Configuration settings are swopped with the website, so logging settings will be swopped.

2. File logging.

3. **Log Files/application/[Instance Id]-[PID]-[EventTickCount].txt - Instance Id, Process ID**.

4. Open the filter options using the double-chevron button on the right-hand side of the streaming log output toolbar and enter a filter string.

5. `System.Diagnostics.Trace`.

6. **Error**: This will allow us to catch or log any errors but minimize storage with additional information.

7. `TraceInformation (string, object[])`.

8. This is because the controller doesn't swallow the exception and allows the error to be handled globally by the default `FilterConfig`.

9. 12 hours.

10. Table and blob storage.

11. WCF Data Service filters.

12. Extra information about error response codes `400` or greater.

13. `https://mysite.scm.azurewebsites.net`.

14. No.

15. This is because the **Release** configuration is optimized and cannot be remote debugged.

16. 48 hours.

17. NA.

18. NA.

7
Azure Service Bus Topic Integration

In this chapter, we're going to start implementing an Azure Service Bus topic that allows the subsystems across the three business units to send order status messages to each other and receive them via topic subscriptions.

After a quick introduction to Microsoft Azure Service Bus and topics, we'll create our Service Bus infrastructure, integrate the sales customer website, and create a WPF messaging simulator application, which will introduce some of the Azure Service Bus SDK features and provide us with a useful tool to help us build and test the full enterprise system.

We'll cover the following areas in this chapter:

- An overview of Microsoft Azure Service Bus topics
- Creating a Service Bus topic
- Connecting a website to a topic
- Creating a message simulator
- Exploring the portal's topic workspace

This will give us the foundations for building the rest of the system throughout the remainder of the book.

Introducing Azure Service Bus and topics

Service Bus technology, in general (not specific to Microsoft or Azure), allows multiple subsystem tiers in enterprise systems to communicate with each other in a loosely coupled and resilient manner.

Service Bus queues have a one-to-one relationship between providers and consumers, where a provider posts a message to a queue and it can be removed and processed once by a single consumer. This means we can easily scale up a consumer application without the fear of duplicating work; however, if we have a different application that may be interested in the same message, which is the case in our Azure Bakery system, we will need multiple processing applications to receive the same messages. This is the reason we selected an Azure Service Bus topic.

Service Bus topics handle messages to queues in a similar way, except that we can have multiple subscriptions for a topic that has a one-to-one relationship, where the applications interact in a similar way with a subscription as they do in a queue, in that only a single consumer may remove and process a message from a subscription. This gives us deterministic one-to-many messaging across our system.

In our Azure Bakery system, we have a single Service Bus topic, which spans the whole system, allowing applications to send messages and receive them via their own subscriptions:

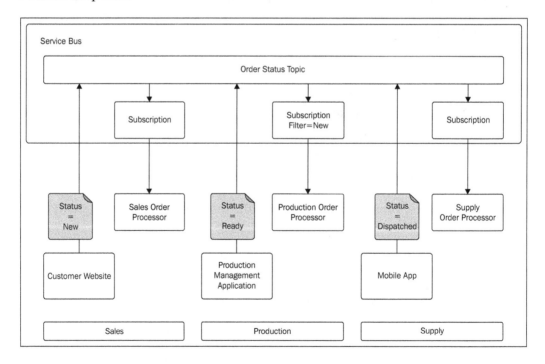

The following is the sequence of an order message life cycle through the topic:

1. A customer creates an order in the sales customer website, where an order message is sent to the topic with the **New** status.

2. The **Production Order Processor** (worker role) consumes the **New** status messages from its filtered **Subscription**, allocating stock and creating batch schedules.

3. The **Supply Order Processor** (worker role) consumes all messages and uses the **New** status messages before production to prepare packaging and address labels.

4. Once the **Production** business unit has finished manufacturing all items of an order, it will mark the order with ReadyToDispatch in the **Production Management Application**, which will send a message to the topic.

5. The **Sales Order Processor** (worker role) consumes all messages and updates the order status in its database, allowing customers to view the status of their orders via the **Customer Website** and **Mobile App**; it also sends push notifications to the mobile application when orders are dispatched.

6. The **Supply Order Processor** uses the ReadyToDispatch status messages to pick up completed orders from production and schedule deliveries.

7. Once the product has been dispatched, an order status message with a **Dispatched** status is sent via the supply mobile application, and the order life cycle is complete.

Queues and topics can help level the workload of a system by effectively buffering work items, allowing worker processes to process them in their own time and scale up, as required.

Disconnected systems in which applications may not always be online to communicate with each other can really benefit from implementing Service Bus messaging, as they can send messages to a topic or queue without continually having to retry the disconnected target system when it is offline; once the target system comes online, it can read and process the messages.

Dead-letter queues

Under various failure conditions, messages can be automatically sent to a topic's dead-letter queue (the same applies to Service Bus queues). We can configure topics and subscriptions to dead-letter messages if their **Time to live (TTL)** expires, if they don't have a matching subscription filter, or if they cannot be delivered.

We need to pay attention to the dead-letter queue as it consumes our storage allocation for the topic, but it can also allow us to administer undelivered messages and diagnose potential performance issues or application problems.

Each subscription has its own dead-letter queue that can be accessed using the `TopicClient` object with `/$DeadLetterQueue` appended to various failure conditions; messages can be automatically sent to a the subscription name, like this:

```
// Create subscription client
var subscriptionClient = SubscriptionClient.Create("TopicName",
  "SubscriptionName");

// Create dead letter client using subscription client TopicPath
var deadLetterClient =
  SubscriptionClient.Create(subscriptionClient.TopicPath,
    "SubscriptionName" + "/$DeadLetterQueue");
```

Creating a Service Bus topic

Once we have a Service Bus namespace in place, Azure Service Bus topics and subscriptions can be created through the portal at design time and in code at runtime (also using the Azure PowerShell console, but we're not covering that). This makes it possible to create everything up front, providing the subsystems with the design details, or have the individual subsystems provision their own messaging infrastructure.

Creating Service Bus components in-code has security implications, as in order to create queues and topics, an application needs to use the namespace **Access Control Service (ACS)** or **Shared Access Signature (SAS)** credentials. System administrators may not want production applications to have this kind of capability, so they don't lose control over the Service Bus infrastructure architecture. If these credentials are compromised, the whole namespace can be at risk of an attack. To create subscriptions in-code, we need the `Manage` permission on a SAS policy in the topic, which is less risky but still gives us full control over the topic.

We're going for a middle-ground approach, where we'll create a topic in the portal so that each subsystem doesn't need namespace authorization and doesn't have to test for the existence of the topic and create it if it doesn't exist at startup. The subsystems will create their own subscriptions at runtime using their own tailored SAS credentials.

We'll get started by creating a topic in the portal with the following procedure (because we don't already have a Service Bus namespace, this will be created too):

1. Click on the **NEW** service button in the **SERVICE BUS** workspace; select **TOPIC** and then **CUSTOM CREATE**:

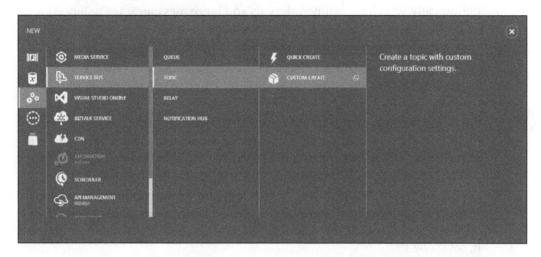

2. Fill in the **TOPIC NAME**, select a **REGION**, choose a **SUBSCRIPTION**, and enter a name in **NAMESPACE NAME** (the **NAMESPACE** field can be used for multiple **TOPIC**, **QUEUE**, **RELAY**, and **NOTIFICATION HUB**, so choose a general name, not specific to the topic) and click on the next arrow:

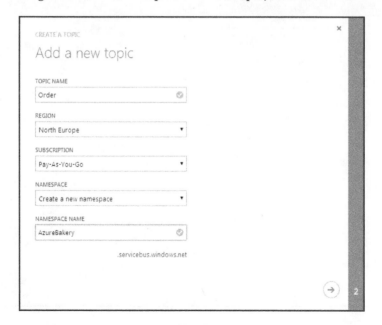

3. Next, we will configure the topic to have the lowest **MAX SIZE** value (this is the maximum total message size the topic can hold) of **1 GB**. Once a message is consumed, it is removed from the topic; we're expecting all our systems to be online all the time and we'll be using small messages, so this should be fine. If we had a disconnected system where consumers come online periodically with long offline intervals and large messages, we will need a larger topic size as messages would build up.

4. Set **DEFAULT MESSAGE TIME TO LIVE**; I left this as **14 days** (default). If you have a disconnected system, you need to be careful with this setting, as messages can be removed from the topic before a consumer has the chance to collect it if the TTL is set too low.

5. I'm setting **Enable duplicate detection** so that any duplicate messages (determined by comparing the `BrokeredMessage.MessageId` property) will be automatically removed from the topic). We need to be careful with this setting too as historical messages form a part of our **MAX SIZE** quota.

6. I'm setting **Enable Partitioning**, which will allow multiple message brokers to process our messages, so we're not limited by the performance of a single broker. This setting can't be changed afterwards, so if you want to implement it, set it now!

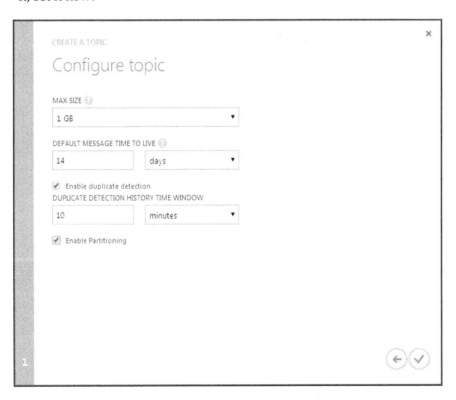

There is no extra cost incurred from using partitioning, so it's definitely worth using it. You can read more about message partitioning at `http://msdn.microsoft.com/en-us/library/dn520246.aspx`.

7. In the topic workspace **CONFIGURE** tab, I've enabled **FILTER MESSAGE BEFORE PUBLISHING** so that a `NoMatchingSubscriptionException` is thrown to the client when messages sent to the topic have no matching subscription. If this is not set, these messages will fall into a black hole or eventually appear in the dead-letter queue once they're expired, if configured to do so:

8. Once the topic is created, navigate to the **CONFIGURE** tab in the **TOPIC** workspace and scroll down to the **shared access policies** section. We're going to create a policy for the sales customer website, so we don't have to use the namespace connection credentials, which would allow the application to have full control over the whole namespace; this is a good practice for security.

9. Add a **NAME** for the new policy and adjust the permissions; I chose **Send** as we only want to send messages to the topic. **Listen** allows messages to be read from the topic, and **Manage** allows full control over the topic. Click on **SAVE** in the toolbar:

10. At the bottom of the page, we should now see keys generated under **shared access key generator**; we can regenerate the keys from here if they were ever compromised:

11. Create another policy called `SalesSimulator` with **Manage** permissions.

Connecting a website to the Service Bus topic

We last saw the sales customer website order controller in *Chapter 5, Building Azure MVC Websites*, with the order status being updated to New in the sales database. Now that we have the service bus topic set up, we can modify this to send an order message for the production business domain to process and start manufacturing and the supply business domain to process and prepare packaging.

Preparing the website

The following procedure walks us through the installation of the `WindowsAzure.ServiceBus` NuGet package and configuration of the connection string, allowing the website to interact with the Service Bus:

1. In the portal, navigate to the **TOPICS** tab in the Service Bus workspace, select the new topic, and click on **CONNECTION INFORMATION** on the toolbar:

2. Here, we can see the **SAS** connection string for the SAS policies we just created. Leave this page open so that we can copy the strings later:

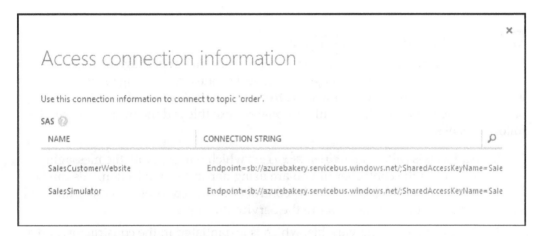

3. In order to interact with the Service Bus from the website, we need to install the `WindowsAzure.ServiceBus` NuGet package, so go to our website solution in Visual Studio and enter the following command in the **Package Manager Console** to install the package:

```
Install-package windowsazure.servicebus
```

4. The package will create a connection string in the `appSettings` section of the `Web.config` file, which allows the application to connect to our newly created Service Bus namespace using ACS. Find the `Microsoft. ServiceBus.ConnectionString` app setting in the `Web.config` file, using the following code:

```
<!-- Service Bus specific app settings for messaging connections
<add key="Microsoft.ServiceBus.ConnectionString"
   value="Endpoint=sb://[your
      namespace].servicebus.windows.net;SharedSecretIssuer=owner;
      SharedSecretValue=[your secret]" />
```

5. Copy the **SAS CONNECTION STRING** value from the portal and paste it into the `value` attribute like this:

```
<add key="Microsoft.ServiceBus.ConnectionString" value="
   Endpoint=sb://azurebakery.servicebus.windows.net/;
   SharedAccessKeyName=SalesCustomerWebsite;
   SharedAccessKey=Z842VTFPrHI/XXXXXXXXXXXXXXXXXXXXXXXXXXXXXXX=" />
```

Creating messaging logic

Now that we've got the `WindowsAzure.ServiceBus` NuGet package installed, we can work on sending order messages. First, we'll create a messaging service class in order to separate our messaging logic from our controller, which will build order messages and send them with optional retries; this is done by completing the following steps:

1. Add a class called `MessagingService`, which will separate the messaging logic from the controller (if you are using dependency injection, this can be abstracted and injected into the controller by the controller factory), and add a method to send the order to the Service Bus topic.

2. Add a `TopicClient` variable, which is instantiated in the constructor, and a `string` variable for the topic name:

```
using System;
using System.Diagnostics;
using System.Threading.Tasks;
using Microsoft.ServiceBus.Messaging;
using AzureBakery.Sales.Model;

namespace AzureBakery.Sales.CustomerWebsite.Services
{
    public class MessagingService
    {
        private readonly TopicClient _topicClient = null;
```

```
        private readonly string _topicName = "Order";

        public MessagingService()
        {
            // Create TopicClient (this uses the
            Microsoft.ServiceBus.ConnectionString app setting
            this._topicClient =
            TopicClient.Create(_topicName);
        }
    }
}
```

The `TopicClient` object allows us to interact with a topic at runtime; you can read more about it at `http://msdn.microsoft.com/en-us/library/microsoft.servicebus.messaging.topicclient.aspx`.

3. Next, we'll add a public `SendOrderAsync` method, which will be used by the `OrderController` to send an order across the system without concerning itself with messaging mechanics. The `TopicClient` object supports `async` operations, which are more efficient with thread resources, so I've used these and made my methods `async Task<T>` typed, so they can be called asynchronously using the `await` operator. The `SendOrderAsync` method takes an `order` parameter and creates a `BrokeredMessage` object (this is the message object that is sent across the Azure Service Bus) with the `Status` property set to `New`, allowing it to be filtered by subscriptions that look for newly created orders and a unique ID:

```
public async Task<bool> SendOrderAsync(Order order, int retires =
0)
{
    Trace.TraceInformation("MessagingService SendOrder -
      Start");

    // Create message with Order body
    BrokeredMessage message = new BrokeredMessage(order);

    // Set status to New
    message.Properties["Status"] = "New";

    // Unique Id
    message.MessageId = Guid.NewGuid().ToString();

    var sent = await this.SendMessageAsync(message,
      retires);

    Trace.TraceInformation("MessagingService SendOrder -
      Start");

    return sent;
}
```

4. Next, we'll implement the `SendMessageAsync` method, which will send a `BrokeredMessage` object with the option for retries. It's a good idea to implement a retry mechanism in case a send fails. There's a helpful `IsTransient` property on the `MessagingException` object, which indicates whether the message has failed due to transient comms conditions and should be retried:

```
private async Task<bool> SendMessageAsync(BrokeredMessage message,
int retires = 0)
{
    Trace.TraceInformation("MessagingService SendMessage -
      Start");

    int retry = 0;
    bool sent = false;

    while (true)
    {
        try
        {
            // Send message
            await this._topicClient.SendAsync(message);
            sent = true;
            break;
        }
        catch (MessagingException ex)
        {
            // If an exception is transient we will retry
            if (ex.IsTransient)
            {
                retry++;

                Trace.TraceInformation("MessagingService
                  SendMessage - Retry: {0}", retry);
            }
            else
            {
                Trace.TraceError("MessagingService
                  SendOrder Error: {0}", ex);

                throw;
            }
        }

        if (retry > retires)
```

```
        break;

        // Back-off for retry
        await Task.Delay(2000);
    }

    Trace.TraceInformation("MessagingService SendMessage -
        End");

    return sent;
}
```

Sending a message from the controller

Now we can modify the behavior of the controller to send an order message and update the order once it is complete. If the send fails (after three retries), the order will be marked as MessageFailed (a new state), which will allow the order to be picked up by the sales business domain order processor worker role to try and resend it later, which means we don't have to ask the customer to try later.

As the SendOrder method is asynchronous, the PayConfirm method is now marked async Task<ActionResult>:

```
public async Task<ActionResult> PayConfirm()
{
    Trace.TraceInformation("OrderController PayConfirm - Start");

    ViewResult vw = null;

    try
    {
        var order = this.GetOpenOrder();

        // At this point we would need to take a card payment or
        setup an invoice
        // But this isn't real so we'll order the item!

        var msgService = new MessagingService();

        if (await msgService.SendOrderAsync(order, 3))
        {
            // Update status to New
            order.Status = OrderStatus.New;
        }
        else
```

```
        {
            // Update status to MessageFailed, which will indicate
            to the Sales order processor that it need resending
            order.Status = OrderStatus.MessageFailed;
        }

        this._uow.SaveChanges();

        vw = View();
    }
    catch (Exception ex)
    {
        Trace.TraceError("OrderController PayConfirm Error: {0}",
        ex);

        throw;
    }

    Trace.TraceInformation("OrderController PayConfirm - End");

    return vw;
}
```

One final tweak I did was to mark the OrderItem class with the
[DataContract(IsReference = true)] attribute, so that it can be serialized. This
needs the System.Runtime.Serialization assembly referencing in the project.

If we run this now, the SendAsync method will throw a
NoMatchingSubscriptionException because we don't have any subscriptions
to consume the message, which is good, as this means we have a deterministic
messaging implementation. If you want to test it now, go to the **CONFIGURATION**
tab of the topic workspace in the portal and disable **FILTER MESSAGE BEFORE
PUBLISHING**, which will stop the exception being thrown; however, we will be
creating a simulator in the next section, which has a subscription that enables itself
and the website to send messages.

The messaging simulator

The customer website is now integrated into the Service Bus, so new order messages
are sent to the topic for the production and distribution business domains to process.
To test the worker roles and load-test the system, we don't want to manually create
orders through the website, as this would be extremely laborious and time-consuming,
so we'll create a simulator application, which can generate orders of varying products
at configurable rates on demand.

We'll create a new WPF application, which will allow us to start and stop messaging; control the order message cycle delay; and decide the quantity range of individual items to be added to the order, and the number of concurrent simulator threads, which will allow us to heavily load the system during testing.

If you don't have access to Visual Studio Professional, Premium, or Ultimate, you can create a new solution using Visual Studio Express for Desktop and add the existing `Model` project instead.

Setting up the project

First, we'll create a new WPF project, install some NuGet packages, and configure the Service Bus and database connection strings in the following procedure:

1. If you're not using Visual Studio Express, add a new WPF application called `OrderSim`.

2. If you're using Visual Studio Express for Desktop, create a new solution with a WPF project called `OrderSim`, and add the existing `Model` project by right-clicking on the solution and navigating to **Add | Existing Project...**.

3. Add a `Model` project reference to the `OrderSim` project.

4. Next, we'll install a number of NuGet packages: MVVM Light, which provides us with a quick-to-implement MVVM architecture, Entity Framework, which we've used in our websites already so far, and Windows Azure Service Bus, which we also used in the customer website. Enter the following commands into the **Package Manager Console** to install these packages:

   ```
   Install-package mvvmlight

   Install-package entityframework

   Install-package windowsazure.servicebus
   ```

5. As with the website, the package will create a connection string in the app settings section of the `app.config` file, which allows the application to connect to our newly created Service Bus namespace using SAS. Find the `Microsoft.ServiceBus.ConnectionString` app setting in the `app.config` file like this:

   ```
   <!-- Service Bus specific app settings for messaging
     connections
   <add key="Microsoft.ServiceBus.ConnectionString"
     value="Endpoint=sb://[your
     namespace].servicebus.windows.net;SharedSecretIssuer=owner;
     SharedSecretValue=[your secret]" />
   ```

6. Copy the `OrderSim` SAS connection string from the portal and paste it into the `value` attribute like this:

```
<add key="Microsoft.ServiceBus.ConnectionString" value="
  Endpoint=sb://azurebakery.servicebus.windows.net/;
  SharedAccessKeyName=SalesSimulator;
  SharedAccessKey=Z842VTFPrHI/XXXXXXXXXXXXXXXXxxxxxxxxxxxxxx=" />
```

7. Copy the connection string from the website and paste it into the `app.config` file under the `appSettings` block like this:

```
</appSettings>
<connectionStrings>
  <add name="DefaultConnection" connectionString="Data
    Source=localhost;Initial Catalog=
      AzureBakerySales;Integrated Security=True"
        providerName="System.Data.SqlClient" />
</connectionStrings>
```

We're just going to use the local database as we're only interested in reading the product list. If the Azure database had more products, we could use that instead.

Creating a data service

MVVM Light comes with a built-in SimpleIoc, which means we can easily create services (application domain logic, not web services) and register them along with the view models in the IoC container, which will automatically inject them into the view models when we request them.

This approach makes it really easy to separate the view model from the business; in a large application, it's best to separate the service layer into its own assembly, so it can easily be tested independently, and the application view models can be tested against mock services; however, we'll keep things in the same project for simplicity and for the benefit of having clean and easy-to-understand code. We'll create a data service to access product data:

1. First, create an `ApplicationDbContext` EF `DbContext` implementation class (I put mine under a solution folder called `DataAccess`):

```
namespace AzureBakery.Sales.DataAccess
{
    public class ApplicationDbContext : DbContext
    {
        public ApplicationDbContext()
            : base("DefaultConnection")
        {
```

```
base.Configuration.ProxyCreationEnabled =
    false;

Database.SetInitializer<ApplicationDbContext>(null);
}

public DbSet<Product> Products { get; set; }
    }
}
```

 Notice that the database initializer is set to null to stop EF from trying to create the database from the model because the website controls the database migrations.

2. Create an interface called IDataService under a Services/Interfaces folder with a single GetProducts method:

```
using AzureBakery.Sales.Model;
using System.Collections.Generic;

namespace AzureBakery.Sales.OrderSim.Services.Interfaces
{
    public interface IDataService
    {
        IEnumerable<Product> GetProducts();
    }
}
```

3. Now create a class called DataService under the Services folder, which implements the IDataService interface and returns products from the database on the GetProducts method:

```
using AzureBakery.Sales.DataAccess;
using AzureBakery.Sales.OrderSim.Services.Interfaces;
using System.Collections.Generic;

namespace AzureBakery.Sales.OrderSim.Services
{
    public class DataService : IDataService
    {
        private readonly ApplicationDbContext _ctx = new
            ApplicationDbContext();

        public IEnumerable<Model.Product> GetProducts()
        {
```

```
            return this._ctx.Products;
        }
    }
}
```

4. Finally, register the service in the IoC container within the constructor of the `ViewModelLocator` class (notice that the `MainViewModel` class is already registered):

```
public ViewModelLocator()
{
    ServiceLocator.SetLocatorProvider(() =>
        SimpleIoc.Default);

    SimpleIoc.Default.Register<IDataService,
        DataService>();

    SimpleIoc.Default.Register<MainViewModel>();
}
```

Creating a messaging service

We'll now create a `MessagingService` that is similar to the one we implemented in the sales customer website, which will allow us to send messages, create a subscription, and purge messages from the subscription:

1. Create an interface called `IMessagingService` under a `Services/ Interfaces` solution folder with the following methods:

```
using AzureBakery.Sales.Model;
using System.Threading.Tasks;

namespace AzureBakery.Sales.OrderSim.Services.Interfaces
{
    public interface IMessagingService
    {
        Task CreateSubscriptionAsync();

        Task<int> PurgeSubscriptionAsync();

        Task SendOrderAsync(Order order, int retires = 0);
    }
}
```

2. Next, create a class called `MessagingService`, which implements `IMessagingService` under the `Services` solution folder, and add the `topic` and `subscription` name constants and a `TopicClient` variable during instantiation:

```
using AzureBakery.Sales.Model;
using AzureBakery.Sales.OrderSim.Services.Interfaces;
using Microsoft.ServiceBus;
using Microsoft.ServiceBus.Messaging;
using System;
using System.Linq;
using System.Threading.Tasks;

namespace AzureBakery.Sales.OrderSim.Services
{
    public class MessagingService : IMessagingService
    {
        private readonly TopicClient _topicClient = null;
        private const string _topicName = "Order";
        private const string _subscriptionName =
          "SalesSimSubscription";

        public MessagingService()
        {
            this._topicClient =
              TopicClient.Create(_topicName);
        }
    }
}
```

3. Now, implement the `CreateSubscription` method with a check to see if it exists, before creating it:

```
public async Task CreateSubscriptionAsync()
{
    var namespaceManager = NamespaceManager.Create();

    // Look for topic
    if (! await
      namespaceManager.TopicExistsAsync(_topicName))
        return;

    var topic = await
      namespaceManager.GetTopicAsync(_topicName);
```

```
if (!await
  namespaceManager.SubscriptionExistsAsync(_topicName,
    _subscriptionName))
{
    var newOrderFilter = new SqlFilter("Status =
      'New'");
    await
      namespaceManager.CreateSubscriptionAsync(_topicName,
        _subscriptionName, newOrderFilter);
}
}
```

4. Implement the `PurgeSubscription` method, which loops around receiving batches of messages using the `ReceiveBatchAsync` method until there are no more messages (the methods will time out when the topic is empty and will not return any messages). By default, `SubscriptionClient` has `PeekLock RecieveMode`, which allows the consumer to commit the message if it successfully processes it, removing it from the subscription; otherwise, if it cannot process it, the message is not removed. This method keeps trying indefinitely to send in the event of transient exceptions:

```
public async Task<int> PurgeSubscriptionAsync()
{
    var agentSubscriptionClient =
      SubscriptionClient.Create(_topicName,
        _subscriptionName, ReceiveMode.ReceiveAndDelete);
    int count = 0;

    while (true)
    {
        bool backOff = false;

        try
        {
            // Get a batch of 100 messages
            var messages = await
              agentSubscriptionClient.ReceiveBatchAsync(100,
                TimeSpan.FromSeconds(5));

            // If there are no messages, we're done
            if (messages.Count() == 0)
                break;

            count += messages.Count();
        }
        catch (MessagingException e)
        {
```

```
            if (!e.IsTransient)
                throw;
            else
                backOff = true;
        }

        // Wait for transient fault to clear
        if (backOff)
            await Task.Delay(2000);
    }

    agentSubscriptionClient.Close();

    return count;
}
```

5. Now, create a `SendMessageAsync` method, which sends `BrokeredMessage` with a retry on the transient fault mechanism:

```
private async Task SendMessageAsync(BrokeredMessage message, int
retries = 0)
{
    int retry = 0;

    while (true)
    {
        try
        {
            await this._topicClient.SendAsync(message);
            break;
        }
        catch (MessagingException e)
        {
            if (!e.IsTransient)
                throw;
            else
                retry++;
        }

        if (retry > retries)
            break;

        // Back-off for retry
        await Task.Delay(2000);
    }
}
```

6. Next, implement the `SendOrderAsync` method, which creates an order message with a `Status` property set to `New` and sends it using the `SendMessage` method:

```
public async Task SendOrderAsync(Order order, int retries =
    0)
{
    var message = new BrokeredMessage(order);
    message.Properties["Status"] = "New";
    message.MessageId = Guid.NewGuid().ToString();

    await this.SendMessageAsync(message, retries);
}
```

7. Finally, register the service with the IoC container in the `ViewModelLocator` constructor:

```
public ViewModelLocator()
{
    ServiceLocator.SetLocatorProvider(() => SimpleIoc.Default);

    SimpleIoc.Default.Register<IDataService, DataService>();
    SimpleIoc.Default.Register<IMessagingService,
    MessagingService>();

    SimpleIoc.Default.Register<MainViewModel>();
}
```

Completing the simulator

There's not enough space in this book to go through the entire main view and view model, so go and get them from the code samples.

As we've separated all the data and messaging logic from the view models, there's actually no reference to `Microsoft.ServiceBus` or our `DbContext`, so we're not missing anything directly related to this subject!

Running the simulator

When we first run the simulator, we have a **1000** ms delay between orders, **1** thread, and between **0** and **10** products per order, as shown in the following screenshot:

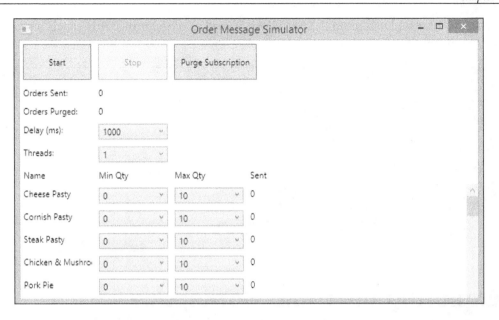

This will give us a slow throughput of orders into the system. If we increase the number of **Threads** and set the **Delay** to **0**, meaning each thread will send orders as fast as the topic will take them, we can put large volumes of messages into the system in a short period of time, which is great for load testing and testing scaling capabilities. This was achieved in a few seconds:

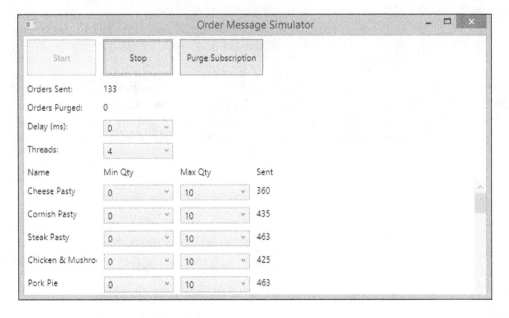

Now, if we take a look at the **DASHBOARD** section of the topic workspace, we can see the metrics for the messages we sent:

Exploring the topic workspace

If we navigate to our Service Bus namespace workspace in the portal and click on the **TOPICS** tab, we can see a quick overview of our topics, including their status, stored message size (**CURRENT SIZE**), and capacity (**MAX SIZE**):

Now, if we click on the topic and navigate to its workspace, we have a **DASHBOARD** section, which gives us a quick overview of the topic status with a graph that shows the messaging metrics, and a usage overview, which shows us how much of our storage allowance we're using along with some quick glance information.

The MONITOR tab

The **MONITOR** tab shows us the same metrics graph as the **DASHBOARD** section with more details of the tabular statistics underneath:

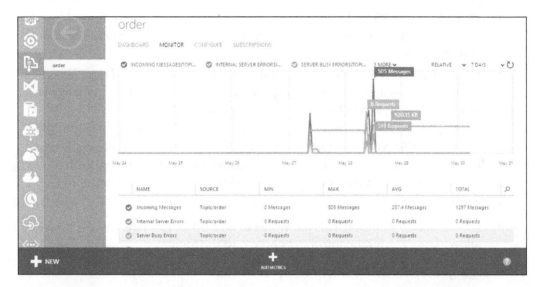

If we click on the **ADD METRICS** button, we can add and remove metrics from the display:

The CONFIGURE tab

The **CONFIGURE** tab allows us to configure the following settings that we originally set up when we created the topic:

- **DEFAULT MESSAGE TIME TO LIVE**: This is the amount of time elapsed between a message being sent and it expiring and being deleted or sent to the dead-letter queue.

- **DUPLICATE DETECTION HISTORY**: This is the amount of time for which the topic stores messages for duplicate detection. If a duplicate message is detected during this period, it will be deleted or moved to the dead-letter queue. If it is outside this period, it will appear on the topic for consumption.

- **FILTER MESSAGE BEFORE PUBLISHING**: This prevents messages that have no matching subscription filter from being sent to the topic with a NoMatchingSubscriptionException being thrown at the client.

- **TOPIC STATE**: This allows us to enable or disable the topic.

- **shared access policies**: This allows us to add up to 12 shared access policies, allowing us granular control over access to the topic.

These settings are shown in the following screenshot:

The SUBSCRIPTIONS tab

The **SUBSCRIPTIONS** tab shows us an overview of our registered subscriptions and allows us to manually **CREATE**, **EDIT**, and **DELETE** them from the toolbar:

Clicking on **EDIT** allows us to modify the following settings for the topic:

- **DEFAULT MESSAGE TIME TO LIVE**: This is the amount of time elapsed between a message being sent and it expiring and being deleted or sent to the dead-letter queue (the default is **14 days**—there seems to be a bug in the portal).

- **MOVE EXPIRED MESSAGES TO THE DEAD-LETTER SUBQUEUE**: This setting allows messages that have exceeded their TTL to be moved to the dead-letter queue.

- **MOVE MESSAGES THAT CAUSE FILTER EVALUATION EXCEPTIONS TO THE DEAD-LETTER SUBQUEUE**: When we have the **FILTER MESSAGE BEFORE PUBLISHING** setting enabled in the topic, this setting allows messages with no matching subscription filter to be sent to the dead-letter queue.

- **LOCK DURATION**: This is the duration of time `PeekLock` is allowed before a lock is lost, causing a `MessageLockLostException` to be thrown in the client, and allowing another consumer to consume the message.

- **MAXIMUM DELIVERY COUNT**: This is the maximum number of times a message is received by a consumer but not completed (failed to process) before it is sent to the dead-letter queue.

- **TOPIC SUBSCRIPTION STATE**: This allows us to enable and disable the subscription.

The settings to edit a subscription are shown in the following screenshot:

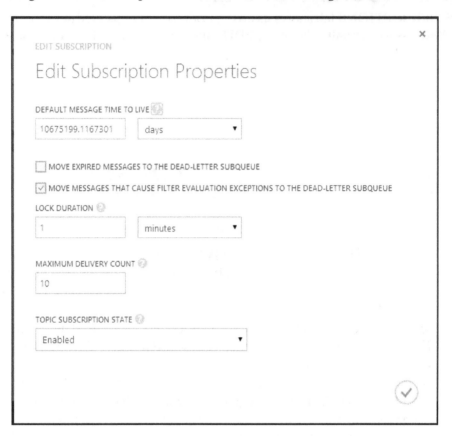

Summary

We've successfully implemented our Azure Service Bus Topic, which is the messaging layer of our entire enterprise system, integrated the Sales Customer website, and built a messaging simulator application, which will help us develop and test the rest of the system.

In the next chapter, we're going to be creating worker roles for the business units that will have their own subscriptions to consume and process Order Status messages.

Questions

1. What is the path of a subscription dead-letter queue?

2. What are the security implications of creating queues and topics in code?

3. What does the **Enable Partitioning** setting do when we create a topic?

4. What does the **FILTER MESSAGE BEFORE PUBLISHING** setting in the portal do?

5. Where can we find topic SAS connection strings?

6. In which config block does the Service Bus connection string appear when we install the `WindowsAzure.ServiceBus` package?

7. Which object do we use to send messages to a topic?

8. What does the `IsTransient` property on `MessagingException` tell us?

9. Which exception is thrown if a client tries to send a message with no matching subscription and **FILTER MESSAGE BEFORE PUBLISHING** is enabled?

10. What is the default `ReceiveMode` for a `SubscriptionClient`?

11. What is the message type we send to the Service Bus?

12. How many shared access policies can one topic have?

13. Create a simple WPF application, which creates a Service Bus queue itself, and then posts simple messages to the queue on a timer.

14. Create a second WPF application, which consumes messages from the queue and displays them on the UI.

Answers

1. Subscription name along with /$DeadLetterQueue.

2. The code needs to use the Service Bus namespace security credentials, which puts the whole namespace at risk if the credentials are compromised.

3. Allows the Service Bus broker to scale up.

4. Prevents messages without a matching subscription filter being sent.

5. Under the topic **CONNECTION INFORMATION** in the **TOPICS** tab of the Service Bus workspace.

6. appSettings.

7. TopicClient.

8. If true, it tells us that an exception was caused by a transient fault and should be retried.

9. NoMatchingSubscriptionException.

10. PeekLock.

11. Brokered message.

12. **12**.

13. NA.

14. NA.

8
Building Worker Roles

In this chapter, we're going to start looking at Microsoft Azure Cloud services and building our production order processor worker role. By the end, we'll have a scalable worker role that consumes order messages from the Service Bus topic subscription we created previously. Orders will be stored in the production database, and periodic tasks will create batch schedules to manufacture the products and allocate the stock.

We'll cover the following topics:

- Introduction to cloud services
- Creating a worker role
- Running a worker role locally
- Publishing a worker role
- Building the production order processor
- Creating a scheduled work activity
- Testing the production order processor
- Deleting idle cloud services

Along with looking at worker roles, we'll be revisiting Service Bus topics and building databases. We'll also be introducing scheduled tasks and storage queues, which we've not looked at yet.

Introducing cloud services

Cloud services are PaaS Azure services that allow us to create highly available applications (99.95 percent monthly SLA) and deploy them to dedicated virtual machines of various image sizes, which can be scaled out to meet the demands of the system.

There are two types of cloud services, worker roles and web roles. Worker roles are similar to Windows Services; they are unattended applications with no user interface which that long-running tasks. Web roles are websites deployed in IIS and run on dedicated cloud service VMs; they are very similar to normal Azure websites, with the additional configuration and diagnostic capabilities of a cloud service.

Cloud services come with production and staging deployment slots that run on dedicated VM instances so that staged deployments don't impact the performance of the production deployment (unlike staging slots in websites). Cloud services can be debugged remotely (with IntelliTrace), run start-up tasks, and allow remote desktop sessions to allow advanced configuration and debugging.

Cloud service projects hold one or more roles, which run on their own virtual machines, and allow them to be logically grouped, making them easier to deploy together rather than having a separate cloud service per role. It is not cost effective to split every single task you want to perform into dedicated roles (particularly if they're not highly resource-intensive), so we'll look at a neat pattern to do this using async tasks within a single role later on.

Exploring worker roles

To begin with, we're going to create a boiler-plate worker role in Visual Studio, run it locally, then publish it, and run it on Azure. It's possible to create a cloud service in the portal, then publish a project to it or upload a package.

It's also possible to automatically provision a cloud service during the first publish from Visual Studio, which is the approach we'll take.

Creating a worker role

We'll create the role using the following procedure:

1. I've created a blank solution called `AzureBakery.Production`, which is the start of our production business unit solution for the worker role, production data model, WPF management application, and Web API service.

2. To create a worker role, right-click on the solution root in Visual Studio and go to **Add | New Project**, then select **Windows Azure Cloud Service** under the **Cloud** templates, choose **Name**, and click on **OK**:

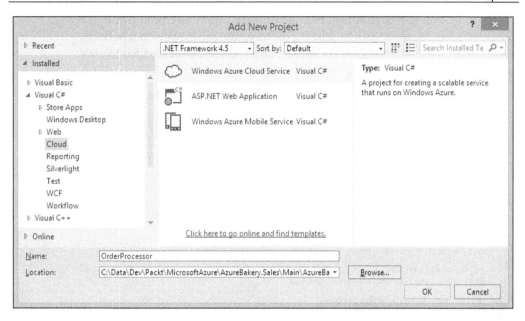

3. Select **Worker Role** (notice that there is a template for a **Worker Role with Service Bus Queue** option, which is a good starting point if you are creating a worker role that is consuming messages from a queue) and click on the right-arrow to add it to the list (you can add and remove multiple web and worker roles to the cloud service from here):

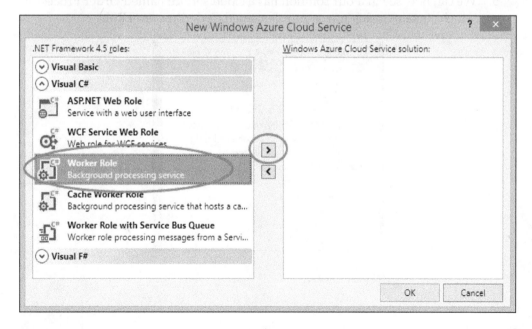

4. Click on the **Edit** button to change the name (I've called mine
    `OrderProcessorRole`, but if you have multiple roles in a service,
    you may want to give different names to the cloud service to save
    confusion), and click on **OK**:

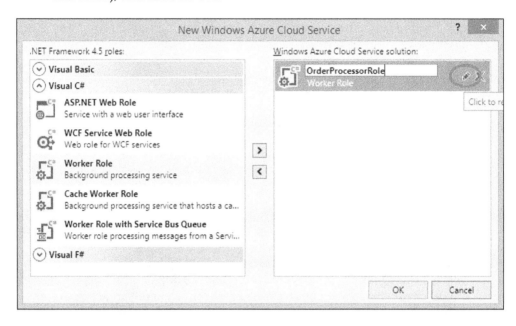

5. We can now see that our solution has a cloud service named **Order Processor**,
    which contains a single worker role named **OrderProcessorRole**:

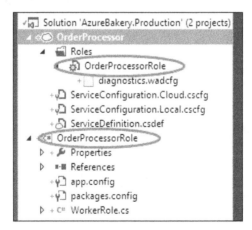

Examining the worker role

If we take a quick look at the worker role we just created, there's not much in there; it's a class library that looks pretty similar to a Windows service. We have an App.config file, which just contains the trace listener configuration that allows the application diagnostics to be logged. The WorkerRole class itself (I've tidied up the using keyword to save space) is derived from RoleEntryPoint, which provides methods for the role's starting, stopping, and running:

```
using Microsoft.WindowsAzure.ServiceRuntime;
using System.Diagnostics;
using System.Net;
using System.Threading;

namespace OrderProcessorRole
{
    public class WorkerRole : RoleEntryPoint
    {
        public override void Run()
        {
            // This is a sample worker implementation. Replace with
            your logic.
            Trace.TraceInformation("OrderProcessorRole entry point
                called");

            while (true)
            {
                Thread.Sleep(10000);
                Trace.TraceInformation("Working");
            }
        }

        public override bool OnStart()
        {
            // Set the maximum number of concurrent connections
            ServicePointManager.DefaultConnectionLimit = 12;

            // For information on handling configuration changes
            // see the MSDN topic at
            http://go.microsoft.com/fwlink/?LinkId=166357.

            return base.OnStart();
        }
    }
}
```

The following are the worker role's life cycle methods:

- OnStart: When a worker role starts, the OnStart method is called, which is used to perform initialization tasks, for example, creating resources such as messaging clients and database contexts

- Run: If OnStart returns true, the Run method will then be called, which begins the worker role's work activity

- OnStop: When a worker role is signaled to stop, the OnStop method is called, which can be used for clearing up resources and finalizing the role

The OnStart method sets the ServicePointManager.DefaultConnectionLimit property (without setting this, the default value is 2), which is the number of concurrent connections the worker role instance is allowed for things such as database connections, messaging clients, and HTTP requests. If this is not set correctly, we will get undesirable behavior from connections being dropped if the connection limit is exceeded.

The Run method simply sits in a loop with a 10s delay and traces a Working info message. Once the method returns, the role will recycle, so it needs to be blocked or stay in a loop while the role is running. The example Run method is synchronous, so it can be held in a simple loop and delayed using Thread.Sleep, which blocks the thread; in our production order processor worker role (we'll be looking at it shortly), we're going to implement some tasks to service the topic and two storage queues, which are async and will need a different approach to stop the Run method from terminating early and recycling the role.

Examining the cloud service

The cloud service is a special project type (.ccproj — the cloud configuration project), which consists of a number of configuration files that describe the features and behavior of all the roles within the service. The files have the following functions:

- Diagnostics.wadcfg: This is the diagnostics configuration for each role; it appears under a RoleNameContent folder in the directory structure

- ServiceConfiguration.cloud: This contains the configuration settings for the role in the cloud service configuration (published to Azure); these configurations settings can be changed in the portal

- ServiceConfiguration.local: This contains the configuration settings for the role in the local service configuration (running in the compute emulator)

- ServiceDefinition.csdef: This defines the roles within the cloud service and the role modules included

All the settings can be configured from within the role UI, which can be opened by double-clicking a role under the cloud service's `role` folder.

Running locally

We know that we can easily run Azure websites locally while we're developing them because they're normal websites and will run in IIS and IIS Express without any difficulty. Cloud services aren't normal executables, which can run on Windows, but they can be run locally on the Windows Azure compute emulator and storage emulator. We have a full and express emulator available to us in the SDK; we'll start with the default express version and look at the full version when we need it later.

To get started, put some break points in the application in the `OnStart` and `Run` methods, one at the start and one inside the `while` loop. Run the debugger in Visual Studio and we'll see a progress dialog that notifies us of the compute emulator, storage emulator, and worker role initialization progress:

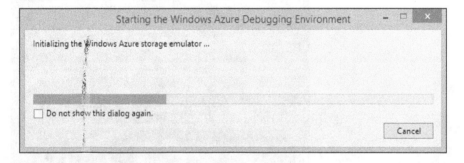

Once this is completed, the worker role should break on the `OnStart` method, and we notice that we have a new Windows icon in the system tray; if we right-click on it, we have a number of options for the Azure emulators:

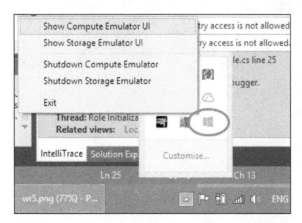

We have options to see the UIs for the emulators and options to shut down the emulators.

When we continue to run the debugger, we will break on the Run method, which will continue to loop until we stop the debugger.

The compute emulator UI

If we select **Show Compute-Emulator UI**, we'll see the cloud service, worker role, and instances in the tree diagram on the left-hand side, and if we drill down to our single instance **0**, we can see the diagnostics output running live:

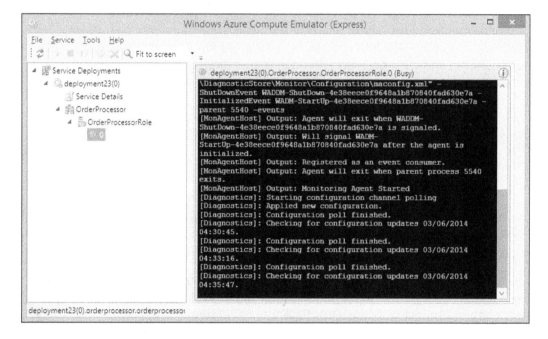

We can change the tracing level by going to the **Tools** | **Logging level** menu:

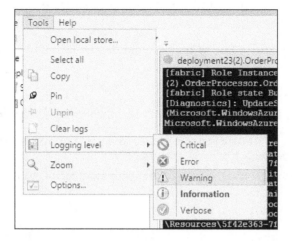

We can also get to the logfile directory quickly by clicking on the **Open log store...** menu item, which will open Windows Explorer in the temporary log directory, where we can drill into `\directory\DiagnosticStore\Monitor\Tables` to find our log table data.

The storage emulator UI

Now, open the storage emulator UI by selecting the **Show Storage-Emulator UI** option from the context-sensitive menu; when I do this, I see a dialog box that tells me that the UI is deprecated, and gives an option to use the **New Command Line** interface or **Old Interface (UI)**; if you see this option, select **New Command Line**.

We'll now see a standard command console appear at the storage emulator path:

```
C:\WINDOWS\System32\cmd.exe

Windows Azure Storage Emulator 3.2.0.0 command line tool
Usage:
    WAStorageEmulator.exe init            : Initialize the emulator database and
configuration.
    WAStorageEmulator.exe start           : Start the emulator.
    WAStorageEmulator.exe stop            : Stop the emulator.
    WAStorageEmulator.exe status          : Get current emulator status.
    WAStorageEmulator.exe clear           : Delete all data in the emulator.
    WAStorageEmulator.exe help [command]  : Show general or command-specific hel
p.

See the following URL for more command line help: http://go.microsoft.com/fwlink
/?LinkId=392235

C:\Program Files (x86)\Microsoft SDKs\Windows Azure\Storage Emulator>
```

We have some basic commands listed from the help option to initialize, start, and stop the emulator. Also, commands for getting the status and clearing the emulator's data store are available.

We can quickly play with some of the commands; the following command shows the status:

```
WAStorageEmulator.exe status
```

This command displays the running status and the storage endpoints:

```
C:\Program Files (x86)\Microsoft SDKs\Windows Azure\Storage
Emulator>WAStorageEmulator.exe status
Windows Azure Storage Emulator 3.2.0.0 command line tool
IsRunning: True
BlobEndpoint: http://127.0.0.1:10000/
QueueEndpoint: http://127.0.0.1:10001/
TableEndpoint: http://127.0.0.1:10002/
```

> In a command console, to save typing the whole exe name, type the first few characters, and then press *Tab* to cycle through the matching files. In this case, if you type was and hit *Tab* once, it'll find `WasStorageEmulator.exe` straightaway.

The following command clears all the emulator storage, which is useful if it's been running for a while:

```
WAStorageEmulator.exe clear all
```

Publishing a worker role

To test the worker role that just runs the boiler-plate code on Azure, we'll publish it using the following procedure:

1. Right-click on the cloud service in the **Solution Explorer** window and select **Publish...** from the context-sensitive menu:

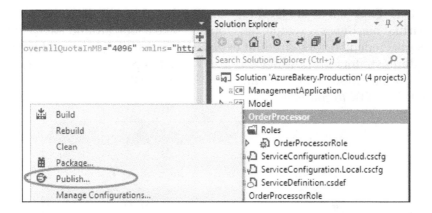

2. Choose **Subscription** and click on **Next**; if you've not got any worker roles configured in the portal, you'll get a dialog that prompts you to create one with a storage account.

3. Choose **Name** and select **Region or Affinity Group**. The **Enable Geo-Replication** option is for the storage account. Click on **Create** to complete.

4. Choose a **Cloud Service** option to publish to Azure, select the **Environment** option (I chose **Staging**, so we can test the service before swopping to production), and leave **Build configuration** as **Release** and **Service configuration** as **Cloud**:

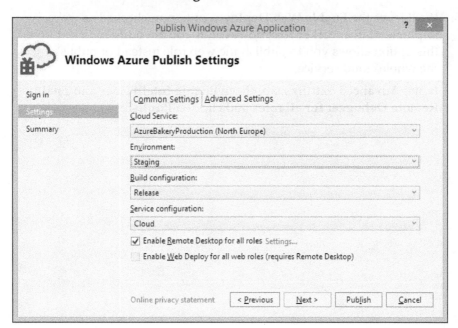

5. Check **Enable Remote Desktop for all roles** (this will allows us to access the virtual machine via remote desktop and take a look around later). Enter your login credentials (the **Account expiration date** setting is useful for system administrators to allow developers to have temporary access to a cloud service to do some fault finding without giving them long-term access). Click on **OK** to complete:

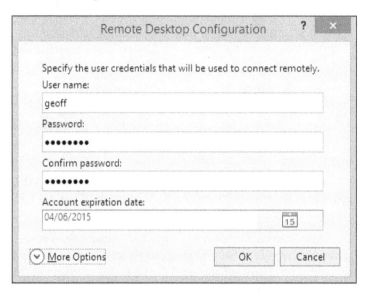

6. We'll leave the **Enable Web Deploy...** option unchecked as we're implementing a worker role; however, if you are building a web role, this option allows you to publish the web role instead of publishing the whole cloud service.

7. In the **Advanced Settings** tab, check **Enable IntelliTrace** and **Enable Remote Debugger for all roles** and click on **Publish**:

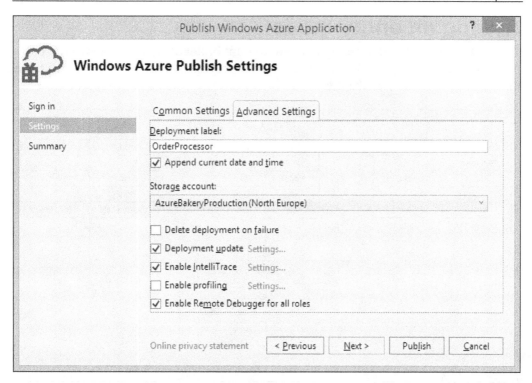

8. The publishing process may take a while as a new VM instance is provisioned for the cloud service to run on.

Building the production order processor

We're going to start working on the production business domain order processor worker role, which first subscribes to the OrderStatus.New status order messages on the topic, then adds the orders to its own database, creates batch schedules, and allocates stock for the products requested in the orders. The worker role will be structured with separate tasks and business logic to perform the individual messaging and business domain activities.

Adding an entity model

We've already built a data model in a fair amount of detail, so we'll go through the process pretty quickly for the production order processor. The entity model for the production system looks like this:

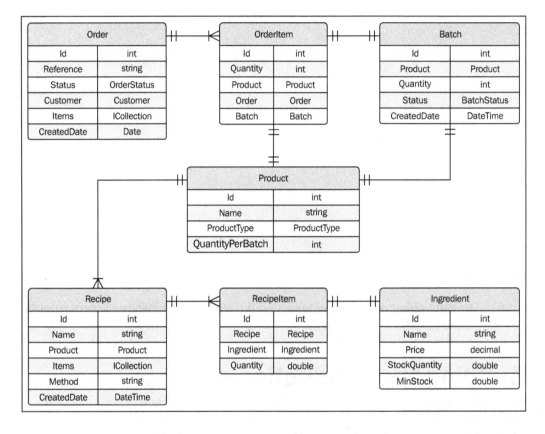

Get the `AzureBakery.Production.Model` project, which contains all the entities from code, and add it to the solution, and then perform the following procedure to implement it in the worker role, which will manage the database migrations:

1. Add a `Model` project reference to the `OrderProcessorRole` project.

2. Install the Entity Framework NuGet package into the `OrderProcessorRole` project using the following command in the **Package Manager Console**:

   ```
   install-package entityframework
   ```

3. Add an `ApplicationDbContext` class to a `DataAccess` solution folder (use the code samples).

4. Add a connection string to the `App.Config` file:

```
<connectionStrings>
    <add name="DefaultConnection" connectionString="Data
       Source=localhost;Initial Catalog= AzureBakeryProduction;
       Integrated Security=True"
       providerName="System.Data.SqlClient" />
</connectionStrings>
```

5. Enter the following command in the **Package Manager Console** to enable migrations:

`enable-migrations`

6. Enter the following command in the **Package Manager Console** to add an initial migration:

`add-migration initial`

7. Add the seeding code to the `Configuration.Seed` method to seed the database (use the code samples).

8. Enter the following command in the **Package Manager Console** to update (create) the database:

`update-database`

Preparing the Service Bus topic

We're going to create a new SAS policy for the order processor, which will allow it to create its own subscription and read messages from it. We'll then install the `WindowsAzure.ServiceBus` package and configure its connection string using the following steps:

1. Create a new SAS policy called `ProductionOrderProcessor` with the **Manage** and **Listen** permissions in the topic's **CONFIGURE** tab, the same as we did in the previous chapter when we created the simulator application.

2. Install the `WindowsAzure.ServiceBus` NuGet package with the following command:

`install-package WindowsAzure.ServiceBus`

3. Locate the `Microsoft.ServiceBus.ConnectionString` appSetting in the `app.config` file and change the value to use our new SAS connection string. It should look something like this when you're done:

```
<appSettings>
    <!-- Service Bus specific app settings for messaging
       connections -->
```

```
    <add key="Microsoft.ServiceBus.ConnectionString"
      value="Endpoint=sb://azurebakery.servicebus.windows.net/;
        SharedAccessKeyName=ProductionOrderProcessor;
          SharedAccessKey=XXXXXXXXXXXXXXXxxxxxxxxxxxxxxxxxx=" />
  </appSettings>
```

 You can get the connection string from the **CONNECTION INFORMATION** setting on the **TOPICS** tab in the toolbar.

Adding an order processor task

To start with, we'll create a reusable base class to consume messages from a subscription and hand them off to some business logic to process the message; once we've got this, we'll implement it to consume our order status topic.

Creating TopicProcessorBase

The following class encapsulates a mechanism to poll a topic subscription and then process messages in the abstract `ProcessMessage` method, which will be implemented in a derived class. I've left out the `CreateSubscription` code as this was covered in the previous chapter. The mechanics of the `ProcessSubscriptionAsync` method is pretty much the same as the `PurgeSubscriptionAsync` method in the `AzureBakery.Sales.OrderSim.Services.MessagingService`; there is a `retry` mechanism on transient fault:

```csharp
using Microsoft.ServiceBus;
using Microsoft.ServiceBus.Messaging;
using System;
using System.Net;
using System.Threading.Tasks;

namespace OrderProcessorRole.Messaging
{
    public abstract class TopicProcessorBase : IDisposable
    {
        private SubscriptionClient _subscriptionClient = null;
        private string _topicName = null;
        private string _subscriptionName = null;
        private string _sqlFilter = null;

        public bool IsRunning { get; private set; }
```

```csharp
public TopicProcessorBase(string topicName, string
  subscriptionName, string sqlFilter)
{
    this._topicName = topicName;
    this._subscriptionName = subscriptionName;
    this._sqlFilter = sqlFilter;

    // Set the maximum number of concurrent connections
    ServicePointManager.DefaultConnectionLimit = 12;

    // Create subscription
    this.CreateSubscription();

    // Create subscription client
    this._subscriptionClient =
      SubscriptionClient.Create(_topicName, _
      subscriptionName);
}

private void CreateSubscription()
{
    // Code omitted for brevity
}

public async Task ProcessSubscriptionAsync()
{
    this.IsRunning = true;

    while (this.IsRunning)
    {
        bool delay = false;

        try
        {
            // Get a message. The serverWaitTime parameter
            will give us a delay in our processing loop
            // when there are no messages
            var message = await
              this._subscriptionClient.ReceiveAsync(TimeSpan.
              FromSeconds(5));

            // Parse message
            if (message != null)
```

```
                {
                    await this.ProcessMessage(message);
                }

            }
            catch (MessagingException e)
            {
                if (!e.IsTransient)
                    throw;
                else
                    delay = true;
            }

            // Wait for transient fault to clear
            if(delay)
                await Task.Delay(2000);
        }
    }

    public void Stop()
    {
        this.IsRunning = false;
    }

    protected abstract Task ProcessMessage(BrokeredMessage
        message);

    public void Dispose()
    {
        if (this._subscriptionClient != null)
            this._subscriptionClient.Close();
    }
    }
}
```

The `ProcessTopicAsync` method is asynchronous (as the naming convention suggests), which means it is more efficient with thread resources, which is good in a multithreaded application (or a client application with a threading context such as a WPF application, where the UI thread is not blocked when performing activities such as making web requests or data access, which may take some time). It's fairly easy to implement .NET 4.5 async tasks to get performance benefits rather than having to create async code with async callbacks, which can be difficult to write and follow.

Implementing TopicProcessorBase

Now that we have a base class for creating and processing topic subscriptions, we can implement it in a derived class to override the `ProcessMessage` method:

```
using Microsoft.ServiceBus.Messaging;
using OrderProcessorRole.Business;
using System;
using System.Diagnostics;
using System.Threading.Tasks;

namespace OrderProcessorRole.Messaging
{
    public class OrderTopicProcessor : TopicProcessorBase
    {
        public OrderTopicProcessor()
            : base("Order", "ProductionSubscription", "Status =
              'New'")
        {

        }

        protected override async Task
          ProcessMessage(BrokeredMessage message)
        {
            Trace.TraceInformation("OrderProcessorRole.Messaging.
              OrderTopicProcessor.ProcessMessage - Begin");

            try
            {
                var order =
                  message.GetBody<AzureBakery.Sales.Model.Order>();
                await new OrderProcessor().Process(order);

                await message.CompleteAsync();
            }
            catch (Exception ex)
            {
                Trace.TraceError("OrderProcessorRole.Messaging.
                OrderTopicProcessor.
                 ProcessMessage - Error: {0}", ex);
            }
        }
    }
}
```

We can see that this implementation is very simple and simply parses an order object from the message body and then hands it off to the `OrderProcessor` business logic, so we have a clear separation of concerns.

> In this case, I've actually borrowed the sales model from the sales domain so that it can be easily parsed; if we wanted complete separation or we didn't have access to the model, we could use the JSON serialization, which is less fussy about namespaces, rather than the standard `DataContractSerializer`, or strip the namespaces from the originating model and have a replica on the consuming side.

As we get a `PeekLock ReceiveMode` by default, the message must be completed with `Complete` or `CompleteAsync` once it has been successfully processed so that it is removed from the subscription.

I'm not showing the business logic here to save space, so go and grab it from the code. As with the other projects, it's a good idea in the long run to use a dependency injection for binding components together to help in testing and maintenance, so it would be nice to abstract the processors and business logic further and have them bind and inject into the worker role using an IoC container; however, we'll not cover this as it's not in the scope of this book.

Using OrderTopicProcessor in the worker role

Now that we have the mechanics in place to subscribe to and process the order status messages on the topic, we can implement it in our worker role. In the `OnStart` method, we have some tracing, so we can see what's going on in the diagnostics and then instantiate our `OrderTopicProcessor`, which creates the subscription if required:

```
public override bool OnStart()
{
    Trace.TraceInformation("OrderProcessorRole.WorkerRole.OnStart
      - Begin");

    try
    {
        // Create processors
        this._orderTopicProcessor = new OrderTopicProcessor);

        Trace.TraceInformation("OrderProcessorRole.WorkerRole.OnStart
          - End");

        return true;
```

```
    }
    catch (Exception ex)
    {
        Trace.TraceError("OrderProcessorRole.WorkerRole.OnStart -
            Error: {0}", ex);
    }

    return false;
}
```

As I mentioned before, we need to stop the Run method from exiting by blocking it; otherwise, the role will recycle. We can run the task using Task.Run, which queues the processor task to run on the thread pool and returns a proxy for the task, which we can then wait to complete blocking the calling thread using the Task.WaitAll method. This is a nice pattern as we can quickly add in extra tasks to run on the thread pool in the Task.WaitAll parameters, which we will do shortly:

```
public override void Run()
{
    Trace.TraceInformation("OrderProcessorRole.WorkerRole.Run -
        Begin");

    try
    {
        Task.WaitAll(
            Task.Run(() =>
                this._orderTopicProcessor.ProcessSubscriptionAsync()),
    }
    catch(Exception ex)
    {
        Trace.TraceError("OrderProcessorRole.WorkerRole.Run -
            Error: {0}", ex);
    }
}
```

The ProcessSubscriptionAsync method will stay in a loop until Stop is called; however, if we didn't use Task.WaitAll, the Run method will terminate as it's asynchronous.

The OnStop method is very simple; we call the Stop method, which causes the processing loop to terminate, and the Run method exits once the waited tasks complete:

```
public override void OnStop()
{
    this._orderTopicProcessor.Stop();

    base.OnStop();
}
```

As we've separated our messaging and business logic from the worker role, we can see that we don't have much code in the `WorkerRole` class itself, which makes it nice and clean and easy to see what's going on.

Creating a scheduled work activity

We've got most of the production worker role completed with orders safely being inserted into the production database, but there's a bit missing, and we have a slight problem with it.

The production order processor must create product batch schedules and allocate stock for the production management application. We don't want to perform this operation every time an order message comes in, as it will put too much load on the system. Also, when we have multiple roles running as we scale out, we don't want to get database contention from multiple instances trying to work on the same records in the database. Pessimistic and optimistic concurrency will not even help us here as we need to create single new batches when existing batches are full as well as adding to existing incomplete batches.

To solve this problem, we need a way of only one role performing these activities at any one time and a way of requesting the scheduled activities. Azure gives us a number of options, which can help achieve this:

- We're already using a topic, which allows multiple worker roles to receive order messages and prevents them from processing the same message, so we can use something similar to queue scheduled work activities. The Azure Scheduler allows us to send messages to a storage queue, so our worker role instances can consume this, and only one instance will process a single message.

- We can use a storage blob leasing to effectively create a lock, where one role obtains a lock on a blob (we could have a single lock or multiple locks across product types to make the approach less contentious), allowing it to perform a scheduled activity triggered by a timing mechanism within the role while the other role(s) attempts to get the same lock and fails to tell them that another role is working on the scheduled activity and they should back off.

- In-role cache allows us to share cached memory across role instances, so we can write a locking mechanism similar to the blob leasing approach without having to create blobs and communicate with storage.

To keep things simple and to give us an opportunity to explore the Azure Scheduler and storage queues, we'll use the first option.

Creating a scheduled job and queue

The following procedure details how to set up two scheduled jobs and storage queues to create batches and allocate stock (separating the scheduled tasks helps to distribute the work load):

1. Click on the **+ NEW** service button in the portal, and go to **APP SERVICES | SCHEDULER | CUSTOM CREATE**:

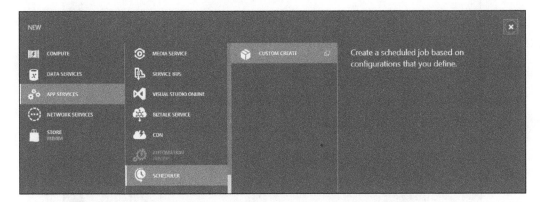

2. Choose a **SUBSCRIPTION** and **REGION**; if you haven't got a **JOB COLLECTION** or don't want to add it to an existing collection, select **Create New** (default), choose a **NEW JOB COLLECTION NAME** (if you're creating a new one), and click on the next arrow:

3. Next, choose **NAME** for the job, select **Storage Queue** from the **ACTION TYPE** options, choose a **STORAGE ACCOUNT**, select **Create New** from the **QUEUE NAME** options, choose a **NEW QUEUE NAME** (lowercase), and click on the next arrow (I've left the **BODY (TEXT/PLAIN)** section blank as we're only interested in using the message to trigger an action in the roles):

4. Next, select **Recurring Job** from the **RECURRENCE** options, enter a recurrence period in the **RECUR EVERY** options (I've chosen 10 minutes; in the code, I'm going to be careful to poll at least twice this rate and disregard messages that are 10 minutes old or more as these could indicate a scheduling or processing failure, which may result in duplicated work by the roles). You can set an **ENDING ON** time, and optionally set it to never end once the job is created. Click on the tick button to complete:

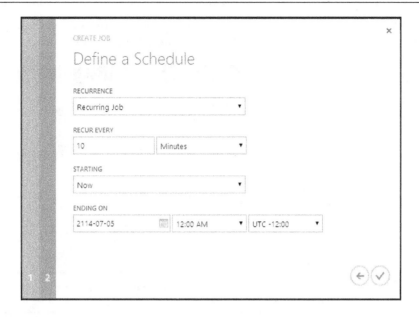

5. Repeat the procedure for the stock allocation job using the same container.

Configuring a connection string

We're going to add a storage connection string to the cloud service settings, which can be accessed by the worker role and changed at runtime in the portal. This can be done by performing the following steps:

1. In the **Settings** tab of the worker role properties, click on **Add Setting** (for **All Configurations**):

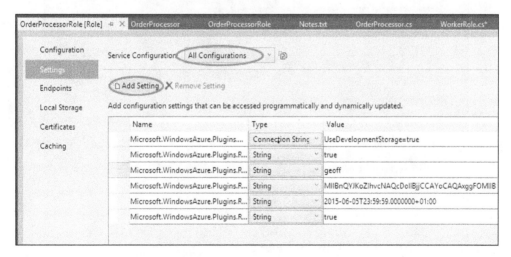

2. Next, enter **Name** for the connection string, select **Connection String** as **Type**, and click on the ellipsis button to create a connection string:

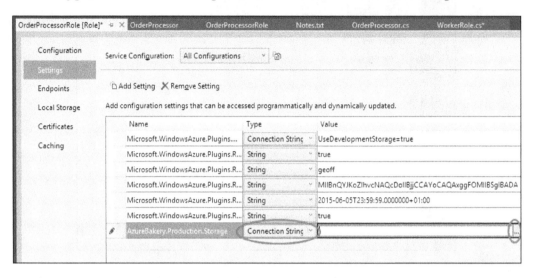

3. Sign in to your account when prompted.

4. Choose the **Subscription** and **Account name** options for the queue that we just configured from the scheduler, and click on **OK**:

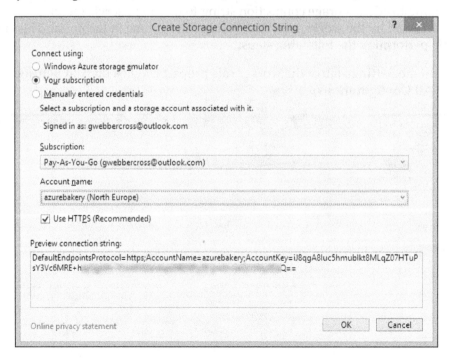

Adding batch processor tasks

As with the order processor, we'll create tasks to encapsulate our batch-processing logic, which will be neatly slotted into the task pattern we've started. Before we do anything, we need to install the `WindowsAzure.Storage` NuGet package, which will allow us to interact with the storage queue by entering the following command into the NuGet **Package Manager Console**:

```
Install-package WindowsAzure.Storage
```

Creating a storage queue processor base

We'll create a common base class to process these queues, which allow us to run tasks on a single role instance in a scaled-out worker. The `StorageQueueProcessorBase` class follows a pattern similar to the `TopicProcessorBase` class, where we create a client on construction, then have a `ProcessQueueAsync` task, which continually polls the queue for messages and then hands off messages that have not expired (remember we talked about failure modes when we created the scheduled task?) to the abstract `Process` method for the derived classes to implement:

```
using Microsoft.WindowsAzure;
using Microsoft.WindowsAzure.Storage;
using Microsoft.WindowsAzure.Storage.Queue;
using OrderProcessorRole.Business;
using System;
using System.Collections.Generic;
using System.Linq;
using System.Text;
using System.Threading.Tasks;

namespace OrderProcessorRole.Messaging
{
    public abstract class StorageQueueProcessorBase
    {
        private CloudQueue _batchQueue = null;

        private string _queueName = null;
        private string _cnString = null;
        private int _delay = 60000;

        public bool IsRunning { get; private set; }

        public StorageQueueProcessorBase(string queueName, string
          cnString)
```

```
    {
        this._queueName = queueName;
        this._cnString = cnString;

        this.CreateQueueClient();
    }

    private void CreateQueueClient()
    {
        // Retrieve storage account from connection string
        var storageAccount =
          CloudStorageAccount.Parse(this._cnString);

        // Create a queue client to get refs from
        var queueClient =
          storageAccount.CreateCloudQueueClient();

        this._batchQueue =
          queueClient.GetQueueReference(this._queueName);
    }

    public async Task ProcessQueueAsync()
    {
        this.IsRunning = true;

        while (this.IsRunning)
        {
            bool delay = true;

            try
            {
                var msg = await
                  this._batchQueue.GetMessageAsync();
                if (msg != null)
                {
                    // Check the message is not expired which
                    // may occur after a failure and cause
                    // concurrent processing
                    if (DateTimeOffset.Now - msg.InsertionTime
                      < TimeSpan.FromMinutes(10))
                    {
                        await this.Process();
                    }
```

```
                    else
                    {
                        // We have a message but it's expired
                        so get next
                        delay = false;
                    }

                    // Delete message now we're finished with
                    it
                    await
                        this._batchQueue.DeleteMessageAsync(msg);
                }
            }
            catch (Exception ex)
            {

            }

            // Wait for a minute
            if(delay)
                await Task.Delay(this._delay);
        }
    }

    public void Stop()
    {
        this.IsRunning = false;
    }

    protected abstract Task Process();
    }
}
```

Implementing StorageQueueProcessorBase

Now that we have a base class that provides common messaging logic for both queues, it couldn't be simpler to implement them:

```
using Microsoft.WindowsAzure;
using OrderProcessorRole.Business;
using System.Threading.Tasks;

namespace OrderProcessorRole.Messaging
```

```
{
    public class BatchQueueProcessor : StorageQueueProcessorBase
    {
        public BatchQueueProcessor()
            : base("batchqueue",
                CloudConfigurationManager.GetSetting("AzureBakery.
                Production.Storage"))
        {

        }

        protected override async Task Process()
        {
            Trace.TraceInformation("OrderProcessorRole.Messaging.
            BatchQueueProcessor.Process - Begin");

            try
            {
                // Process stock
                await new BatchProcessor().Process();
            }
            catch(Exception ex)
            {
                Trace.TraceError("OrderProcessorRole.Messaging.
                BatchQueueProcessor.Process - Error: {0}", ex);
            }
        }
    }
}
```

As with the order processor, we separated out the processing business logic, which you can get from the code.

 Make sure the scheduled tasks have run at least once; otherwise, the storage queues will not be created.

Completing the worker role

We now have all the tasks we need, so we can add them to the role:

```
using Microsoft.WindowsAzure.ServiceRuntime;
using OrderProcessorRole.Messaging;
using System;
```

```
using System.Diagnostics;
using System.Threading.Tasks;

namespace OrderProcessorRole
{
    public class WorkerRole : RoleEntryPoint
    {
        private OrderTopicProcessor _orderTopicProcessor = null;
        private BatchQueueProcessor _batchQueueProcessor = null;
        private StockQueueProcessor _stockQueueProcessor = null;

        public override void Run()
        {
            Trace.TraceInformation("OrderProcessorRole.WorkerRole.Run
              - Begin");

            try
            {
                // WaitAll tasks will block Run until they have
                all completed, otherwise the role will recycle
                itself
                Task.WaitAll(
                    Task.Run(() =>
                      this._orderTopicProcessor.
                      ProcessSubscriptionAsync()),
                    Task.Run(() =>
                      this._batchQueueProcessor.ProcessQueueAsync()),
                    Task.Run(() =>
                      this._stockQueueProcessor.ProcessQueueAsync()));
            }
            catch(Exception ex)
            {
                Trace.TraceError("OrderProcessorRole.WorkerRole.Run -
                Error: {0}",
                  ex);
            }
        }

        public override bool OnStart()
        {
            Trace.TraceInformation("OrderProcessorRole.WorkerRole.
            OnStart - Begin");
```

```
        try
        {
            // Create processors
            this._orderTopicProcessor = new
               OrderTopicProcessor();
            this._batchQueueProcessor = new
               BatchQueueProcessor();
            this._stockQueueProcessor = new
               StockQueueProcessor();

            Trace.TraceInformation("OrderProcessorRole.WorkerRole.
            OnStart - End");

            return true;
        }
        catch (Exception ex)
        {
            Trace.TraceError("OrderProcessorRole.WorkerRole.
            OnStart - Error:
              {0}", ex);
        }

        return false;
    }


    public override void OnStop()
    {
        this._orderTopicProcessor.Stop();
        this._batchQueueProcessor.Stop();
        this._stockQueueProcessor.Stop();

        base.OnStop();
    }
  }
}
```

We can see that the pattern we've used makes it very simple to extend the tasks, which the worker role performs.

Testing the production order processor

Now that we've completed our worker role, we need to test whether it is behaving as expected, as a single instance to start with, and then multiple instances once we're happy with its behavior.

If the worker role cannot run in a scaled out configuration with multiple instances, it won't be able to cope with a large volume of work and will not run in a resilient configuration.

Testing a single instance

We can start testing locally, and once we're happy, publish and test on Azure. Running as a single instance, we need to check the following:

- The worker role starts and runs
- It doesn't recycle on its own
- There are no exceptions being logged
- Orders and order items are being inserted by the order processor tasks
- Batches are created and assigned to order items
- Order items have stock allocated
- Batches are not fragmented (there must never be more than one incomplete batch per product)

The following T-SQL script can be used to help you do the fragmentation checks on our data (this is really domain-specific, but shows the kind of checks you need to do on your data); it shows the total and incomplete items per batch per product:

```
SELECT
  b.[Product_Id],
  COUNT(b.[Id]) [Total Count],
  SUM(CASE WHEN p.QuantityPerBatch = b.Quantity THEN 1 ELSE 0 END)
[Complete Count],
  SUM(CASE WHEN p.QuantityPerBatch = b.Quantity THEN 0 ELSE 1 END)
[Incomplete Count]
FROM [AzureBakeryProduction].[dbo].[Batches] b INNER JOIN
[AzureBakeryProduction].[dbo].[Products] p ON
  b.Product_Id = p.Id

GROUP BY [Product_Id]
```

 Use the order simulator we created in *Chapter 7, Azure Service Bus Topic Integration*, to send messages to the topic.

Testing multiple instances

First, we need to configure our worker role to run with multiple instances; to do this, right-click on the role in the solution and select **Properties** from the menu, and then click on the **Configuration** tab:

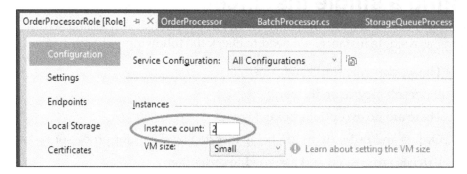

We also need to change the project to use the full Azure compute emulator rather than the default express version, which will allow multiple instances to run. In the **Web*** tab of the cloud service project properties, select **Use Full Emulator**:

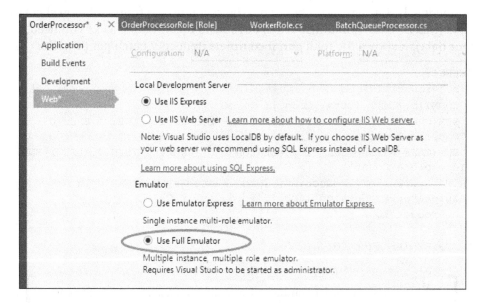

To run the full Azure compute emulator, you must be running Visual Studio with elevated privileges (**Run as administrator**). If you are already running the express emulator, make sure you fully close it first.

We need to test the same things as with a single instance, with the following additions:

- Check that the storage queue processors, which are redesigned to perform an action periodically on a single instance, only call their business logic once across all instances per schedule slot. This can be checked in diagnostics or by putting a breakpoint on the business logic `Process` method.

- Check that both roles are processing orders by examining the tracing in the logs.

Deleting idle cloud services

When we're developing systems, we may have a number of cloud services that we've finished working on and may be sitting idle for a period of time, so it's a good idea to delete them, as we're not paying for them to just sit there doing nothing.

We can delete a cloud service from the toolbar of a cloud service's workspace; however, we need to be careful to delete instances and not the full service, as we would lose our entire cloud service including the DNS name, which would require a completely new publishing profile and may cause configuration issues with other systems, relying on the allocated DNS name if someone else takes it, and we cannot use it again:

Summary

In this chapter, we've gone from examining and running a boiler-plate cloud service to building our production order processor worker role, which runs multiple concurrent tasks to process orders, create batches and assign order items to them, and allocate stock for new items.

There are two other worker roles for the sales and dispatch business domains in the system, which we're not going to look at in this book as they're less complex and cover fewer features than the production worker role, but you can get them from the code files of this chapter.

In the next chapter, we're going to take a deeper dive into cloud service debugging and diagnostics to help us develop and maintain our worker and web roles.

Questions

1. What are the two types of cloud services?

2. What is the difference between a website and a web role?

3. What is the base class of a worker role?

4. Name the three worker role life cycle methods.

5. What happens if the `Run` method is not blocked?

6. How can we find the status of the storage emulator?

7. What method must we call on a `BrokeredMessage` object to delete it from a subscription when we use `PeekLock ReceiveMode`?

8. When we use async tasks in a worker role, why do we need to implement `Task.Wait` or `Task.WaitAll` in the `Run` method?

9. Which NuGet package do we need to interact with a storage queue and what command do we use to install it?

10. How do we remove a storage queue message when we're finished with it?

11. What extra steps do we need to take to run multiple role instances locally?

12. When is it a good idea to delete a cloud service and why must we only delete the instances?

Answers

1. Web role and worker role.

2. Web roles run on dedicated virtual machines, which can be debugged remotely using IntelliTrace and allow advanced configuration and debugging with remote desktop and start-up tasks available on the virtual machines.

3. `RoleEntryPoint`.

4. `OnStart`, `Run`, and `OnStop`.

5. The role will recycle.

6. Use the `WAStorageEmulator.exe status` command.

7. `Complete` or `CompleteAsync`.

8. As the tasks are asynchronous, they are queued onto the thread pool and not called immediately, so the calling method continues and is not blocked. We need to use `Task.Wait` or `Task.WaitAll` to block the thread while the tasks(s) complete; otherwise, the role will recycle.

9. `WindowsAzure.Storage` and `Install-package WindowsAzure.Storage`.

10. Call the `CloudQueue.Delete` method.

11. Set the role instances in the role config and switch to using the full emulator in the project config.

12. If we're not currently using a role instance during development, it's a good idea to delete it during development as we will be incurring charges for it. If we delete the whole service, we lose our DNS name, which could mean that we might not get it back if someone else takes it.

9

Cloud Service Diagnostics, Debugging, and Configuration

In the previous chapter, we introduced cloud services and created a worker role for our production order processor. We're going to continue with cloud services in this chapter, taking a closer look at diagnostics, debugging, and configuration.

We'll be covering the following topics:

- Configuring diagnostics
- Remote debugging
- Debugging with IntelliTrace
- Remote desktop
- Configuration change
- Start-up tasks

We've already covered a lot about the fundamentals of application logging and diagnostics in *Chapter 6, Azure Website Diagnostics and Debugging*, which applies to cloud services too, so we'll go straight into taking a look at cloud service diagnostic configuration options here.

Configuring diagnostics

Cloud services can log application diagnostics using the `Trace` object in the code in worker and web roles and server diagnostics from the virtual machine instances that are hosting the roles.

We can configure a role's diagnostics in the role properties by double-clicking on the role in Visual Studio and looking at the **Configuration** tab:

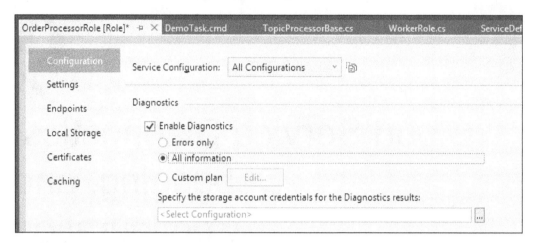

We have options to enable and disable diagnostics with the **Enable Diagnostics** setting; then we have basic diagnostic levels of **Errors only**, which only logs errors, **All information** logs everything, and **Custom plan** gives us more fine-grained control over what we log with options for **Application logs**, **Event logs**, **Performance counters**, **Infrastructure logs**, and **Log directories**:

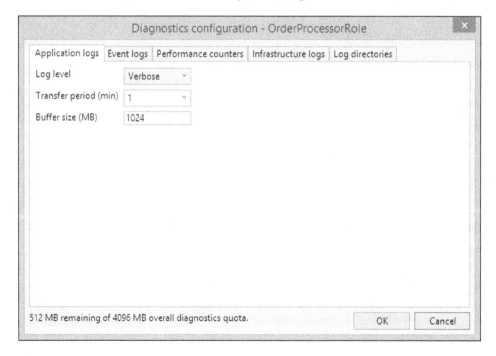

Adding local diagnostics

Cloud services have the facility to attach local storage, which can be used as a temporary data store, which is only available locally to the instance. Local diagnostics can be useful for development and debugging as we can access them easily through the Visual Studio **Server Explorer** window, and we will not incur costs for storing data in cloud storage.

To enable logging to local storage, we need to first add some storage by selecting **Local Storage** and clicking on **Add Local Storage**:

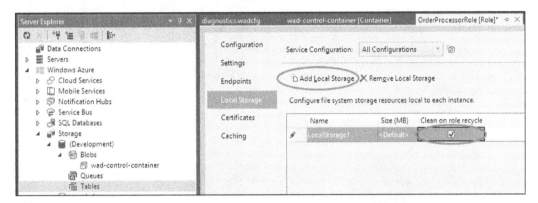

We also have the option to clear the storage when the role is recycled, which is fairly self-explanatory and will delete all the stored data on recycle.

To configure the role to use local storage, choose a **Service Configuration** to apply it to (I've used **Local**, so I'm not storing debug diagnostics on the cloud) and click on the ellipsis button under **Specify the storage account credentials for the Diagnostics results** and choose **Windows Azure storage emulator**:

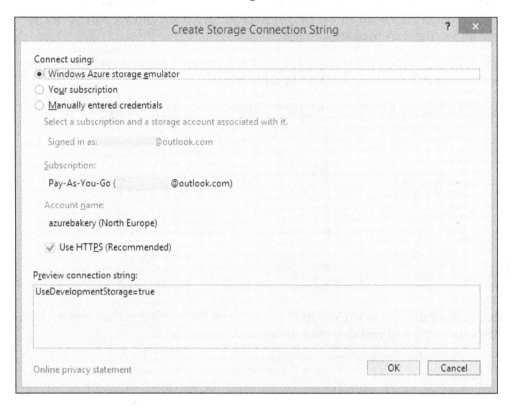

Now, when we debug the worker role, we see a **WADLogsTable** appear in the **Storage | (Development) | Tables** folder, which we can open to see our diagnostic data:

Configuring Azure storage diagnostics

To configure the role to use cloud storage, choose a **Service Configuration** to apply it to (I've used **Cloud**, so I'm storing production diagnostics on the cloud) and click on the ellipsis button under **Specify the storage account credentials for the Diagnostics results** and choose **Your subscription** and select the storage account you wish to use:

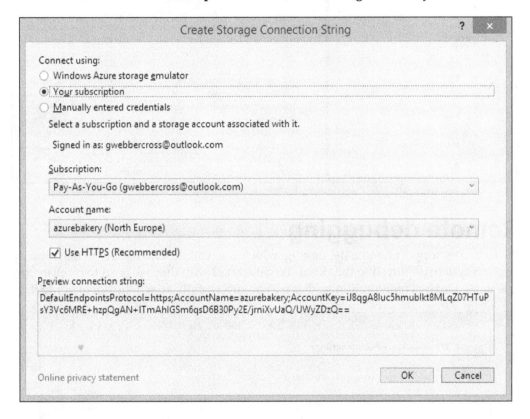

Once the role is published and running, we'll see the **WADLogsTable** appear in the
Server Explorer window, which we can open to see diagnostics data:

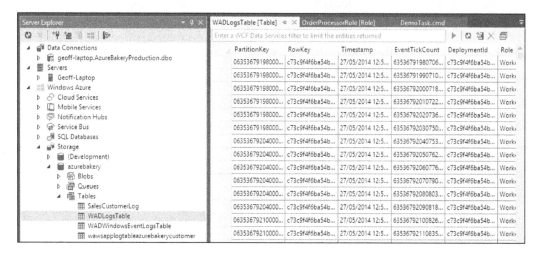

Remote debugging

Worker roles support remote debugging, which is a really useful feature to help you
debug a system deployed to the cloud. To get started with this, we need to publish our
role in the **Debug** configuration so that we can successfully attach the debugger to it:

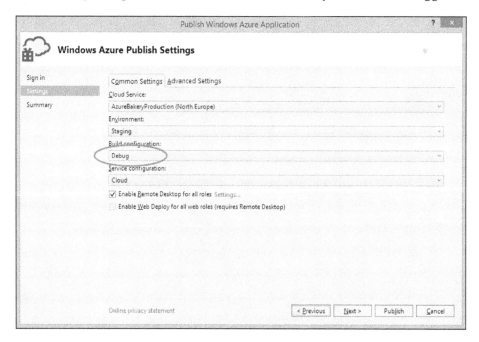

In the **Advanced Settings** tab, check **Enable Remote Debugger for all roles**. I've also checked **Enable IntelliTrace**, so we can look at this too:

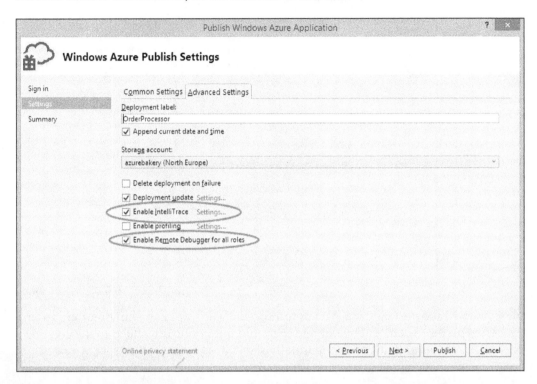

We can debug an entire role or an individual instance from the Visual Studio **Server Explorer** window. If we choose to debug an entire role, the debugger will break on the first instance to run into the break point; debugging multiple instances is similar to debugging multithreaded applications, which can sometimes be a little confusing, so if you're not debugging a concurrency issue, it's probably easier to debug a single instance.

To start debugging in Visual Studio from the **Server Explorer** window, choose a role or an instance, right-click on it, and select **Attach Debugger...**:

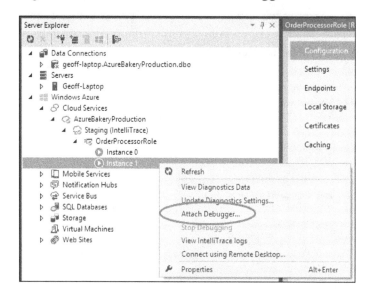

Next, we will see the standard **Attach to Process** dialog appear, showing the running processes on our instance. The debugger should automatically attach to the correct process, but I found that I had to manually select it, so for a worker role, we need `WaWorkerHost.exe` (`WaIISHost.exe` for web roles):

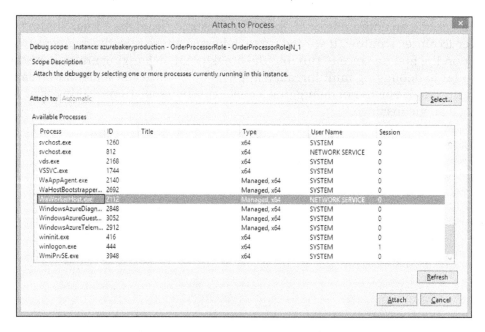

If we debug multiple instances, we will see an indication of the number of processes being debugged in brackets after the process name.

Click on **Attach**, and we'll see the attached process appear in the **Server Explorer** tree, and the debugger will break on the break points in code:

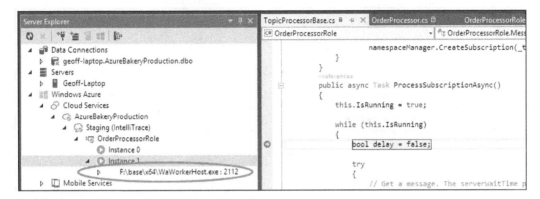

 We need to be careful in using remote debugging as it can cause a role to become unstable, so in a production environment, it should be used with caution.

Stopping the debugger

To stop the debugger, right-click on the process under the instance and select **Stop Debugging**:

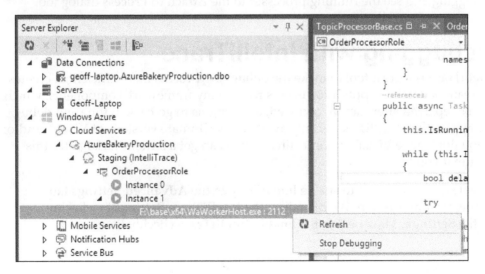

Examining how remote debugging works

When we enable diagnostics, IntelliTrace, remote desktop, or remote debugging during publishing, our virtual machines are provisioned with the appropriate plugins installed, which can be seen by browsing to the `plugins` folder on the machine:

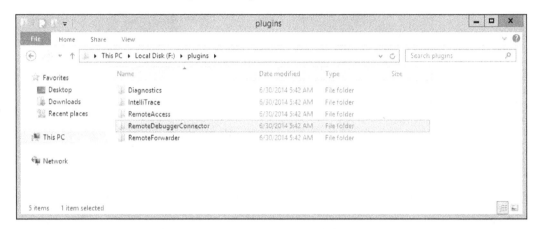

These plugins provide an extra server-side functionality to the roles. Remote debugging uses the connector to listen to commands from Visual Studio such as `start` and `get processes` and the `Forwarder` command to send debug data between the remote debugging monitor (`msvsmon.exe`) on the VM and Visual Studio of the client machine. If you start remote debugging and have a remote desktop connection to the machine (we will cover this in a bit) and open the task manager, you can see all these processes running. You can actually start remote debugging and see the running processes in the **Attach to Process** dialog too.

Debugging with IntelliTrace

IntelliTrace is a great tool to make the debugging process more efficient; it creates a stream of detailed application events from many framework components, which can be replayed after they've occurred, allowing us to go back in time and debug the application. IntelliTrace is only available in Ultimate versions of Visual Studio; if you don't have Visual Studio Ultimate, you can get a 3-month trial to try this feature if you like.

To get started, we need to enable IntelliTrace in the **Advanced Settings** tab during the publish step. We can adjust the **IntelliTrace Settings** by clicking on the **Settings...** link next to the **Enable IntelliTrace** checkbox:

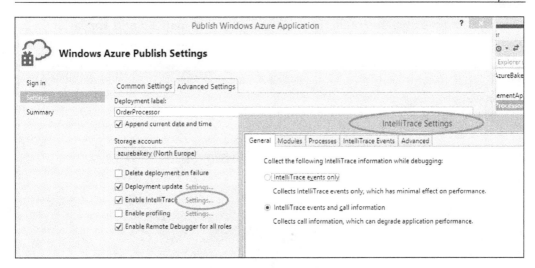

 As with all diagnostic data, we need to be careful while using IntelliTrace as we can quickly build up large amounts of data in storage, which we will be charged for. We can control the maximum amount of data stored by navigating to the **IntelliTrace Settings | Advanced** tab, and the default value is 250 MB.

To view the IntelliTrace logs, we can right-click on an instance and select **View IntelliTrace logs** from the context-sensitive menu:

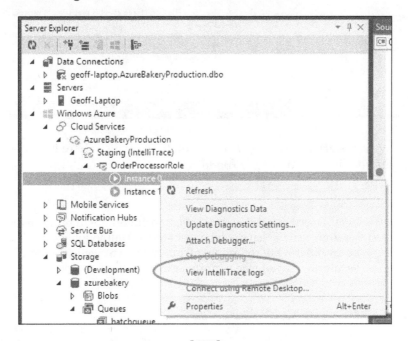

Once we've done this, the IntelliTrace file will start to download and appear in the **Windows Azure Activity Log** pane, and will then open automatically once complete:

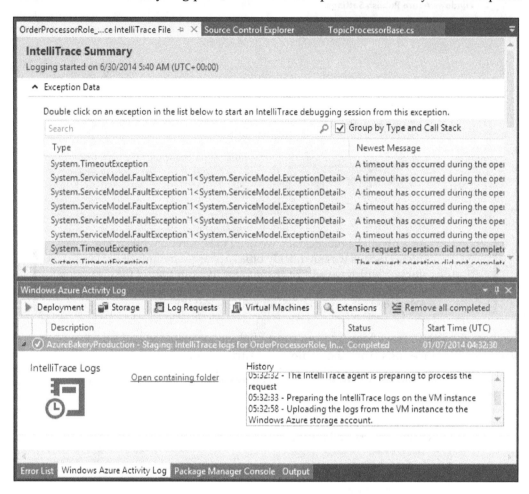

From here, we can start debugging with the IntelliTrace file. There is a good guide to getting started with this at `http://msdn.microsoft.com/en-us/library/dd264963.aspx`.

 IntelliTrace is a good way of debugging intermittent problems as we don't need to have a debugger attached, although we need to be careful if we're collecting call information as well as events, as this can degrade the performance of a role.

Remote desktop connection

As cloud services run on dedicated virtual machines (per deployment environment), it's possible to remote desktop to them to perform advanced diagnostics and configuration, although generally, it's not the best practice to do manual modifications to the environment as these will not be applied to roles when they are initially created during a scale out or re-imaged on a guest-OS upgrade, which happens every few months (there's a great article about OS upgrades here: `http://blogs.msdn.com/b/kwill/archive/2012/09/19/role-instance-restarts-due-to-os-upgrades.aspx`). To implement environment customizations, it's recommended that you use start-up tasks, which we will be covering shortly.

In the previous chapter, we configured remote desktop during the publish step with a username and password. We can connect using a `.rdp` file downloaded from the portal, which is useful for system administrators or via the Visual Studio **Server Explorer** window, which can be more convenient for developers.

Downloading a Remote Desktop Protocol (RDP) file

When we click on an instance in the portal, we should see the **CONNECT** button enabled (if it is not, check that remote desktop is enabled in the publish settings). Choose an environment and an instance to connect to and click on the **CONNECT** button to download the `.rdp` file:

Before we make a connection, if we open the `.rdp` file in Notepad, we can see some interesting details about the cloud service endpoints and how we connect to an instance:

```
full address:s:80c247175c3b4ea9ad4e002bb0a5cb8a.cloudapp.net
username:s:geoff
LoadBalanceInfo:s:Cookie:
  mstshash=OrderProcessorRole#OrderProcessorRole_IN_0
```

The cloud services are on an internal network and cannot be connected to directly. The `full address` setting is the DNS name of the load-balanced endpoint, and the `LoadBalanceInfo` setting tells the load balancer which role and instance within the service we want to connect to.

Establishing an RDP connection

We'll establish a **Remote Desktop Protocol (RDP)** connection via the Visual Studio **Server Explorer** window using the following procedure (the procedure is pretty much the same using a `.rdp` file):

1. Choose a role instance, right-click on it, and select **Connect using Remote Desktop...**:

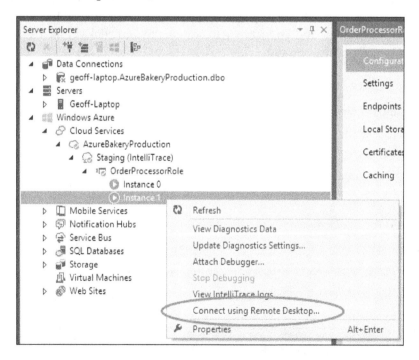

2. The **Remote Desktop Connection** dialog will appear like this:

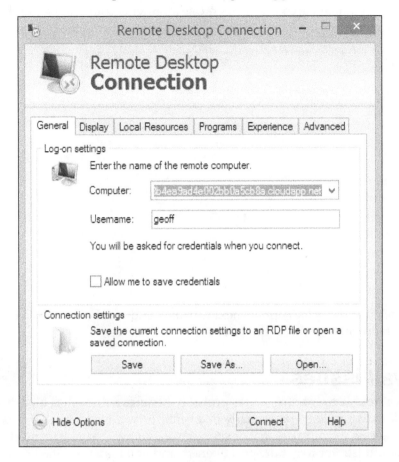

3. Click on **Connect** and accept the untrusted publisher warning.

4. Click on **Connect**, and a login prompt will appear. If you get an option to use a domain account, click on **Use another account** and enter the credentials for the local account we configured during the publish:

5. Click on **OK** and accept the next warning, and we should connect to the instance and see the desktop for the virtual server.

Firewall issues

If you have trouble connecting it, it is probably because a firewall is blocking the default RDP port 3389 particularly in an enterprise environment. If you don't have access to your personal or site firewall, you will need to contact your network administrator to get the port opened, and you may need the IP address of the virtual machine for the firewall policy, which can be found on the cloud service **DASHBOARD** tab in the quick glance section:

Detecting configuration changes in code

When we use configuration settings in our roles, such as the `AzureBakery.Production.Storage` setting we created in the previous chapter, we can change these at runtime in the role's **CONFIGURATION** tab in the portal:

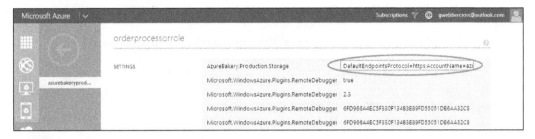

To detect config changes in code, we can attach event handlers to the `RoleEnvironment.Changing` event, which is fired before a config change is applied to the role and the `RoleEnvironment.Changed` event, which is fired after the change has been applied:

```
public override bool OnStart()
{
    Trace.TraceInformation("OrderProcessorRole.WorkerRole.OnStart
      - Begin");

    RoleEnvironment.Changing += RoleEnvironment_Changing;
    RoleEnvironment.Changed += RoleEnvironment_Changed;
}
```

Using the `Changing` event, we can set the `e.Cancel` flag to `true`, which will cause the role to recycle, and the new changes are applied on the next start:

```
private void RoleEnvironment_Changing(object sender,
    RoleEnvironmentChangingEventArgs e)
{
    // Implements the changes after restarting the role instance
    if ((e.Changes.Any(change => change is
    RoleEnvironmentConfigurationSettingChange)))
    {
        e.Cancel = true;
    }
}
```

Using the `Changed` event, we can write code to handle configuration changes (first, test for the `RoleEnvironmentConfigurationSettingChange` type). In the following example from our production order processor, we're stopping and reinstantiating our queue processors:

```
private void RoleEnvironment_Changed(object sender,
  RoleEnvironmentChangedEventArgs e)
{
    // Implements the changes after the config has changed
    if ((e.Changes.Any(change => change is
    RoleEnvironmentConfigurationSettingChange)))
    {
        this._batchQueueProcessor.Stop();
        this._stockQueueProcessor.Stop();

        this._batchQueueProcessor = new BatchQueueProcessor();
        this._stockQueueProcessor = new StockQueueProcessor();
    }
}
```

Using configuration settings and implementing these events is a great way of making roles dynamically configurable so that we don't need to change settings in a config file and republish the whole role, or manually restart the role to apply changes made through the portal.

Start-up tasks

Start-up tasks are command-line scripts that can be added to a role in the `ServiceDefinition.csdef` file, allowing the role to perform activities before the role has started. These activities might be things such as installing a third-party package or making environmental or configuration changes. Start-up tasks are the best way of customizing a server rather than making manual changes using a remote desktop. We're going to have a very brief look at this area, so it's worth doing some additional reading around this area yourself.

Creating a batch script

To get started, we need to create a `.cmd` batch script to perform a task (you can also write PowerShell `.ps1` scripts) called `DemoTasks.cmd` and put it in a solution folder called `Tasks`:

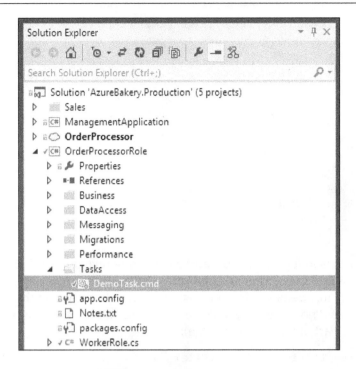

Before we write the script, we'll set the **Build Action** property of the file to **Content** so that the file along with the Tasks folder is copied to the output (bin) folder, and **Copy to Output Directory** to **Copy if newer** so that the file is copied if it changes:

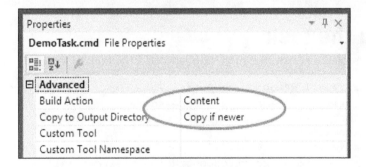

My script simply writes some details about the start-up date and time to a logfile, which is a good starting point for any script:

```
REM Demo Start-up Tasks to log the start-up date and time

REM Output variable
SET OutputFile="%TEMP%\StartupLog.txt"
```

```
ECHO DemoTask.cmd: >> %OutputFile% 2>&1
ECHO Current date and time: >> %OutputFile% 2>&1
DATE /T >> %OutputFile% 2>&1
TIME /T >> %OutputFile% 2>&1

REM Error block
IF ERRORLEVEL EQU 0 (
    REM   No errors occurred. Exit cleanly with /B 0
    EXIT /B 0
) ELSE (
    REM   Log error
    ECHO Error - ERRORLEVEL = %ERRORLEVEL%.  >> %OutputFile% 2>&1
    EXIT %ERRORLEVEL%
)
```

The best practice is to log the `stderr` and `stdout` streams to a logfile for debugging purposes; this following command echos the `DemoTask.cmd` text and pipes the `stderr` and `stdout` streams using the `2>&1` operation to the file in the `OutputFile` variable (be careful not to use spaces when defining variables as you would in C# as they become part of the variable name):

```
ECHO Startup1.cmd: >> %OutputFile% 2>&1
```

We've used the `%TEMP%` variable, which is an environmental variable for the `temporary` folder on the machine. You can find a list of environmental variables at `http://technet.microsoft.com/en-us/library/cc749104(v=ws.10).aspx`.

Adding the task

Once we've created a script, the next step is to add the task to the `csdef` file like this:

```xml
<?xml version="1.0" encoding="utf-8"?>
<ServiceDefinition name="OrderProcessor"
  xmlns="http://schemas.microsoft.com/ServiceHosting/2008/10/
    ServiceDefinition"
    schemaVersion="2014-01.2.3">
  <WorkerRole name="OrderProcessorRole" vmsize="Small">
    <Startup>
      <Task commandLine="Tasks\DemoTask.cmd"
        executionContext="limited" taskType="simple" />
</Startup>
```

There are three attributes we can set: `commandLine`, `executionContext`, and `taskType`. The `commandLine` attribute is pretty straightforward; it's the command we want to execute; we can use a `.cmd` batch file or even write a batch command in-line; `executionContext` is used to control the privileges the script executes under; the options are as follows:

- `limited`: This is used for normal privileges
- `elevated`: This is used for administrator privileges

The `taskType` attribute controls the type of task and the options, which are as follows:

- `simple`: Simple tasks run synchronously, allowing you to control the sequence of the tasks in the `Startup` element. If a simple task ends with a non-zero error code, the role will not start.
- `foreground`: Foreground tasks run asynchronously, so tasks can be executed concurrently. The role will wait for all tasks to complete with a non-zero error code before starting.
- `background`: Background tasks also run asynchronously but the role will start without the tasks completing.

Environmental variables

We use the `%TEMP%` environmental variable in our script, which is a built-in variable, but it's also possible to add custom environmental variables to the `Task` folder in the `csdef` file, like this:

```
<Task commandLine="Tasks\DemoTask.cmd" executionContext="limited"
  taskType="simple">
  <Environment>
    <Variable name="Simple" value="Hello startup task!" />
    <Variable name="ComputeEmulatorRunning">
      <RoleInstanceValue
        xpath="/RoleEnvironment/Deployment/@emulated" />
    </Variable>
  </Environment>
</Task>
```

Here, we've created a simple variable called `Simple`, which we can use in the script with the `%Simple%` variable. We've also created a more useful variable called `ComputeEmulatorRunning`, which uses an `xPath` value to determine whether the role is running in the emulator. We can add the following script to use these variables:

```
REM Test Simple environment variable works
ECHO Simple Environment Variable: %Simple% >> %OutputFile% 2>&1

REM Check if we're in the emulator
IF "%ComputeEmulatorRunning%" == "true" (
  ECHO Running in emulator >> %OutputFile% 2>&1
) ELSE (
    ECHO Running in Azure cloud >> %OutputFile% 2>&1
)
```

There are some examples of other `xPath` variables at `http://msdn.microsoft.com/en-us/library/hh404006.aspx`.

Summary

We've now completed the cloud services topic we started in the previous chapter, and we've taken a closer look at using diagnostics, remote debugging, and IntelliTrace, to help us debug our applications that run in the cloud. We've also looked at detecting configuration change so that our cloud services can dynamically respond to changes without the need to redeploy or manually recycle. Finally, we looked at start-up tasks, which allow us to customize the cloud service environment before a role starts.

In the next chapter, we're going to look at building an ASP.NET Web API web service and a production management application, which we will integrate into our system using Azure Active Directory.

Questions

1. Which connection string is used for local storage?
2. What is the name of the storage table where diagnostic data is stored?
3. What publish settings must we apply to enable remote debugging?
4. What process do we attach to when remote debugging a worker role?
5. What happens if we debug a role rather than an instance?
6. Is it possible to use IntelliTrace on cloud services in Visual Studio Express?
7. Which is the default RDP port?

8. What is the difference between the `RoleEnvironment.Changed` and `RoleEnvironment.Changing` events?

9. Where are start-up tasks defined?

10. What properties must we apply to a task script so that it is copied when we publish?

11. What is the `%TEMP%` variable an example of and what does it do?

12. What is the difference between limited and elevated `executionContext`?

Answers

1. `UseDevelopmentStorage` should be set to `true`.

2. `WADLogsTable`.

3. The **Debug** configuration and **Enable Remote Debugger for all roles** in the **Advanced Settings** tab.

4. `WaWorkerHost.exe`.

5. We start debugging all role instances simultaneously.

6. No, unfortunately it's only available in Visual Studio Ultimate.

7. `3389`.

8. The `RoleEnvironment.Changed` event allows us to detect when config has changed in code and deal with it accordingly at runtime. `RoleEnvironment.Changing` allows us to recycle the role if the config is changing using the `e.Cancel` flag so that new settings are applied on start.

9. They are defined on a per-role basis in the cloud service's `ServiceDefinition.csdef` file.

10. **Build action** is set to **Content** and **Copy to Output Directory** is set to **Copy if newer**.

11. It's a standard environmental variable, which gives us the path of the `temp` directory.

12. Limited runs the script with normal privileges while elevated runs the script with administrator privileges.

10
Web API and Client Integration

In this chapter, we'll create an on-premise production management client Windows application allowing manufacturing staff to view and update order and batch data and a web service to access data in the production SQL database and send order updates to the Service Bus topic.

The site's main feature is an ASP.NET Web API 2 HTTP service that allows the clients to read order and batch data. The site will also host a SignalR (`http://signalr.net/`) hub that allows the client to update order and batch statuses and have the changes broadcast to all the on-premise clients to keep them synchronized in real time. Both the Web API and SignalR hubs will use the Azure Active Directory authentication.

We'll cover the following topics in this chapter:

- Introducing a Web API
- Introducing SignalR
- Building a Web API service
- Creating a SignalR hub
- Publishing a Web API
- Modifying the Web API AD manifest
- Adding a client application to AD
- Building a client application

Introducing a Web API

Using web services with client applications is common practice in many systems, as it allows clients to interact with data sources and other resources indirectly, allowing greater control over security and also allowing us to present data to applications in an application-domain friendly format.

The Web API (currently Version 2) is an ASP.NET framework for building RESTful HTTP web services (`http://en.wikipedia.org/wiki/Representational_state_transfer`) for a wide range of client applications, including websites, desktop applications, and mobile applications (although Azure also offers dedicated mobile services that we'll look at in the next chapter). A Web API is simple to implement compared to other web service technologies such as WCF, which is designed for SOAP and requires complicated configuration. A Web API is similar to MVC, where we have controllers with HTTP methods routed to actions, but where MVC is used to build websites that interact with a web browser and a Web API provides services for applications to interact with data in JSON and XML formats.

An example of where we benefit from using a web service such as ASP.NET Web API is when we have a client application that needs to get data from a SQL Server Database. If the client application accesses the database directly, it needs to use SQL Server or Windows authentication. If we choose SQL Server authentication, we need to hardcode a connection string with the credentials, which is not ideal, as it means we cannot change it without recompiling the application and reissuing it to our users; also, the application can be decompiled by a malicious user to retrieve the connection details. Alternatively, we can put the connection string in a config file, which allows us to change the connection string, but this directly exposes it to anyone with access to the filesystem. Using Windows authentication is much better, as we can use the user's credentials to connect to the database; however, there is an administrative overhead as users must be added directly to the SQL Server security or to an AD group that has access to the database, and the user and group privileges need configuring in the database.

Using a web service allows us to use any authentication method we choose, as the user has no direct access to the server filesystem; this is particularly important for Azure databases as they don't currently support Windows authentication. We authenticate users and control authorization to resources in the client application, which then accesses the database via a web service.

Introducing SignalR

SignalR is a library for .NET developers to help build real-time web-connected applications. SignalR makes use of WebSockets (`http://en.wikipedia.org/wiki/WebSocket`) where available, which provide duplex (two-way) communications over TCP sockets, allowing clients to send data to a server; but more importantly, it allows the server to push data back to the client, which means that clients don't need to continually poll the server for updates.

SignalR can have issues with scalability when deployed on load-balanced web servers because clients will have a connection to a single website instance and will not receive messages from other instances, which means that we end up with multiple hubs rather than just one.

There are a number of solutions to deal with scalability with SignalR using a backplane; where each hub forwards messages to the backplane rather than directly to the client, the backplane then updates all hub instances, which then forwards the message to the client. There are three backplane options:

- **Microsoft Azure Service Bus**: The Service Bus is used to allow hub instances to message each other via redundant topics
- **Redis**: This is an in-memory solution with a publish/subscribe pattern, where hub instances can update each other directly
- **SQL Server**: Hub instances are updated via SQL database tables with the option to use a service broker

We'll implement the Microsoft Azure Service Bus backplane in our solution.

Building a Web API service

We'll create a new web project for the production system that hosts the Web API HTTP service and the SignalR hub. Since we already have Azure AD authentication in place across the other internal systems, we'll configure this website to use Azure AD authentication, too.

If you've not already done so, read the *Adding Azure AD single sign-on to a website* section in *Chapter 5, Building Azure MVC Websites*, which covers creating an Azure AD, which is a prerequisite to creating a website with Azure AD integration.

Creating a Web API project

In the following procedure, we'll create a web project in Visual Studio with a Web API template and configure it to use Azure AD authentication:

1. Add a new web project to your solution, I've called mine ManagementWebApi, select the **Web API** template and make sure **Host in the cloud** is checked:

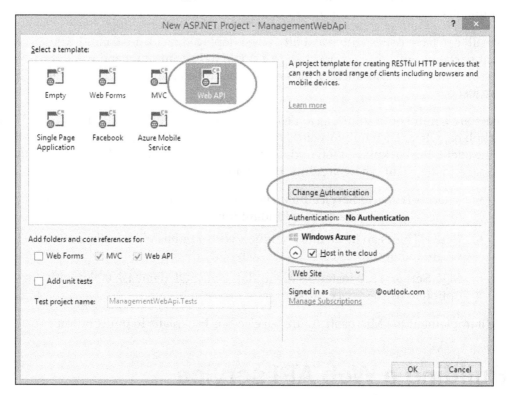

2. Click on **Change Authentication**, then select **Organizational Accounts**, fill in the Azure AD **Domain** field, and click on **OK**:

3. Sign in using the new AD user, then click on **OK** in the previous dialog
    (be careful to change the user to your Azure portal account when prompted
    to sign in to Azure).

4. Enter a value against **Site name**, and choose **Region** and **Database Server**
    (select **No database** because we're using the existing one):

5. Click on **OK**; this will provision the website, set up an AD application, and create our Web API project for us. If we take a look at the **APPLICATIONS** tab in our AD workspace in the portal, we can see that our application has been added to the list:

6. If we take a look at the `App_Start/Startup.Auth.cs` class, we can see how AD authentication is implemented using the `IAppBuilder` interface. The `UseWindowsAzureActiveDirectoryBearerAuthentication` method with the `ida:Audience` (our Web API application) and `ida:Tenent` (our AD) app settings from the `Web.config` file is as follows:

```
public void ConfigureAuth(IAppBuilder app)
{
    app.UseWindowsAzureActiveDirectoryBearerAuthentication(
        new
          WindowsAzureActiveDirectoryBearerAuthenticationOptions
        {
            Audience =
              ConfigurationManager.AppSettings["ida:Audience"],
            Tenant =
              ConfigurationManager.AppSettings["ida:Tenant"]
        });
}
```

7. As with the sales admin website, we can test this locally by simply running the project (which has a built-in website) from Visual Studio. You will get a security warning due to the implementation of a temporary SSL certificate on your local web server (in IE), as shown in the following screenshot:

8. Accept the warning and we will see the home page of the Web API. Unlike the MVC website, the Web API home page does not need authorization by default; this allows us to create a public API reference, which doesn't need to use authorization (we can change this by adding the `Authorization` attribute to `HomeController`).

9. If we navigate to the `api/values` URL, which is the path of the `Values` API controller that is created for us in the project, we will see an error response (**401 Unauthorized**) telling us we're not authorized to use the service (I used Chrome here as it shows the response better than IE, and you can hit *F12* to see the developer console for more information about the request and response):

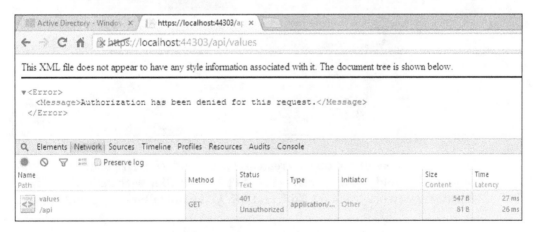

This shows us that the authorization is working; we'll be able to use the API once we have an authorized request from our client application.

Creating API controllers

Next, we'll add a couple of controllers for order and batch data using scaffolding to quickly create DbContext and a set of REST actions to create, read, update, delete, and list data. You've probably got the idea by now, but as I keep mentioning, it's always good to use a dependency injection and a repository/UoW pattern to build our data service tiers. However, this is a quick way of getting us to where we need to be. To create OrderController, use the following procedure:

1. Before we add the controllers, we need to add a project reference to the ProductionModel project so that the scaffold can see the entities we want to use. So, right-click on the References folder, select **Add Reference**, check **ProductionModel** by navigating to the **Solution | Projects** tab, and click on **OK**.

2. Right-click on the Controllers folder and go to **Add | Controller** to open the **Add Scaffold** dialog:

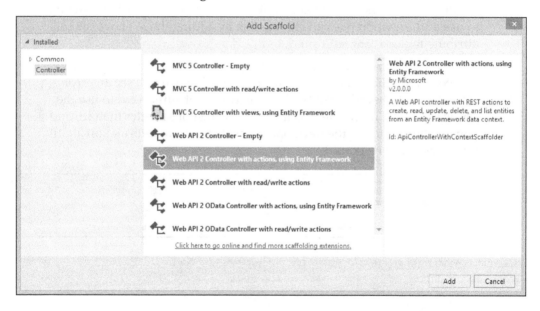

3. We see a number of options to create the MVC and Web API controllers with different scaffold options; select **Web API 2 Controller with actions, using Entity Framework**, click on **Add**, and the **Add Controller** dialog will appear:

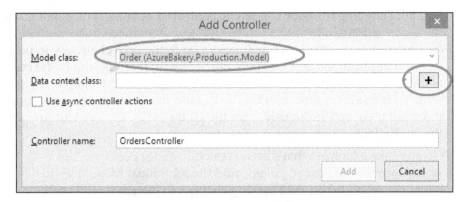

4. Select the order model from the **Model class** picker, then click on the
    + button next to **Data context class** to create a new DbContext (if you're
    onto BatchController, select the existing DbContext from the picker):

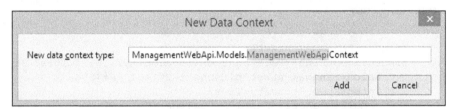

5. At this point, you can change the name of the data context (I'm going
    to leave it to the default); click on **Add** and we'll see the details in the
    Add Controller dialog:

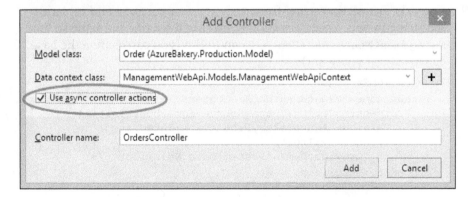

6. Finally, I'm going to check **Use async controller actions**, which will mark the `async` actions, allowing us to use the `async` methods in `DbContext` (we've used `async Tasks` a few times so far in the project already to help us build applications that are more efficient with threads, and in the case of client applications, which we're looking at again in this chapter, help us write code to access resources that will cause the UI to become unresponsive if we call them synchronously from the UI thread). Click on **Add** to scaffold the controller.

7. Go and take a look at what's been created in `OrdersController`, `ManagementWebApiDataContext`, and the additional EF sections in `Web.config`, and then start making changes to integrate with our existing database.

8. We need to change the database connection string to point to our existing SQL express database so that it can share data with the order processor. So, in the `Web.config` file, locate the database connection string, using the following code:

```
<connectionStrings>
  <add name="ManagementWebApiContext"
    connectionString="Data Source=(localdb)\v11.0; Initial
      Catalog=ManagementWebApiContext-20140708044804;
        Integrated Security=True;
          MultipleActiveResultSets=True;
            AttachDbFilename=|DataDirectory|ManagementWebApiConte
            xt-20140708044804.mdf"
              providerName="System.Data.SqlClient" />
</connectionStrings>
```

9. Copy the connection string from `OrderProcessorRole` and replace the string in `Web.config` as shown, leaving the name the same so that `ManagementWebApiDataContext` can find it (you can change the base constructor if you want):

```
<connectionStrings>
    <add name="ManagementWebApiContext"
      connectionString="Data Source=localhost;Initial
        Catalog= AzureBakeryProduction;Integrated
          Security=True"
            providerName="System.Data.SqlClient" />
    </connectionStrings>
```

10. Add the following line of code to the `ManageMentWebApiDataContext` constructor to disable the EF proxy creation:

```
public ManagementWebApiContext() :
  base("name=ManagementWebApiContext")
{
    base.Configuration.ProxyCreationEnabled = false;
}
```

11. Now, we'll modify the `OrdersController` `GetOrders` method to return only the `open` status orders:

```
public IQueryable<Order> GetOrders()
{
    return db.Orders
        .Where(o => o.Status == OrderStatus.Open)
}
```

12. You might not have noticed, but the controller is not decorated with the `Authorize` attribute, which means it is unsecured; this is bad because anybody can access it, but is good for now as we can give it a quick test!

13. Debug the Web API project, and then navigate to `/api/orders` (or whatever your IIS express port is), as shown in the following code:

```
https://localhost:44303/api/orders
```

14. I used Chrome because it shows the results nicely in the browser. If you're doing the same, you'll notice the data coming back as XML because the browser has the application/XML option in the `accept` header by default.

15. Once you're happy with the way the controller is working, put the `Authorize` attribute on the controller class, as shown:

```
[Authorize]
public class OrdersController : ApiController
```

16. For `BatchController`, use the same procedure, but use `DbContext` we created before instead.

   To further test the controller, we can use the browser for most HTTP GET actions, use a tool such as Fiddler (`http://www.telerik.com/fiddler`), or use cURL (`http://curl.haxx.se/`) to construct other actions such as POST or PUT, which require data to be inserted into the `request` body.

Creating a SignalR hub

We'll implement a SignalR hub to allow clients to update order and batch statuses as they are changed by a user, and we'll receive updates from other clients in the system as they are updated by other users. Create the hub in the following procedure:

1. Enter the following command into the NuGet **Package Manager Console** to install the `Microsoft.AspNet.SignalR` package:

   ```
   Install-Package Microsoft.AspNet.SignalR
   ```

2. Enter the following command into the NuGet **Package Manager Console** to install the `Microsoft.AspNet.SignalR.ServiceBus` package:

   ```
   Install-Package Microsoft.AspNet.SignalR.ServiceBus
   ```

3. Finally, enter the following command to install the `windowsazure.servicebus` package (do this at last because the `Microsoft.AspNet.SignalR` command installs its own version, which might not be compatible with partitioned brokered messages):

   ```
   install-package windowsazure.servicebus
   ```

4. Modify the `Microsoft.ServiceBus.ConnectionString` app setting, which was added by the `Microsoft.AspNet.SignalR.ServiceBus` package, and add an ACS key for the Service Bus namespace (get it from the portal). Unfortunately, the library requires full control over the namespace as it needs to create its own topics. The connection string should look like this:

   ```
   <add key="Microsoft.ServiceBus.ConnectionString"
     value="Endpoint=sb://azurebakery.servicebus.windows.net/;
       SharedSecretIssuer=owner;SharedSecretValue=
         vxaQFgh8zGFtsqnAemCcv/NTCtLNM2qhYslQq7TIQsI=" />
   ```

5. Modify the `Startup` class in the `App_Start/Startup.Auth.cs` file, as shown:

   ```
   using Microsoft.AspNet.SignalR;
   using Microsoft.Owin;
   using Microsoft.Owin.Security.ActiveDirectory;
   using Owin;
   using System.Configuration;
   ```

```
[assembly: OwinStartup(typeof(ManagementWebApi.Startup))]
namespace ManagementWebApi
{

    public partial class Startup
    {
        // For more information on configuring authentication,
        please visit http://go.microsoft.com/fwlink/?LinkId=301864
        public void ConfigureAuth(IAppBuilder app)
        {
            app.UseWindowsAzureActiveDirectoryBearerAuthentication(
            new WindowsAzureActiveDirectoryBearerAuthenticationOptions
                {
                    Audience = ConfigurationManager.
                    AppSettings["ida:Audience"],
                    Tenant = ConfigurationManager.
                    AppSettings["ida:Tenant"]
                });

            // SignalR startup
            var connectionString = ConfigurationManager.
            AppSettings["Microsoft.ServiceBus.ConnectionString"];
            GlobalHost.DependencyResolver.
            UseServiceBus(connectionString, "ManagementApi");

            app.MapSignalR();
        }
    }
}
```

6. It's important to note the OwinStartup attribute, which is used to mark the class that's needed for automatic startup. The last three lines, which retrieve the Service Bus connection string from config, tells SignalR to use Service Bus to message and configures the signal routing to api/signalr.

7. Next, add a hub class to the project; I put mine under a solution folder called `SignalR`. Right-click on the solution folder and go to **Add | New Item**, and then select **SignalR Hub Class (v2)** from the **SignalR** tab, give it a name, and click on **OK**:

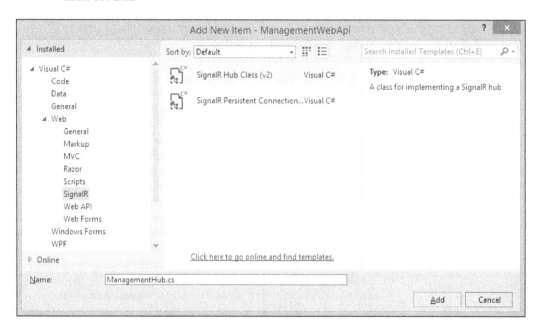

8. Add the `UpdateOrder` and `UpdateBatch` methods that a client calls and updates to all connected clients. I've abstracted the database and messaging logic into service classes to make the code easier to read, so get this from the samples. The class is decorated with the `Authorize` attribute, which uses the same AD authentication mechanism as the Web API:

```
[Authorize]
public class ManagementHub : Hub
{
    private readonly DataService _dataService = new
      DataService();
    private readonly MessagingService _messagingService =
      new MessagingService();

    public void UpdateOrder(Order order)
    {
        // Update database
        this._dataService.UpdateOrder(order);

        // Send order message to Topic
        this._messagingService.UpdateOrder(order);
```

```
        // Notify all clients
        Clients.All.updateOrder(order);
    }

    public void UpdateBatch(Batch batch)
    {
        // Update database
        this._dataService.UpdateBatch(batch);

        // Notify all clients
        Clients.All.updateBatch(batch);
    }
}
```

Publishing a Web API

We can publish a Web API straight to the website that was provisioned when we created it using the normal website publish procedure; however, we need to pay particular attention to the publish settings:

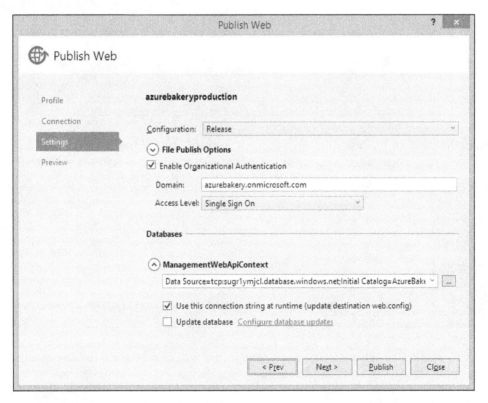

Check **Enable Organizational Authentication**, enter the AD tenant **Domain** name, make sure to set the database connection string of the Azure database, and check **Use this connection string at runtime (update destination web.config)**.

When we publish, we need to enter our AD tenant login credentials:

When the publish process is complete, we'll see our website has been created, but we also see a new application appear in the AD tenant workspace **APPLICATIONS** tab:

The `ida:Audience` setting in the `Web.config` file will also be updated to have the ID of our new Azure Web API application.

Modifying the Web API AD manifest

Before we create an AD application for our client, we need to modify the manifest of the local and Azure `ManagementWebApi` (my Azure application is called `webapp-azurebakeryproduction.azurewebsites.net`) applications so that other applications can be given permission to access them using the AD authorization. We'll do this in the following procedure:

1. Go to **MANAGE MANIFEST** | **Download Manifest** on the toolbar for the AD application in the portal:

2. Open the downloaded `json` manifest file; the start should look something like this:

```
{
    "appId": "0a2141c3-566f-4d52-98c6-9cb249224868",
    "appMetadata": null,
    "appPermissions": [],
    "availableToOtherTenants": false,
    "displayName": "ManagementWebApi",
    "errorUrl": null,
    "homepage": "https://localhost:44303/",
    "identifierUris": [
       "https://azurebakery.onmicrosoft.com/ManagementWebApi"
    ],
```

3. Replace the empty `"appPermissions": []` section with the following code, and save the file:

```
"appPermissions": [
    {
       "claimValue": "user_impersonation",
       "description": "Allow the application full access to
       the service on behalf of the signed-in user",
       "directAccessGrantTypes": [],
       "displayName": "Have full access to the service",
       "impersonationAccessGrantTypes": [
         {
            "impersonated": "User",
            "impersonator": "Application"
```

```
            }
        ],
        "isDisabled": false,
        "origin": "Application",
        "permissionId":
            "B4B3BA55-0770-47D0-A447-C55BB6A371DF",
        "resourceScopeType": "Personal",
        "userConsentDescription": "Allow the application full
          access to the service on your behalf",
        "userConsentDisplayName": "Have full access to the
          service"
    }
],
```

4. Upload the saved manifest by navigating to the **MANAGE MANIFEST |
   Upload Manifest** menu item.

5. Repeat the steps for the second manifest.

Adding a client application to AD

Before we can connect to the Web API from our client application, we need to add it
to our Azure AD with permissions to access the Web API application. We'll do this in
the following procedure:

1. Navigate to the AD workspace in the Azure portal.

2. Click on **ADD** on the **APPLICATIONS** toolbar of our Azure Bakery tenant:

3. Then, select **Add an application my organization is developing**:

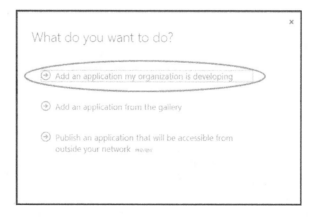

4. Enter the application **NAME**, select **NATIVE CLIENT APPLICATION** (the other option is for web applications), and click on the next arrow:

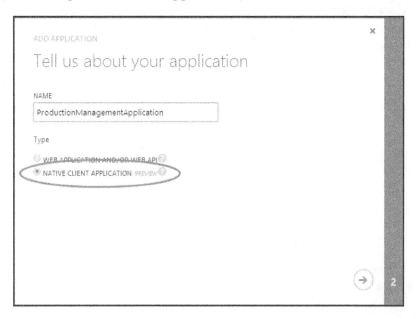

5. Next, enter a value for **REDIRECT URI** (this just needs to be a valid URI for the redirect after the OAuth2 request and is not used in this implementation), and click on the tick button to complete:

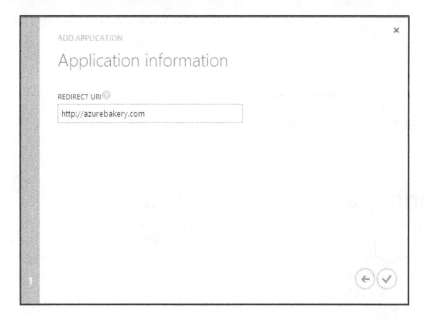

6. Now, we need to add permission to `ManagementWebApi`, so scroll to the **permissions to other applications** section at the bottom of the **CONFIGURATION** tab and add a new permission for `ManagementWebApi`, which should now appear in the list after our manifest modification. Now, choose **Have full access to the service** as the delegated permission, which is the display name we used:

7. Change the delegated permissions for the default **Windows Azure Active Directory** permission to include **Access your organization's directory (preview)**:

8. Add permissions for the Azure Management API.
9. Click on **SAVE** on the toolbar to complete.

Building a client application

For the client application, we'll create a WPF client application to display batches and orders and allow us to change their state. We'll use MVVM Light again, like we did for the message simulator we created in the sales solution, to help us implement a neat MVVM pattern. We'll create a number of data services to get data from the API using Azure AD authentication.

Preparing the WPF project

We'll create a WPF application and install NuGet packages for MVVM Light, JSON.
NET, and Azure AD authentication in the following procedure (for the Express
version of Visual Studio, you'll need Visual Studio Express for desktops):

1. Add a WPF project to the solution called `ManagementApplication`.

2. In the NuGet **Package Manager Console**, enter the following command to
    install `MVVM Light`:

    ```
    install-package mvvmlight
    ```

3. Now, enter the following command to install the `Microsoft.`
    `IdentityModel.Clients.ActiveDirectory` package:

    ```
    install-package Microsoft.IdentityModel.Clients.ActiveDirectory
    ```

4. Now, enter the following command to install JSON.NET:

    ```
    install-package newtonsoft.json
    ```

5. Enter the following command to install the `SignalR` client package
    (note that this is different from the server package):

    ```
    Install-package Microsoft.AspNet.SignalR.Client
    ```

6. Add a project reference to `ProductionModel` by right-clicking on the
    References folder and selecting **Add Reference**, check `ProductionModel`
    by navigating to the **Solution | Projects** tab, and click on **OK**.

7. Add a project reference to `System.Configuraton` and `System.Net.Http` by
    right-clicking on the **References** folder and selecting **Add Reference**, check
    `System.Config` and `System.Net.Http` navigating to the **Assemblies |
    Framework** tab, and click on **OK**.

8. In the project's `Settings.settings` file, add a string setting called `Token` to
    store the user's auth token.

9. Add the following `appSettings` block to `App.config`; I've put comments
    to help you understand (and remember) what they stand for and added
    commented-out settings for the Azure API:

    ```
    <appSettings>
      <!-- AD Tenant -->
      <add key="ida:Tenant" value="azurebakery.onmicrosoft.com" />

      <!-- The target api AD application APP ID (get it from
        config tab in portal) -->
      <!-- Local -->
    ```

```
      <add key="ida:Audience"
        value="https://azurebakery.onmicrosoft.com/ManagementWebApi"
    />
      <!-- Azure -->
      <!-- <add key="ida:Audience"
        value="https://azurebakery.onmicrosoft.com/
          WebApp-azurebakeryproduction.azurewebsites.net" /> -->

      <!-- The client id of THIS application (get it from
        config tab in portal) -->
      <add key="ida:ClientID" value=
        "1a1867d4-9972-45bb-a9b8-486f03ad77e9" />

      <!-- Callback URI for OAuth workflow -->
      <add key="ida:CallbackUri"
        value="https://azurebakery.com" />

      <!-- The URI of the Web API -->
      <!-- Local -->
      <add key="serviceUri" value="https://localhost:44303/" />
      <!-- Azure -->
      <!-- <add key="serviceUri" value="https://azurebakeryproduction.
    azurewebsites.net/" />
      -->
    </appSettings>
```

10. Add the MVVM Light `ViewModelLocator` to `Application.Resources` in `App.xaml`:

```
    <Application.Resources>
      <vm:ViewModelLocator x:Key="Locator"
        d:IsDataSource="True" xmlns:vm=
          "clr-namespace:AzureBakery.Production.
            ManagementApplication.
              ViewModel" />
    </Application.Resources>
```

11. Add a binding to `MainWindow.xaml` `DataContext` with path to the `Main` property, which is the `MainViewModel` we will use:

```
<Window x:Class="AzureBakery.Production.ManagementApplication.
    MainWindow"
          xmlns="http://schemas.microsoft.com/winfx/2006/xaml/
            presentation"
          xmlns:x="http://schemas.microsoft.com/winfx/2006/xaml"
          DataContext="{Binding Source={StaticResource
            Locator}, Path=Main}"
          Title="Production Management Application"
            Height="350" Width="525">
```

Creating an authentication base class

Since the Web API and SignalR hubs use Azure AD authentication, we'll create services to interact with both and create a common base class to ensure that all requests are authenticated. This class uses the `AuthenticationContext.AquireToken` method to launch a built-in login dialog that handles the OAuth2 workflow and returns an authentication token on successful login:

```csharp
using Microsoft.IdentityModel.Clients.ActiveDirectory;
using System;
using System.Configuration;
using System.Diagnostics;
using System.Net;

namespace AzureBakery.Production.ManagementApplication.Services
{
    public abstract class AzureAdAuthBase
    {
        protected AuthenticationResult Token = null;

        protected readonly string ServiceUri = null;

        protected AzureAdAuthBase()
        {
            this.ServiceUri =
              ConfigurationManager.AppSettings["serviceUri"];
#if DEBUG
            // This will accept temp SSL certificates
            ServicePointManager.ServerCertificateValidationCallback +=
            (se, cert, chain, sslerror) => true;
#endif
        }

        protected bool Login()
        {
            // Our AD Tenant domain name
            var tenantId =
              ConfigurationManager.AppSettings["ida:Tenant"];

            // Web API resource ID (The resource we want to use)
            var resourceId =
              ConfigurationManager.AppSettings["ida:Audience"];

            // Client App CLIENT ID (The ID of the AD app for this
            client application)
```

```
var clientId =
  ConfigurationManager.AppSettings["ida:ClientID"];

// Callback URI
var callback = new
  Uri(ConfigurationManager.AppSettings["ida:CallbackU
  ri"]);

var authContext = new
  AuthenticationContext(string.Format("https://login.
  windows.net/{0}", tenantId));

if(this.Token == null)
{
    // See if we have a cached token
    var token = Properties.Settings.Default.Token;
    if (!string.IsNullOrWhiteSpace(token))
        this.Token = AuthenticationResult.
        Deserialize(token);
}

if (this.Token == null)
{
    try
    {
        // Acquire fresh token - this will get user to
        login
        this.Token =
          authContext.AcquireToken(resourceId,
            clientId, callback);
    }
    catch(Exception ex)
    {
        Debug.WriteLine(ex.ToString());

        return false;
    }
}
else if(this.Token.ExpiresOn < DateTime.UtcNow)
{
    // Refresh existing token this will not require
    login
    this.Token =
      authContext.AcquireTokenByRefreshToken(this.Token.
      RefreshToken, clientId);
}
```

```
        if (this.Token != null && this.Token.ExpiresOn >
          DateTime.UtcNow)
        {
            // Store token
            Properties.Settings.Default.Token =
              this.Token.Serialize(); // This should be
              encrypted
            Properties.Settings.Default.Save();

            return true;
        }

        // Clear token
        this.Token = null;

        Properties.Settings.Default.Token = null;
        Properties.Settings.Default.Save();

        return false;
      }
    }
  }
```

The token is stored in user settings and refreshed if necessary, so the users don't have to log in to the application every time they use it. The `Login` method can be called by derived service classes every time a service is called to check whether the user is logged in and whether there is a valid token to use.

Creating a data service

We'll create a `DataService` class that derives from the `AzureAdAuthBase` class we just created and gets data from the Web API service using AD authentication. First, we'll create a generic helper method that calls an API GET action using the `HttpClient` class with the authentication token added to the `Authorization` header, and deserializes the returned JSON object into a .NET-typed object `T`:

```
private async Task<T> GetData<T>(string action)
{
    if (!base.Login())
        return default(T);

    // Call Web API
    var authHeader = this.Token.CreateAuthorizationHeader();
    var client = new HttpClient();
```

```
var uri = string.Format("{0}{1}", this.ServiceUri,
  string.Format("api/{0}", action));
var request = new HttpRequestMessage(HttpMethod.Get, uri);
request.Headers.TryAddWithoutValidation("Authorization",
  authHeader);

// Get response
var response = await client.SendAsync(request);
var responseString = await response.Content.ReadAsStringAsync();

// Deserialize JSON
var data = await Task.Factory.StartNew(() =>
  JsonConvert.DeserializeObject<T>(responseString));

return data;
}
```

Once we have this, we can quickly create methods for getting order and batch data like this:

```
public async Task<IEnumerable<Order>> GetOrders()
{
    return await this.GetData<IEnumerable<Order>>("orders");
}

public async Task<IEnumerable<Batch>> GetBatches()
{
    return await this.GetData<IEnumerable<Batch>>("batches");
}
```

This service implements an `IDataService` interface and is registered in the `ViewModelLocator` class, ready to be injected into our view models like this:

```
SimpleIoc.Default.Register<IDataService, DataService>();
```

Creating a SignalR service

We'll create another service derived from the `AzureAdAuthBase` class, which is called `ManagementService`, and which sends updated orders to the SignalR hub and receives updates from the hub originating from other clients to keep the UI updated in real time.

First, we'll create a `Register` method, which creates a hub proxy using our `authorization` token from the base class, registers for updates from the hub, and starts the connection:

```
private IHubProxy _proxy = null;

public event EventHandler<Order> OrderUpdated;
public event EventHandler<Batch> BatchUpdated;

public ManagementService()
{

}

public async Task Register()
{
    // Login using AD OAuth
    if (!this.Login())
        return;

    // Get header from auth token
    var authHeader = this.Token.CreateAuthorizationHeader();

    // Create hub proxy and add auth token
    var cnString = string.Format("{0}signalr", base.ServiceUri);
    var hubConnection = new HubConnection(cnString, useDefaultUrl:
      false);
    this._proxy = hubConnection.CreateHubProxy("managementHub");
    hubConnection.Headers.Add("Authorization", authHeader);

    // Register for order updates
    this._proxy.On<Order>("updateOrder", order =>
    {
        this.OnOrderUpdated(order);
    });


    // Register for batch updates
    this._proxy.On<Batch>("updateBatch", batch =>
    {
        this.OnBatchUpdated(batch);
    });


    // Start hub connection
    await hubConnection.Start();
}
```

The OnOrderUpdated and OnBatchUpdated methods call events to notify about updates.

Now, add two methods that call the hub methods we created in the website using the IHubProxy.Invoke<T> method:

```
public async Task<bool> UpdateOrder(Order order)
{
    // Invoke updateOrder method on hub
    await this._proxy.Invoke<Order>("updateOrder",
      order).ContinueWith(task =>
    {
        return !task.IsFaulted;
    });

    return false;
}


public async Task<bool> UpdateBatch(Batch batch)
{
    // Invoke updateBatch method on hub
    await this._proxy.Invoke<Batch>("updateBatch",
      batch).ContinueWith(task =>
    {
        return !task.IsFaulted;
    });

    return false;
}
```

This service implements an IManagementService interface and is registered in the ViewModelLocator class, ready to be injected into our view models like this:

```
SimpleIoc.Default.Register<IManagementService,
  ManagementService>();
```

Completing the application

As with other applications we created in the book, there's not enough space to go through a lot of code in detail. I missed out creating the views and view models, so refer to the code samples of this chapter to complete the application.

Testing the application

To test the application locally, we need to start the Web API project and the WPF client application at the same time. So, under the **Startup Project** section in the **Solution Properties** dialog, check **Multiple startup projects**, select the two applications, and click on **OK**:

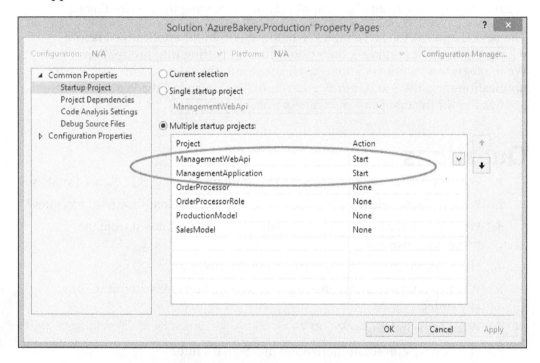

Once running, we can easily debug both applications simultaneously.

To test the application with the service running in the cloud, we need to deploy the service to the cloud, and then change the settings in the client app.config file (remember we put the local and Azure settings in the config with the Azure settings commented-out, so swap them around). In the final chapter, we'll look at transforming the app.config file, which is a bit trickier than Web.config to do automatically. To debug the client against the Azure service, make sure that only the client application is running (select **Single startup project** from the **Solution Properties** dialog). To debug the Azure Web API, follow the procedure to debug websites in *Chapter 6, Azure Website Diagnostics and Debugging*.

Summary

We covered a lot of topics in this chapter. Further, we explored providing a unified authentication system across the whole solution using Azure AD. We learned how to use a Web API to enable the production management Windows client application to access data from our production database and a SignalR hub to handle order and batch changes, keeping all clients updated and messaging the Service Bus topic.

The next chapter is the last chapter, where we will build applications before we start looking at preparing our systems before getting into production. We'll integrate a Windows Phone application into the sales system with push notifications and the Azure notifications hub. We'll also build a Windows Store application for the distribution business unit.

Questions

1. Why is a web service particularly important when using SQL Azure Database?
2. What is the problem with implementing SignalR in load-balanced websites?
3. What solution can we use to solve this problem (as known from the preceding answer)?
4. How can we enforce authorization in a controller?
5. What techniques can we use to test a Web API service without writing any code?
6. What is the hub SignalR URL?
7. How do we enforce authorization in a SignalR hub?
8. What does the **Enable Organizational Authentication** setting achieve during publishing?
9. Why must the `appPermissions` section of Web API AD application's manifest be modified?
10. In the client application's config, what are the `ida:Audience ida:ClientID` settings?
11. If a user's authentication token has expired, what can be done to authenticate the users without them logging in again?
12. How does a client call a SignalR hub method, and how can we tell if it was successful?

Answers

1. SQL Azure only supports SQL authentication, which means that the client application needs access to the login details, which can pose a security risk.

2. SignalR clients maintain connections to a single hub, which means that they will not send data to or receive data from other hub instances.

3. Implement a backplane system such as Azure Service Bus to keep hubs updated in real time.

4. Use the `Authorize` attribute at the controller or individual action level.

5. If we temporarily remove the `Authorize` attribute, we can use the browser to make HTTP GET requests or a tool such as Fiddler or cURL to make other requests.

6. The hub SignalR URL is `api/signalr`.

7. We use the same `Authorize` attribute.

8. An AD application will be provisioned for the new site and the site's `Web. config` file will be updated with the new `ida:Audience` ID.

9. Client applications need to be given permission to access them.

10. The `ida:Audience` ID is the ID of the target application, that is, the Web API, and `ida:ClientID` is the ID of the client application.

11. Use the `RefreshToken` token with the `AuthenticationContext. AcquireTokenByRefreshToken` method; the token can be refreshed without having to log in again.

12. Use the `IHubProxy.Invoke<T>` method to call the hub method, and then use the `.ContinueWith` continuation, which provides a task object with an `IsFaulted` flag.

11
Integrating a Mobile Application Using Mobile Services

In this chapter, we're going to build a Windows Phone application and an Azure mobile service for the sales business unit that will allow customers to view orders they've placed and receive notifications when the order status changes and when new products are added to the system. In the supply business unit, we'll create a Windows Store application and Azure mobile service for the warehouse staff to use on a tablet device in order to view which orders are waiting for dispatch while they are working without having to return to a central terminal. We'll be implementing the notification hub (from the Service Bus family of services) into the sales system so that when the order status changes and new products are created, customers will receive toast and tile push notifications to alert them.

Once we've finished, the sales system will have an architecture like this:

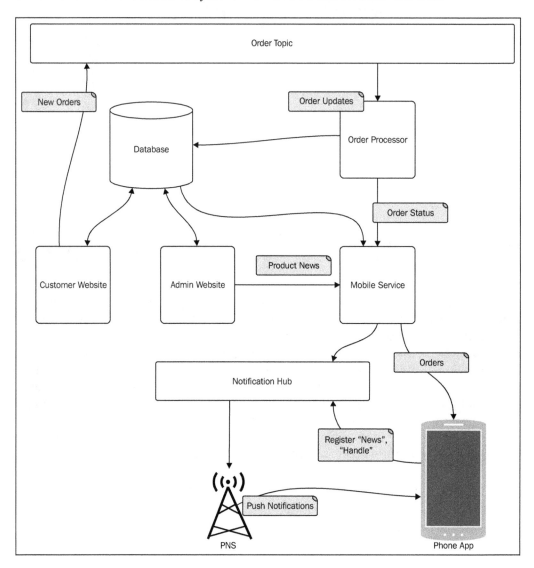

I also add another **Order Processor** Cloud service to the supply system, which will add order addresses to the supply table storage and barcode address labels to blob storage ready for the **Mobile Services** to use. We've covered a lot on cloud services, so I'll leave this out of the book, but of course, you can see all the code in the accompanying samples. Once we've finished, the supply system will have an architecture like this:

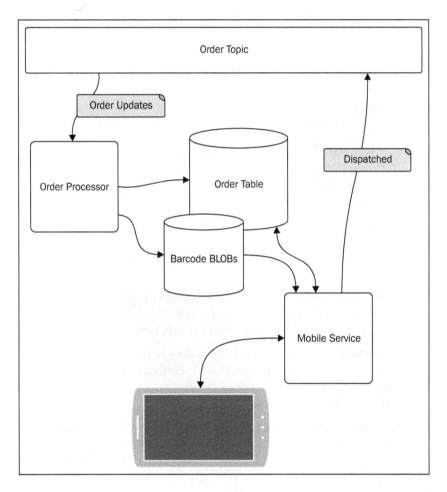

Introducing Azure mobile services

Azure mobile services is a great platform for mobile developers to quickly create backend services for their applications to store data and create custom APIs to interact with their own data or external resources via HTTP. Along with data and custom APIs, there is great support for push notifications, and there are push notification service APIs for all the major platforms. Mobile services also have fine-grained authorization control that allows different authorization levels to be applied to individual service methods and more recently, support for custom authorization providers.

Mobile services have benefits over other service types such as Web API, WCF, and services on other platforms because of the flexible authorization model, notifications' integration, and also excellent SDKs for taking care of authorization with built-in OAuth workflow and table and API-specific data access methods.

Azure mobile services can be used by pretty much any mobile platform such as Android and iOS and not just Windows Phone and Windows Store apps because there are full native SDKs for each platform, and there is also support for Xamarin, which can be used for cross-platform development using C#.

Mobile services offer four authorization levels (.NET/Node.js):

- **Anonymous/Everyone**: This is unauthenticated, so anybody on the Internet with the service URL can access it.

- **Application/Anybody with the application key**: All services have an application key, which allows secure access to services. Requests require an X-ZUMO-APPLICATION header bearing this key.

- **User/Only authenticated users**: User access is allowed to users authenticated via a permitted authenticated provider including Twitter, Facebook, Google, Microsoft, and Azure AD. Requests require an X-ZUMO-AUTH header bearing an OAuth2 authentication token.

- **Admin/Only scripts and admins**: This is the top authorization level, which overrides all other levels with the master key; requests require an X-ZUMO-MASTER header bearing this key. Master keys should not be distributed with client applications as they allow unlimited service access and would make the service vulnerable to misuse.

We will implement the **User** level authentication with the Twitter identity provider for the sales customer phone application, as this is already used by the customer website, so the customer can use the same credentials to log in. We'll implement the **User** level authentication using Azure AD for the supply Windows Store app because it's an internal system and we've used AD for all other internal systems. We'll use the **Admin** authorization level for the admin website and order processor because these are backend services and we don't want anything else to use these services.

Node.js is the original backend platform that allows developers to write scripts to modify table behavior, and create custom APIs and scheduled tasks in the portal itself with a fantastic script editor. Scripts can be pulled locally using Git (`http://git-scm.com/`) to create backups and allow local development in the developer's preferred IDE. Node.js scripts can make use of NPM packages, which are the Node.js equivalent of NuGet packages used by .NET developers, and allow third-party libraries to be utilized.

The Web API backend was introduced early in 2014 and offers much the same functionality; however, there is no editor in the portal (this is possible for Node.js because scripts are interpreted at runtime; however, this is not the case for Web API .NET as code needs to be compiled first). The Web API backend is an obvious choice for .NET developers as it will be the most familiar. Also, in our case study, it allows us to reuse our data model and gives us a more unified development experience.

Creating the customer Azure mobile service

We need to create a mobile service that matches customers to the existing customers in the sales system, allowing them to see their orders and receive notifications when an order status changes and receive news about things such as new product launches.

To retrieve the data, we can use a Windows Azure mobile services custom controller, which is pretty much the same as the Web API controllers we've already used, or remap the data from our own data schema to be consumed by data services, which implement an `ITableData` interface, which enforces a number of default table requirements using a tool such as AutoMapper (`https://github.com/AutoMapper/AutoMapper`). In our application, we don't have a large amount of interaction with the database; we're only retrieving orders, and so I've taken the approach of using a custom controller rather than mapping the schema to `ITableData`, which, in this case, is an unnecessary overhead. If we were creating a new database specifically for the mobile service, we would benefit from using the `EntityData` models, which implement `ITableData` and offer us full **Create, Read, Update, and Delete (CRUD)** database operations.

Push notifications in Web API backend services can only use the notifications hub and cannot directly interact with a **Push Notification Service (PNS)** as you can with a Node.js backend. We'll use a unique push handle created in the app as a tag, which the app subscribes to, so when we want to send an order update, we tag it with the user's unique handle and only they will get it. When we send product news, we will mark it with a news tag, which everyone subscribes to. In your own applications, it's a good idea to allow the user to control what they subscribe to by using a settings page to enable and disable tags for the types of notifications they wish to receive.

The mobile service will allow the phone app to register a handle for the user and retrieve order data using Twitter OAuth authentication. It will also act as a central point to send notifications for the order processor worker role when an order update appears on the Service Bus, and for the admin website, when a new product is created; the internal processes will use the **Admin** authentication with a master key.

Creating a mobile services project

If you're using a Premium version of Visual Studio, it's a lot easier to do this as you can add a mobile service into the existing sales solution; however, if you're an Express user, you'll need to switch to Visual Studio Express for Windows and add the existing Model project used by the other solutions.

To get started, right-click on the solution root in the **Solution Explorer** window and go to **Add | New Project**:

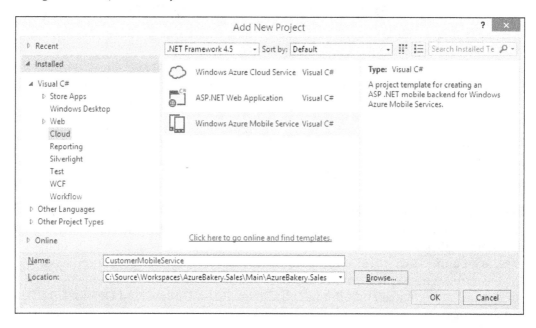

Add **Name** for the project and click on **OK**. The next dialog has all the options disabled, and we notice that we have a **Windows Azure Mobile Service** template selected and core references for Web API, which is what the .NET backend mobile services are built on. Then, click on **OK** to create the service and take a look at the sample code.

Exploring the mobile service sample project

The mobile service project has a similar structure to our MVC projects and more so the Web API project because it's built on the same technology. We have an App_Start folder with a WebApiConfig class, which takes care of initializing and configuring the application, and a Controllers folder with a TodoItemController sample class, which is a special type of API controller that is strongly bound to the EntityData type models, which have a number of default fields enforced by the ITableData interface:

```
public interface ITableData
{
    [JsonProperty(PropertyName = "__createdAt")]
    DateTimeOffset? CreatedAt { get; set; }
    [JsonProperty(PropertyName = "__deleted")]
    bool Deleted { get; set; }
    string Id { get; set; }
    [JsonProperty(PropertyName = "__updatedAt")]
    DateTimeOffset? UpdatedAt { get; set; }
    [JsonProperty(PropertyName = "__version")]
    [SuppressMessage("Microsoft.Performance",
    byte[] Version { get; set; }
}
```

The project structure should look like this:

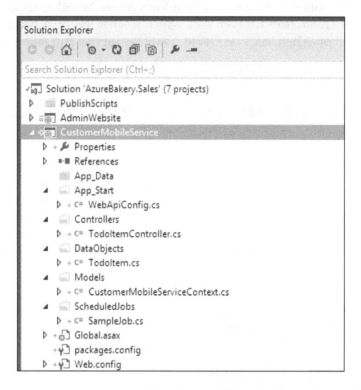

The project uses Entity Framework Code First Migrations to build its database in the same way as we used for the sales and production databases.

The sample table controller

The `TodoItemController` is a `TodoItem` typed `TableController`, which is scaffolded by Visual Studio using an entity from the projects `DbContext` (similar to when we scaffolded MVC controllers in the admin website and Web API). The controller gives us a CRUD method matched to the HTTP actions specified by the method name's prefix convention and commented above each method.

Table controllers can be created by right-clicking on the **Controllers** folder and navigating to **Add | Controller**, and then selecting **Windows Azure Mobile Services Table Controller** from the **Add Scaffold** dialog.

The sample data entity

The `DataObjects` folder contains a `TodoItem` class, which has a number of properties defined, but it will also pick up all the properties enforced by `ITableData` with the `EntityData` base class so that it can be used with `TableControllers`.

There is no wizard to create the `EntityData` classes; just add a class normally and implement the `EntityData` base class manually.

A sample scheduled job

Scheduled jobs implement the `IScheduledJob` interface with the `ScheduledJob` base class. The interface enforces a single task called `ExecuteAsync`, which performs a task with no return value:

```
public interface IScheduledJob
{
    Task ExecuteAsync(ScheduledJobDescriptor
        scheduledJobDescriptor, CancellationToken cancellationToken);
}
```

The task has access to the mobile services resources via the `Services` property in the `ScheduledJob` base class.

Scheduled jobs can be called via a simple HTTP POST request (bearing the correct authentication header — in this sample, there is no authentication). They are scheduled from the **SCHEDULER** tab in the mobile service workspace in the portal.

There is no wizard for creating `ScheduledJob` classes; just add a class normally and implement the `ScheduledJob` base class manually.

Mobile service DbContext

The `Models` folder contains the `DbContext` for the project, which is responsible for providing access to the `DataSet` properties and mapping entities using attribute annotation on the entities with the `AttributeToColumnAnnotationConvention`.

WebApiConfig

This `WebApiConfig.Register` method is called by `Global.asax` when the application starts and is responsible for configuring the Web API service specifically for mobile services and initializes the database using an initializer for the `DbContext`, which implements `DropCreateDatabaseIfModelChanges` (this is one to watch as it drops the database every time the model changes: `http://msdn.microsoft.com/en-us/library/gg696323(v=vs.113).aspx`) and has a `Seed` method, which inserts some `TodoItems` into the `TodoItems` table.

Cleaning up the project

As we've seen, the project has a load of demo code and EF configuration to create and seed a new database, so we'll clean all this out before we get started since we've already got a database and a full set of entities.

Delete the following demo files:

- `Controllers/TodoItemController.cs`
- The `DataObjects` folder (we already have a `Model` project with all our data entities)
- `ScheduledJobs/SampleJob.cs`

Now, do the following code modifications:

- Delete the `using CustomerMobileService.DataObjects;` lines from `CustomerMobileServicesContext.cs` and `App_Start/WebApiConfig.cs`
- Delete the following block of code from `CustomerMobileServicesContext.cs` because we no longer have a `TodoItem` entity and we're using an existing database created by EF Code First Migrations in the customer sales website (the mechanics of this are the same for mobile services projects if we wanted to create a new database):

```
public DbSet<TodoItem> TodoItems { get; set; }

protected override void OnModelCreating(DbModelBuilder
  modelBuilder)
{
    string schema =
      ServiceSettingsDictionary.GetSchemaName();
    if (!string.IsNullOrEmpty(schema))
    {
        modelBuilder.HasDefaultSchema(schema);
    }
```

```
modelBuilder.Conventions.Add(
    new
        AttributeToColumnAnnotationConvention<
            TableColumnAttribute,
        string>(
            "ServiceTableColumn", (property, attributes) =>
                attributes.Single().ColumnType.ToString()));
}
```

- Delete the following line from `App_Start/WebApiConfig.cs` again because we're using an existing database:

```
Database.SetInitializer(new
    CustomerMobileServiceInitializer());
```

- Delete the `CustomerMobileServiceInitializer` class

Now, build the project and check that there are no errors.

Integrating with the sales database

We need to modify the project to integrate with our existing sales database created by the customer website; we'll do this now, so first add a project reference to the `SalesModel` project by right-clicking on the **References** folder, selecting **Add reference**, then checking the **SalesModel** project in the **Solution/Projects** tab, and clicking on **OK**.

Add the following `DbSet` declarations to `CustomerMobileServiceContext`:

```
public DbSet<Customer> Customers { get; set; }

public DbSet<Product> Products { get; set; }

public DbSet< Order> Orders { get; set; }
```

Configuring development app settings

The mobile service website has a number of application settings for authentication, which can be used to debug the application locally and are overridden by portal settings when the service is published. Change the `MS_MasterKey` and `MS_Application` keys (I've used new GUIDs for both) and fill in the `MS_TwitterConsumerKey` details, which we obtained way back when we built the customer website (I've missed out the ones we don't need):

```
<add key="MS_MobileServiceName" value="CustomerMobileService" />
    <add key="MS_MasterKey" value="1560E6FF-0C32-4374-95DF-
    4CCEBD20B1FC" />
```

```
<add key="MS_ApplicationKey" value="4E2D5547-FEC4-4870-8060-
CB1736D4529A" />
<add key="MS_TwitterConsumerKey"
  value="BdYXYPBuRkFSwjZxxxxxyyyyy" />
<add key="MS_TwitterConsumerSecret"
  value="KIyLklCxFbGIq1nnyVAU0wxFQBUTw5xxxxxxxxxxyyyyyyyyyy" />
```

When we test the admin website and order processor locally, they will use the `MS_MasterKey` details for authenticating their requests against the mobile service.

Integrating authentication with the sales website

We have a slight problem as we need to associate a Twitter-authenticated user with the `Microsoft.WindowsAzure.Mobile.Service.Security` authentication, with our existing user in the sales website, which is authenticated using ASP.NET authentication. The MVC project has a special `IdentityDbContext` database context that has base properties to interact with the ASP.NET authentication tables; mobile services don't support this context as it allows a number of different authentication options, so we need to do a bit of work to match the user credentials.

Basically, what we need to do is get the OAuth identity and match it to the customer's OAuth identity stored in the `AspNetUserLogins` table, which relates to the `AspNetUser` table, which holds our `Customer_Id` related to our customer entity. We'll manually add the ASP.NET table entities (which is where the MVC project stores user credential details) to our `DbContext` to allow us to do this.

Add the following code to the `DbContext` (mine's called `CustomerMobileServiceContext`), which will map the `AspNetUser` and `AspNetUserLogin` tables into our EF model (this mimics part of what the `IdentityDbContext` does for us in the sales customer website in the `ApplicationDbContext`:

```
public class AspNetUser
{
    public string Id { get; set; }
    public string UserName { get; set; }
    public string PasswordHash { get; set; }
    public string SecurityStamp { get; set; }
    public string Discriminator { get; set; }
    public int Customer_Id { get; set; }
}
```

```
public class AspNetUserLogin
{
    [ForeignKey("AspNetUser")]
    public string UserId { get; set; }
    [Column(Order = 1), Key]
    public string LoginProvider { get; set; }
    [Column(Order = 2), Key]
    public string ProviderKey { get; set; }
    public virtual AspNetUser AspNetUser { get; set; }
}


    public DbSet<AspNetUserLogin> AspNetUserLogins { get; set; }
```

Notice the navigation property to relate AspNetUser to the AspNetUserLogins table. If you were using the EF-fluent API, you could map the entities with that instead of data annotations, but we've let EF do all the work for us so far and only need some minor tweaks to get it to understand the composite key in AspNetUserLogins and the foreign key relationship, so I've just used data annotation's attributes.

Next, add a helper class called AuthHelper to a Helpers solution folder, which takes care of getting us a user from the ASP.NET auth tables, and can be used in various controllers that we'll create to save duplication of code. We pass in the DbContext so that we can work on the Customer entity it returns, without having conflicts with the entity being used in multiple contexts:

```
public class AuthHelper
{
    public static async Task<Customer> GetCustomer(ServiceUser
      serviceUser, CustomerMobileServiceContext ctx)
    {
        // Find Twitter Id, of form Twitter:123456789
        var idParts = serviceUser.Id.Split(':');
        var key = idParts[1];
        var provider = idParts[0];

        // We now need to manually get the Customer_Id from the
        AspNetUser table
        var userLogins =
            await
                ctx.AspNetUserLogins.SingleOrDefaultAsync(
                    l => l.LoginProvider == provider &&
                        l.ProviderKey == key);

        if (userLogins != null)
```

```
        {
                var id = userLogins.AspNetUser.Customer_Id;

                // Add handle to customer
                var customer = await ctx.Customers.FindAsync(id);

                return customer;
        }

        return null;
    }
}
```

Adding a channel registration API controller

We're going to add a Windows Azure mobile services custom controller, which will allow the push channel handle of the user's phone to be added to their customer details using their Twitter authentication details previously registered via the website so that customers can be notified when their order status changes. We'll do this in the following procedure:

1. Right-click on the **Controllers** folder and go to **Add | Controller**; then select **Windows Azure Mobile Services Custom Controller** from the **Add Scaffold** dialog:

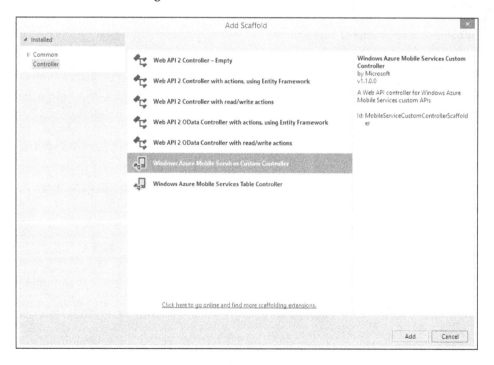

Add the `AuthorizeLevel` attribute and set it to `AuthorizationLevel.User`, which requires the calling HTTP request to have a valid authentication token in the `X-ZUMO_AUTH` header, which in our case will be a Twitter OAuth token, but it can be a token from any other supported OAuth provider including Azure Active Directory:

```
[AuthorizeLevel(AuthorizationLevel.User)]
public class ChannelRegistrationController : ApiController
```

2. Once we have this, we can write a POST method (I chose POST because we are sending data with an action related to the channel registration; we could have added it to a `CustomerController` and used a PUT method, which implies an update, but we don't have any other customer actions):

```
public async Task Post([FromBody]dynamic data)
{
    Services.Log.Info("ChannelRegistrationController -
      Started");

    var handle = (string)data.handle;

    var ctx = new CustomerMobileServiceContext();

    var customer = await AuthHelper.GetCustomer(User as
      ServiceUser, ctx);

    if (customer != null)
    {
        // Add handle to customer
        if (customer.PushHandle != handle)
        {
            customer.PushHandle = handle;
            await ctx.SaveChangesAsync();
        }
        Services.Log.Info("ChannelRegistrationController -
          Completed");
    }
    else
    {
        var message = string.Format("User does not exist");
        Services.Log.Error(message);
        throw new Exception(message);
    }
}
```

3. The `data` parameter is marked with the `FromBody` attribute because the data in a `POST` method is (typically) sent in the `request` body rather than via URL parameters, so this tells the controller where to get the data. I've used a dynamic type, so the caller can pass in a non-typed object, which can be simpler for situations like this where we only have one property (we'll see how it's called in the app later). We use the `AuthHelper.GetCustomer` method to get our customer details, and then update it with the push handle.

Adding an order controller

As I mentioned earlier, we're not going to use table controllers due to the overhead in mapping existing entities to `ITableData`, so we'll use an API controller instead. The `OrderController` is very similar to the `ChannelRegistrationController`; it retrieves the customer details using the `AuthHelper.GetCustomer` method, and then returns all their orders for that customer:

```
[AuthorizeLevel(AuthorizationLevel.User)]
public class OrderController : ApiController
{
    public ApiServices Services { get; set; }

    // GET api/Order
    public async Task<IEnumerable<Order>> Get()
    {
        Services.Log.Info("OrderController - Started");

        var ctx = new CustomerMobileServiceContext();

        var customer = await AuthHelper.GetCustomer(User as
          ServiceUser, ctx);

        if (customer != null)
        {
            var orders = await ctx.Orders.Where(o => o.Customer.Id
              == customer.Id).ToListAsync();

            Services.Log.Info("OrderController - Completed");

            return orders;
        }
    }
```

```
            else
            {
                var message = string.Format("User does not exist");
                Services.Log.Error(message);
                throw new Exception(message);
            }
        }
    }
```

Publishing the mobile service

We need to publish our service before we start working on our application so that we can get the application and master keys along with the details of the notifications hub, which will be provisioned for us during the publish process, so we can use the details in the application. We'll do this in the following procedure:

1. Start the publish process in the same way as for any website, that is, by right-clicking on the project and selecting **Publish**.

2. Click on **Windows Azure Mobile Services** from the **Select a publish target** options, log in, and then click on the **New** button on the **Select Existing Mobile Service** dialog:

3. Choose **Name**, select **Region**, choose the existing database we've joined our data model to, and enter the login credentials for the database.

4. Click on **Create**, which will provision the Azure service portal for us and allow us to publish our service (we could stop here as the notifications hub has been created at this point, but we will continue for completion).

5. The **Connection** tab shows us the connection details for the service we just created.

6. Click on **Next** and we'll see the **Settings** tab, which, when compared with a normal website publish, has little to change.

7. Click on **Publish** to start the publish process.

8. We can now collect the connection details from the portal, so go to the **SERVICE BUS** workspace and we'll see our new namespace:

9. Click on the new namespace name to go into its workspace, then go to the **NOTIFICATIONS HUB** tab, where we will see the new hub, and click on **CONNECTION INFORMATION**:

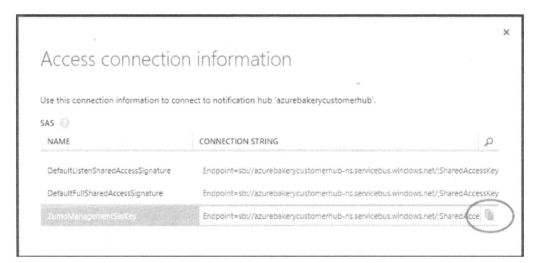

10. There's a **ZumoManagementSasKey** created for our service (Zumo is the mobile service's code name), so copy that.

11. Now, paste the details into the `Microsoft.ServiceBus.Connection` setting in the `Web.config` file and fill in the `MS_NotificationHubName` attribute like this (this will allow us to access the hub from the service):

```
<!-- When using this setting, be sure to add matching
  Notification Hubs connection
string in the connectionStrings section with the name
  "MS_NotificationHubConnectionString". -->
<add key="MS_NotificationHubName"
  value="azurebakerycustomerhub" />
<add key="Microsoft.ServiceBus.ConnectionString"
  value="Endpoint=sb://azurebakerycustomerhub-
    ns.servicebus.windows.net/;SharedAccessKeyName=ZumoManagement
    SasKey;
    SharedAccessKey=KX9kWXakI8JXIH1sRVtmsn2xxxxxxxxxxyyyyyyyyyyy="
/>
```

12. We'll need these details in the application, too.

13. Under the **PUSH** tab, check **Enable unauthenticated push notifications** under the **windows phone notifications settings (mpns)** section and click on **SAVE** (this allows unauthenticated notifications that are throttled to 500 messages a day; you can read more about this at `http://msdn.microsoft.com/en-US/library/windows/apps/ff941099(v=vs.105).aspx`):

Creating a Windows Phone application

We'll now start building our Windows Phone application, which will be very basic in terms of UI but will demonstrate how to set up a push notifications channel, register with the notifications hub, and make authenticated requests to the mobile service. We'll create and set up the application in the following procedure:

1. Right-click on the solution and go to **Add | New project**:

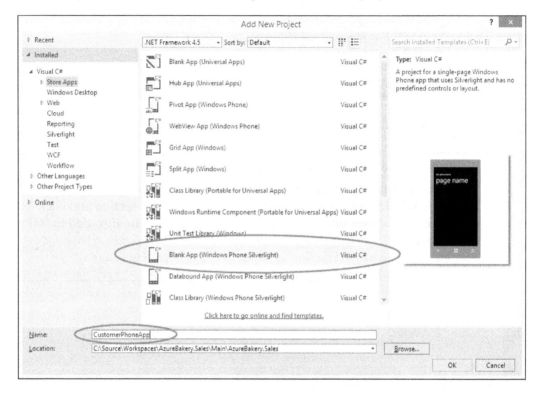

2. Select **Blank App (Windows Phone Silverlight)** from the **Store Apps** tab and click on **OK**. In the next dialog, I've chosen **Windows Phone 8.0** as the target OS version because we're not implementing any 8.1-specific features. Click on **OK** again to create the project.

3. Install the Windows Azure Mobile Service NuGet package by entering the following command into the NuGet **Package Manager Console**:

```
Install-Package WindowsAzure.MobileServices
```

4. Install the `WindowsAzure.Messaging.Managed` NuGet package, which allows us to interact with the notifications hub by entering the following command into the NuGet **Package Manager Console**:

```
Install-Package WindowsAzure.Messaging.Managed
```

5. Install MVVM Light (which we've used on all our XAML apps so far) by entering the following command into the NuGet **Package Manager Console**:

```
install-package mvvmlight
```

Adding data services

In the same style as our other XAML applications, we'll use a service pattern to separate the data access from the view models. To start with, we'll create a `DataServiceBase` class, which has an authentication mechanism built into it to guarantee that all requests to the service are correctly authenticated; then, we'll implement it in a `DataService` class to call the `ChannelRegistrationController` and `OrderContoller`. The user ID and auth token are stored in an isolated storage so that they don't have to log in every time they use the app, unless their token expires.

The DataServiceBase class

The `DataServiceBase` class basically removes the entire authentication overhead from data services that implement it. There is a static instance of `MobileServiceClient` so that multiple implementations get the same instance that contains the authentication credentials:

```
public abstract class DataServiceBase
{
    private const string USER_ID = "USER_ID";
    private const string USER_TOKEN = "USER_TOKEN";

    #if DEBUG
    protected readonly static MobileServiceClient _mobileService =
      new MobileServiceClient(
        "http://localhost:61021",
        "4E2D5547-FEC4-4870-8060-CB1736D4529A"
        );
    #else
    protected readonly static MobileServiceClient _mobileService =
      new MobileServiceClient(
```

```
              "http://azurebakerycustomer.azure-mobile.net/",
              "PopNgBgUnnYsutDBIsHXXXXXXXXXXxxxx"
              );
       #endif

          protected static MobileServiceAuthenticationProvider _provider =
       MobileServiceAuthenticationProvider.Twitter;
```

I have put in a compiler switch, so when we debug locally, we are using the
details of our local service, and when we're in the **Release** mode in Azure, we're
using the details of our Azure mobile service (this is why we published earlier).
The constructor takes two parameters, the first is the mobile service URL and the
second is the application or master key. Only use the application key in the client
applications. The published application key can be found in the mobile services
workspace in the portal, by selecting the service from the service list and clicking
on **MANAGE KEYS** on the toolbar.

The Login method checks storage to see whether we have any credentials
stored (StorageHelper is a basic helper class you can get from the samples);
if there are, we manually create a MobileServiceUser object and apply it to
the MobileServiceClient; if there aren't, we call LoginAsync, which launches
an OAuth login page (browser) for the selected auth provider, allowing the user
to log in and authenticate the client, and then stores the credentials:

```
public static async Task<bool> Login()
{
    var userId = StorageHelper.GetSetting<string>(USER_ID, null);
    var userToken = StorageHelper.GetSetting<string>(USER_TOKEN,
      null);

    bool success = true;

    if (userId != null && userToken != null)
    {
        var user = new MobileServiceUser(userId);
        user.MobileServiceAuthenticationToken = userToken;
        _mobileService.CurrentUser = user;
    }
    else
    {
        try
        {
            var user = await _mobileService.LoginAsync(_provider);
```

```
        StorageHelper.StoreSetting(USER_ID, user.UserId,
            true);
        StorageHelper.StoreSetting(USER_TOKEN,
            user.MobileServiceAuthenticationToken, true);
    }
    catch (InvalidOperationException)
    {
        success = false;
    }
}

return success;
}
```

The `Logout` method basically clears the stored credentials and `CurrentUser` in the client:

```
public static void Logout()
{
    _mobileService.Logout();

    StorageHelper.StoreSetting(USER_ID, null, true);
    StorageHelper.StoreSetting(USER_TOKEN, null, true);
}
```

The main feature is the `ExecutedAuthenticated` method, which allows a function to be passed in so that it can be executed more than once if authentication expires or fails. The number of retries can be set with the optional `retries` parameter:

```
protected async Task<T> ExecuteAuthenticated<T>(Func<Task<T>> t, int
retries = 1)
{
    int retry = 0;
    T retVal = default(T);

    while (retry < retries)
    {
        if (_mobileService.CurrentUser == null)
        {
            // If login fails return default
            if (!await Login())
                return retVal;
        }

        // Try and execute task
        try
```

```
        {
            retVal = await t();
            break;
        }
        catch (InvalidOperationException ioex)
        {
            if (ioex.Message == "Error: Unauthorized")
                _mobileService.CurrentUser = null;

            retry++;
        }
    }
    return retVal;
}
```

The DataService class

The `DataService` class uses the `DataServiceBase` class to manage authenticated service calls, and implements `IDataService` so that it can be registered into the MVVM Light IoC container and automatically injected into the view models:

```
public class DataService : DataServiceBase, IDataService
```

The `RegisterChannel` method passes a function into `ExecuteAuthenticated`, which calls the `MobileServiceClient.InvokeApiAsync<U, T>` method with the API name and a `dynamic` data object that contains the push handle:

```
public async Task RegisterChannel(string handle)
{
    await base.ExecuteAuthenticated(async () =>
    {
        dynamic data = new ExpandoObject();
        data.handle = handle;
        await _mobileService.InvokeApiAsync<object,
          dynamic>("ChannelRegistration", data);
    });
}
```

The `GetOrders` method passes a function into `ExecuteAuthenticated`, which calls the `MobileServiceClient.InvokeApiAsync<U>` method with the API name, the HTTP method (default is POST and we need GET), and `null` for the `parameters` option (this is the best matching overload):

```
public async Task<IEnumerable<Order>> GetOrders()
{
    return await
      base.ExecuteAuthenticated<IEnumerable<Order>>(async () =>
```

```
{
    var orders = await
    _mobileService.InvokeApiAsync<IEnumerable<Order>>("order",
    HttpMethod.Get, null);

    return orders;
});
}
```

 In the samples, I've linked the Model library files because the library can't be directly added since it's a .NET library and the phone app is **Silverlight**. If you wanted, you could create a **Portable Class Library (PCL)** instead, which can support multiple platforms.

Setting up push notifications

We need to do a number of things to get push notifications working in our Windows Phone app; first, modify the manifest to allow push notification's capability and add code to create a push channel and register it with the notifications hub.

Modifying the manifest

Open the WMAppManifest.xml file under the Properties folder and check the **ID_CAP_PUSH_NOTIFICATION** capability under the **Capabilities** tab, and then save the project so that the application is allowed to use notification channels:

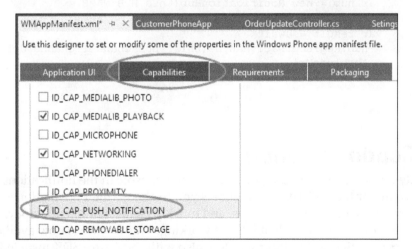

Adding a channel helper

We need to add code to create a push notifications channel using the
`HttpNotificationChannel` object, which has a `ChannelUriUpdated` event, which
is fired when the channel changes (either when it's created or if it changed while
the application is running). I've left most of the code out for this, so grab it from the
samples. When the channel changes, this method is called to register the channel
with the notifications hub:

```
private readonly string HUB_NAME = "azurebakerycustomerhub";
        private readonly string CONNECTION_STRING =
        "Endpoint=sb://azurebakerycustomerhub-
        ns.servicebus.windows.net/;SharedAccessKeyName=ZumoManagem
        entSasKey;
         SharedAccessKey=xxxxxxxxxxxxxxxxxxxxxxxxxxxxxxxxxxxxxxxxxxx
         xx=";

public void Register()
{
    // Stuff onto UI thread because login interacts with UI
    DispatcherHelper.RunAsync(async ()  =>
    {
        // Register with service
        var service = new DataService();
        await service.RegisterChannel(this.GetChannelTag());

        // Register with hub
        var hub = new NotificationHub(this.HUB_NAME,
          this.CONNECTION_STRING);
        var result = await
          hub.RegisterNativeAsync(this._pushChannel.ChannelUri.
          AbsoluteUri,
           new string[] { this.GetChannelTag(), "news" });
    });
}
```

Notifications debug

One really helpful feature in the portal is a debug console in the notifications hub's
workspace under the **DEBUG** tab. It allows you to choose the PNS platform, send a
random broadcast or tagged messages, and quickly create a notification payload to
test whether your registered channels are working. This feature is now available in
the Visual Studio **Server Explorer** window also with the Azure SDK installed.

> The debug console should be used with caution in production environments, as notifications may be sent to real users depending on the tagging.

Completing the app

The data services are injected into the view models by first registering them in the `ViewModelLocator`, and then adding an `interface` parameter to the view model constructor for it to be bound. We covered this in the other XAML applications, and the full code is available in the samples.

> One thing to be careful of is to make sure the `MobileServiceClient.LoginAsync` method is not called before the UI has fully loaded, as it will fail because it needs to be inserted into the root UI element. To ensure this, the view model in the code samples hook into the page loaded event (via a trigger) to initialize, retrieve data, and set up the push channel (which will make an authenticated request when it gets a valid channel).

Updating the order processor

We can update the order processor worker role to call the `Notification/PostOrderUpdate` action when an order status changes. We'll do this in the following short procedure:

1. Install the mobile service NuGet package with the following command in the NuGet **Package Manager Console**:

   `Install-Package WindowsAzure.MobileServices`

2. Add a `mobileServiceUrl` string setting to the role's settings with the URL of our local service for local and the publish service for the cloud.

3. Add a `mobileServiceKey` string setting to the role's settings with the master key of our local service for local and the published service for the cloud.

4. Add a `MobileServiceClient` variable, which is instantiated in the constructor with cloud configurations settings like this:

```
private readonly MobileServiceClient _mobileService;

public OrderProcessor()
```

```
{
    var mobileServiceUrl =
        CloudConfigurationManager.GetSetting("mobileServiceUrl");
    var mobileServiceKey =
        CloudConfigurationManager.GetSetting("mobileServiceKey");

    this._mobileService = new
        MobileServiceClient(mobileServiceUrl, mobileServiceKey);
}
```

5. Add a method called `NotifyHub` to call the `Notification/PostOrderUpdate` action with the updated order ID:

```
private async Task NotifyHub(int orderId)
{
    dynamic data = new ExpandoObject();
    data.orderId = orderId;

    await this._mobileService.InvokeApiAsync<object,
        dynamic>("Notification/PostOrderUpdate", data);
}
```

6. Finally, add a line of code to call the `NotifyHub` method if the order status has changed:

```
public async Task Process(Order order)
{
    // Update status
    var currentOrder = this._ctx.Orders.FirstOrDefault(o =>
        o.Id == order.Id);

    if (currentOrder != null && currentOrder.Status !=
        order.Status)
    {
        currentOrder.Status = order.Status;

        await this._ctx.SaveChangesAsync();

        await this.NotifyHub(order.Id);
    }
}
```

Updating the admin website

As with the order processor, we can do a small modification to the admin website to call the `Notification/PostProductNews` action when a new product is created, which will send push notifications to all customers. The procedure for this is pretty much the same, but here, I created a separate helper class to separate the logic from the controller:

```
private readonly MobileServiceClient _mobileService;

public Notifications()
{
    var mobileServiceUrl = ConfigurationManager.AppSettings["mobileSe
    rviceUrl"];
    var mobileServiceKey = ConfigurationManager.AppSettings["mobileSe
    rviceKey"];

    this._mobileService = new MobileServiceClient(mobileServiceUrl,
    mobileServiceKey);
}

public async Task NotifyPostProductNews(int productId)
{
    dynamic data = new ExpandoObject();
    data.productId = productId;

    await this._mobileService.InvokeApiAsync<object,
dynamic>("Notification/PostProductNews", data);
}
```

This method can be called by the `ProductController.Create` action:

```
[HttpPost]
[ValidateAntiForgeryToken]
public async Task<ActionResult> Create([Bind(Include = "Id,Name,Produc
tType,Price,IsAvailable")] Product product)
{
    if (ModelState.IsValid)
    {
        db.Products.Add(product);
        db.SaveChanges();
```

```
        // Notify users via push notifications
        await new
          Notifications().NotifyPostProductNews(product.Id);
        return RedirectToAction("Index");
    }
    return View(product);
}
```

Creating the supply mobile service

We've not touched the supply business domain yet, so we're going to create a mobile service and a Windows Store application that allows warehouse staff to view orders, which are ready to dispatch, print labels, and mark orders as Dispatched on their tablet devices.

 I've created a full set of supporting samples for the supply business domain, most of which aren't documented as we've not got space in the book, and we've mostly covered its material already; however, there are some interesting bits in the supply order processor, which writes orders to an order table in table storage and automatically generates barcode labels in the JPEG format and writes them to blob storage, so have a look at that!

We'll create the service and install the required NuGet packages in the following procedure:

1. Right-click on the solution and go to **Add | New project** and select the **Windows Azure Mobile Service** template from the **Cloud template** section.

2. Install the WindowsAzure.ServiceBus NuGet package so that we can send the Dispatched order status updates to the Service Bus topic by entering the following command in the NuGet **Package manager Console**:

    `Install-package WindowsAzure.ServiceBus`

3. Install the WindowsAzure.Storage NuGet package so that we can read order entities from the orders' table storage and read the barcode address labeled JPEG images from blob storage:

    `Install-package WindowsAzure.Storage`

Configuring a mobile service for Azure AD auth

As the supply system is an internal system, we're going to integrate it with the Azure Bakery AD. We'll do this in the following procedure:

1. In the **APPLICATIONS** tab of the AD namespace workspace, we'll see our existing AD application, which gives us clues about what type of applications we need to create; click on **ADD** on the toolbar and select **Add an application my organization is developing**.

2. Give it a name and leave the default type of **WEB APPLICATION AND/OR WEB API**.

3. Next, fill in the **SIGN-ON URL** and **APP ID URI** fields; these are the same URLs created when the service is published and can be collected from the **windows azure active directory** section in the **IDENTITY** tab; they should look like `https://azurebakerysupply.azure-mobile.net/signin-aad`, as shown in the following screenshot:

4. Now, in the same way we did for our Web API, we need to modify the manifest to allow other applications (our mobile app) to access it. So, follow the procedure in *Chapter 10, Web API and Client Integration*, to do this.

5. On the application's **CONFIGURE** tag, copy the **CLIENT ID** value:

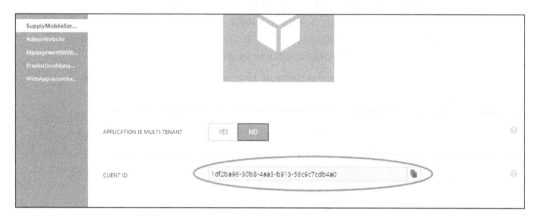

6. Paste it into the **CLIENT ID** setting in the Mobile Service **IDENTITY** tab and also add the AD tenant to **ALLOWED TENANTS** and click on **SAVE**:

 Local debugging of Azure mobile services with a Windows Store app and Azure AD authentication is a bit tricky due to the security restrictions of the Store application. The workaround I came up with is fully implemented in the code samples and explained here: http://webbercross.azurewebsites.net/local-debugging-an-azure-mobile-service-with-ad-auth/.

Creating the barcode controller

The following `ApiController` retrieves a JPEG barcode address labels created by the order processor from blob storage:

```
[AuthorizeLevel(AuthorizationLevel.User)]
public class BarcodeController : ApiController
{
    private readonly CloudStorageAccount _storageAccount;

    public ApiServices Services { get; set; }

    public BarcodeController()
    {
        // Retrieve the storage account from the connection
        string.
        this._storageAccount =
          CloudStorageAccount.Parse(ConfigurationManager.
          ConnectionStrings
            ["StorageConnectionString"].ConnectionString);
    }

    // GET api/Barcode
    public async Task<byte[]> Get(string reference)
    {
        Services.Log.Info("BarcodeController - Patch Start");

        try
        {
            var blobClient =
              this._storageAccount.CreateCloudBlobClient();
            var container =
              blobClient.GetContainerReference("barcodes");
            var blobRef =
              container.GetBlockBlobReference(reference);

            await blobRef.FetchAttributesAsync();
            var buffer = new byte[blobRef.Properties.Length];
            await blobRef.DownloadToByteArrayAsync(buffer, 0);

            Services.Log.Info("BarcodeController - Patch
              Completed");

            return buffer;
        }
```

```
        catch (Exception ex)
        {
            Services.Log.Error("BarcodeController - Get Error",
                ex);
            throw;
        }
    }
}
```

Creating the order controller

The OrderController class has a Get method for returning OrderEntity entities from the Orders table in the table storage, which are created and updated by the order processor:

```
public IEnumerable<OrderEntity> Get()
{
    Services.Log.Info("OrderController - Get Start");

    try
    {
        var tableClient =
          _storageAccount.CreateCloudTableClient();

        var table = tableClient.GetTableReference("orders");

        var query = new TableQuery<OrderEntity>()
            .Where(TableQuery.GenerateFilterCondition("Status",
              QueryComparisons.Equal,
            //OrderStatus.ReadyForDispatch.ToString()));
                OrderStatus.Open.ToString()));

        var data = table.ExecuteQuery(query);

        Services.Log.Info("OrderController - Get Completed");

        return data;
    }
    catch (System.Exception ex)
    {
        Services.Log.Error("OrderController - Get Error", ex);

        throw;
    }
}
```

The `Put` method updates the `OrderEntity` entities using a `TableOperation.` `Replace` operation, and then sends an order update to the Service Bus using a `MessagingService` similar to the one implemented in the admin website:

```
public async Task Put([FromBody] OrderEntity entity)
{
    Services.Log.Info("OrderController - Put Start");

    try
    {
        // Get orders table
        var tableClient =
          _storageAccount.CreateCloudTableClient();
        var table = tableClient.GetTableReference("orders");

        // Update entity
        var updateOp = TableOperation.Replace(entity);
        var updateResult = await table.ExecuteAsync(updateOp);

        // Send to service bus
        var messaging = new MessagingService();
        await messaging.CreateSubscriptionAsync();
        await messaging.DispatchOrder(entity);

        Services.Log.Info("OrderController - Put Completed");
    }
    catch (System.Exception ex)
    {
        Services.Log.Error("OrderController - Put Error", ex);

        throw;
    }
}
```

Creating the supply Windows Store application

We're going to add a Windows Store app to interact with the mobile service. I've selected the **Split App (Windows)** option, which has a group item page and a details page to get us started. We'll do this in the following procedure:

1. Right-click on the solution and go to **Add | New project** and choose a Windows app template from the **Store Apps** templates:

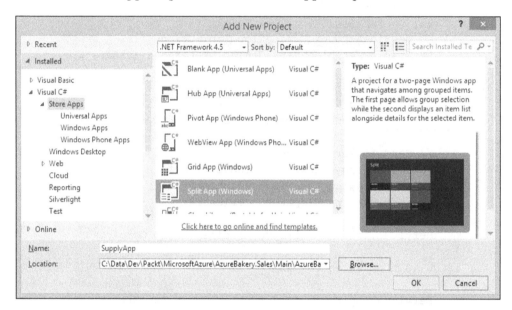

2. Install the `WindowsAzure.MobileServices` NuGet package by entering the following command in the NuGet **Package Manager Console**:

    ```
    Install-package WindowsAzure.MobileServices
    ```

3. Install the `MVVM Light` NuGet package with the following command:

    ```
    Install-package MvvmLight
    ```

4. Install the `Microsoft.IdentityModel.Clients.ActiveDirectory` NuGet package that is needed for Azure AD authentication:

    ```
    Install-package Microsoft.IdentityModel.Clients.ActiveDirectory
    ```

5. Install the `WindowsAzure.Storage` NuGet package so that we can interact with `TableEntity` entities from the service:

    ```
    Install-package WindowsAzure.Storage
    ```

6. Enable **Enterprise Authentication** and **Private Networks (Client & Server)** in the `Package.appxmanifest` file so that the application can use AD authentication:

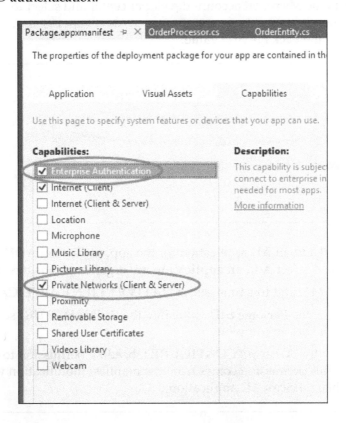

Configuring the Store app for AD authentication

We need to register the application in the Store to get a **Package SID** value and then add an AD application similar to the WPF client application we created. We'll do this in the following procedure:

1. Right-click on the app project and go to **Store | Associate App with the Store**.

2. Click on **Next** on the next screen, and then sign in to your Store account; if you haven't got one, create one here first: `https://appdev.microsoft.com/StorePortals/en-us/Account/Signup/Start`.

3. Enter the app name and click on **Reserve** to reserve it, and then click on **Next**.

4. Click on **Associate** on the next screen to complete the association.

5. Log in to the Microsoft account developer center and select the new application (`https://account.live.com/developers/applications`) and copy the **Package SID** value:

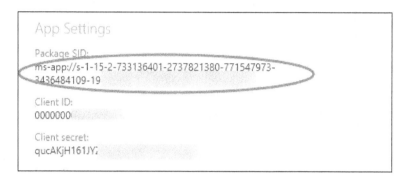

6. Now we'll add an AD application for the app, so click on **ADD** on the toolbar and select **Add an application my organization is developing**.

7. Enter **NAME**, and this time, select **NATIVE CLIENT APPLICATION**.

8. Now, paste the **Package SID** value into the **REDIRECT URI** setting, and click on the tick to complete.

9. Finally, in the AD app's **CONFIGURE** tab, add a permission to the mobile service (this permission comes from the manifest modification we made in the mobile service's AD application):

Creating a DataServiceBase class

The `DataServiceBase` class is very similar to the Windows Phone `DataServiceBase` class we created with Twitter authentication, but there's an extra step to get an access token before the `LoginAsync` method is called:

```
var ac = new AuthenticationContext(authority);
var ar = await ac.AcquireTokenAsync(resourceURI, clientID);
var payload = new JObject();
payload["access_token"] = ar.AccessToken;

user = await client.LoginAsync(_provider, payload);
```

Have a look at the code samples in the code bundle of this chapter to see how this is implemented in the services to interact with the supply system mobile service.

Summary

We've had a really intense look at mobile services in this chapter; it's quite a big subject in its own right, so it's worth doing some more reading yourself, and definitely check out the Node.js backend to compare what it offers to the .NET backend we've looked at in this chapter.

As I've mentioned, there is a lot of code for the supply business domain that has been omitted from the book due to repetition of the topics we've covered and space in this book, but you should definitely have a look, particularly at the order processor worker role, as this has the other half of the table and blob storage for `OrderEntity` and barcode JPEG data.

We have completed the application code now, and we'll be finishing this book in the next chapter by looking at how to prepare our systems to go live.

Questions

1. What benefits do Azure mobile services offer over other type of offer services?
2. What is special about the administrative authorization level?
3. Why might a `TableController` cause us problems with an existing database schema and what options do we have to help us?
4. What base class should scheduled jobs implement and how are they called?
5. How can we relate an OAuth provider authenticated user from a mobile service to a user created by an MVC website?

6. What does the **Enable unauthenticated push notifications under the windows phone notifications settings (mpns)** setting in the mobile service's **PUSH** tab do?

7. Which object contains the user credentials after a successful login from a `MobileServiceClient` instance?

8. In the `DataServiceBase` class, why is the `MobileServiceClient` variable marked `static`?

9. In a Windows Phone app, which capability needs enabling and where is it configured?

10. When we call the `NotificationHub.RegisterNativeAsync` method, what does the `tagExpression` parameter do?

11. Which NuGet package do we need to access tables and blob storages?

12. What step must we perform before attempting a login using AD authentication with a `MobileServiceClient`?

Answers

1. Flexible authentication model, push notifications and notifications hub integration, and client SDKs for all major mobile platforms.

2. This is the highest level of authorization, which overrides all other levels and requires the mobile service master key, which should not be used in client applications.

3. `TableControllers` are typed against the `ITableData` interface, which requires a number of default fields, which an existing table may not have. We can either map the existing entities to a new entity using something like AutoMapper, or use an API controller.

4. `ScheduledJob`; this can be called with an HTTP POST request and configured to run on a schedule in the portal.

5. Add models for the `AspNetUser` and `AspNetUserLogin` users to the `DbContext` with matching `DbSet` properties, and use these to relate the login provider ID and key from the user credentials to the values in the tables.

6. This allows requests without an authentication certificate to make push notifications limited to 500 per day.

7. The `MobileServiceUser` object found in the `MobileServiceClient.CurrentUser` property.

8. This is because there is only one instance, meaning that the user credentials are available for all requests made in the application.

9. **ID_CAP_PUSH_NOTIFICATION** in the `WMAppManifest.xml` file.

10. It allows us to supply a list of tags related to subjects the user wants to subscribe to; these should be user-configurable within the app.

11. `WindowsAzure.Storage`.

12. Call `AuthenticationContext.AcquireTokenAsync` to get an access token.

12
Preparing an Azure System for Production

In this last chapter, we're going to look at deploying our system to various environments for different stages of its life cycle. We'll explore the options for system configuration and create deployment packages manually on the Visual Studio Online Team Foundation build server. We'll finish this chapter by looking at monitoring and maintaining our Azure systems once they are live.

Project configurations for multiple environments

Until now, we've been publishing websites and cloud services straight from Visual Studio and using Entity Framework Code First Migrations to build our databases. Deploying systems to non-development environments from builds on a developer machine is not a good practice as we don't have a controlled way of producing a reproducible, versioned deployment. If we deploy a local build, there is no guarantee that there are no differences between the source control and the local copy of code; even if we build from a fresh branch, so that we think the code is clean and it builds on our development environment, there is no guarantee that it will run on a server as we may have developer SDKs installed, assemblies in the **Global Assembly Cache** (**GAC**) registry modifications, and so on.

Using a build server is a good way of making sure we have a clean build directly from a source control that is not influenced by the development environment and can repeatedly produce deployment packages, which can be versioned and stored. This allows deployments through our environments to be controlled and also easily rolled back to a known version if something goes wrong.

When we're dealing with websites, most of our configuration is in the `Web.config` file (we may sometimes see configs for individual libraries, too) that contains things such as database and storage connection strings, authentication provider keys, and Service Bus connection strings. As we've already seen in an earlier chapter, we can use config transforms to change certain config settings when we publish to a website. When we build a web deployment package on the build server, the packaging process also creates a `MyWebsite.SetParameters.xml` file, which allows us to change secret settings at deployment time, and we can also override config settings in the portal, although it's best to use the correct settings in the first place so that the website doesn't immediately fail on deployment.

With cloud services, we have the choice of configuring settings in the `app.config` file or in the `.cscfg` cloud configuration, which allows us to change configuration at runtime through the portal; generally, the best practice is to put all the settings in the cloud config. However, when it comes to things such as EF (which, by default, reads connection strings from a config file and can't read the cloud configuration without some modification), libraries shared between different types of applications (which have no concept of cloud configurations), we need to use `app.config` for configuration. This could potentially make things difficult as we need to manually modify the `app.config` settings in a package before deployment (the package is a ZIP file, so we can unzip it manually or write a script to automate the process).

Many of these settings contain sensitive information, and we should be careful as to who has access to them, particularly for production environments. In some companies (usually smaller ones, which don't have the requirement for systems administrators), a DevOps or NoOps approach to deployments is taken, where developers are responsible for deploying systems, so they may have access to secret information such as passwords and authentication keys, but still wouldn't want to store them in the source control as this would expose the information to anyone with access to the source code and put the system at risk.

In *Chapter 2*, *Designing a System for Microsoft Azure*, we learned about different system environments for different stages of the application life cycle, and examined typical environment types and choices for different sizes of organizations and systems. We have also seen how we can use transforms in `Web.config` files to modify connection strings and app settings when we publish a website so that we don't have to manually modify them. While I've been writing my samples, I've generally been using the **Release** config transforms to change the settings when I publish, but when we start deploying the system through multiple environments, this strategy no longer meets our requirements as we may have databases, storage accounts, Active Directory namespaces, and Service Bus namespaces for each environment, and we will need to configure the settings for each of them. We'll look at creating Prod, QA, and test configurations, which will be applied when we package our websites and cloud services.

Adding build configurations to a solution

In order to implement configs for each application environment, we need matching build configurations, which we need to create for the solution and for each project. We'll create a new test configuration for the system test environment using the following procedure:

1. Right-click on the solution and select **Properties** and then select **Configuration Properties** in the **Properties** dialog.

2. Click on the **Configuration Manager** button to open the **Configuration Manager** dialog, and then select **<New...>** from the **Active solution configuration** picker (you can see that I've already added **Prod** and **QA**):

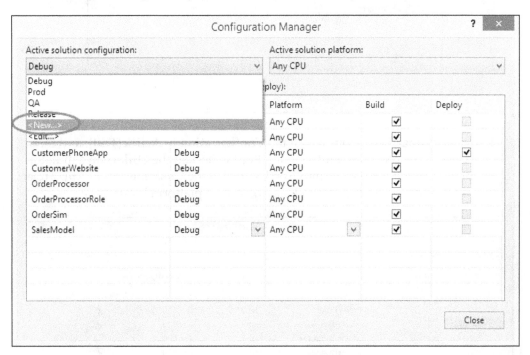

3. Enter the new configuration **Name,** and in the **Copy settings from** picker, select **Release**, so we're copying the settings from the **Release** config and not getting **Debug** symbols in our build. Check **Create new project configurations** so that all the projects get the new config too; otherwise, we'll have to manually create them for each one. Sometimes, it's better to uncheck this if we don't want all our projects to get modified with the new config):

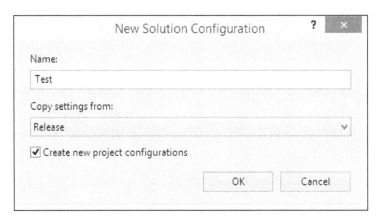

4. In the **Properties** dialog, switch the **Configuration** to **Active(Test)**, and then select the projects we want to build. I've unchecked the **OrderSim** simulator project as that will not be published, and also the **CustomerPhoneApp** project, as it will cause our build to fail later on due to platform limitations:

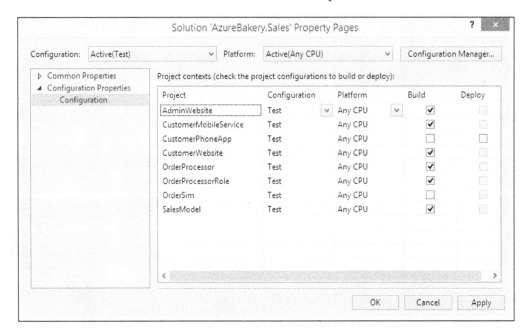

5. Repeat this procedure for all environments.

6. Click on **OK** to save these changes; we'll notice that all our projects and solutions have been modified with these changes.

7. We can do this for each solution we've created.

Website configuration transforms

We've seen that we have a `Web.config` file, which contains all our settings; then, we have `web.debug.config` and `web.release.config`, which contain the transforms we wish to apply when we publish in either the **Release** or **Debug** mode.

 Transforms are only applied during publishing and not during normal build without manually modifying the `.csproj` file.

Now that we have our new build configurations in place, we need to add transforms for them, which we do by simply right-clicking on the `Web.config` file and selecting **Add Config Transform**:

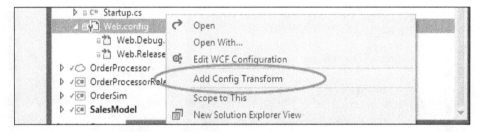

Our new config transform files appear where we can apply configs for each setting that needs transforming per environment:

Application configuration transforms

During publishing, we also need config transforms for our cloud services for any settings that require transformation in the `app.config` files. Unfortunately, there is no built-in support for adding these config transforms or executing them during publishing, so we'll look at manually modifying our cloud service project to do this.

> SlowCheetah (`http://visualstudiogallery.msdn.microsoft.com/69023d00-a4f9-4a34-a6cd-7e854ba318b5`) is a great tool to transform `app.config` automatically, but we'll do it manually here, so that we understand how it works.

First of all, we need to manually add the transform files to the project, so we'll do this in the following procedure:

1. Add a new application config file for each environment (`app.Test.config`, `app.QA.config`,and `app.Prod.config`) in the worker role projects (not the cloud service project), and we will see that they are not arranged under the main `app.config`, like they are for the `Web.config` files:

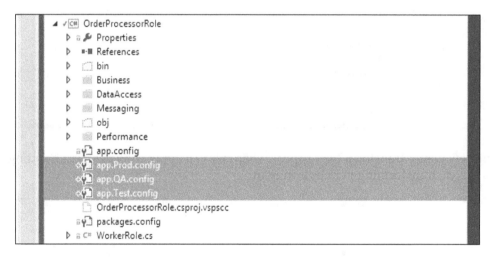

2. Although it's not necessary to fix this, we can easily do it by modifying the `.csproj` file, so right-click on the project and select **Unload Project**, then right-click on the project (now marked unavailable) and select **Edit ProjectName.csproj**, and the `.csproj` XML will load into Visual Studio.

3. Scroll down and look for where the configs are added:

```xml
<ItemGroup>
   <None Include="app.config" />
   <None Include="app.Prod.config" />
   <None Include="app.QA.config" />
   <None Include="app.Test.config" />
   <None Include="packages.config" />
   <None Include="Performance\Microsoft.ServiceBus.
MessagingPerformanceCounters.man" />
</ItemGroup>
```

4. Modify each transform file to have a `DependentUpon` element inside each `None` element like this:

```xml
<ItemGroup>
   <None Include="app.config" />
   <None Include="app.Prod.config">
     <DependentUpon>app.config</DependentUpon>
   </None>
   <None Include="app.QA.config">
     <DependentUpon>app.config</DependentUpon>
   </None>
   <None Include="app.Test.config">
     <DependentUpon>app.config</DependentUpon>
   </None>
   <None Include="packages.config" />
   <None Include="Performance\Microsoft.ServiceBus.
MessagingPerformanceCounters.man" />
</ItemGroup>
```

5. Save the changes, right-click on the project, and select **Reload Project**, and we'll see the files neatly arranged like the `Web.config` files.

6. Copy the contents of one of the `Web.config` transform files and paste it into each `app.config` transform, and fill in all the transforms required.

7. Next, we need to edit the `.csproj` XML again, adding an extra target to transform the `app.config`. Locate this line:

```xml
<Import
   Project="$(MSBuildToolsPath)\Microsoft.CSharp.targets" />
```

8. Now, paste the following block of XML after it:

```
<Import
  Project="$(VSToolsPath)\WebApplications\Microsoft.
WebApplication.
  targets" Condition="'$(VSToolsPath)' != ''" />
<Import
  Project="$(MSBuildExtensionsPath32)\Microsoft\VisualStudio\
    v10.0\
  WebApplications\Microsoft.WebApplication.targets"
Condition="false" />
<UsingTask TaskName="TransformXml"
  AssemblyFile="$(MSBuildExtensionsPath)\Microsoft\VisualStudio\
    v10.0\
    Web\Microsoft.Web.Publishing.Tasks.dll" />
<Target Name="AfterCompile"
  Condition="exists('app.$(Configuration).config')">
  <TransformXml Source="app.config"
    Destination="$(IntermediateOutputPath)$(TargetFileName).
      config"
      Transform="app.$(Configuration).config" />
  <ItemGroup>
    <AppConfigWithTargetPath Remove="app.config" />
    <AppConfigWithTargetPath
      Include="$(IntermediateOutputPath)$(TargetFileName).
        config">
      <TargetPath>$(TargetFileName).config</TargetPath>
    </AppConfigWithTargetPath>
  </ItemGroup>
</Target>
```

9. Unlike the `Web.config` file, the preceding code will transform the `app.config` file on build. This is controlled by the `Target Name="AfterCompile"` line, which is required so that the transform happens before the packaging step; otherwise, the config is copied before it is transformed.

Cloud configuration

We've sorted out the `app.config` files for our cloud services, so now, we need to look at the `.cscfg` cloud configurations. We'll add configurations for each environment in the following procedure:

1. Right-click on a role under the **Roles** folder in the cloud service project and select **Properties**.

2. Select **<Manage...>** from the **Service Configuration** dropdown:

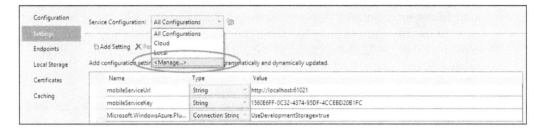

3. Now, select **Cloud** (all our environments are in the cloud, so this is a good starting point) and click on **Create copy**:

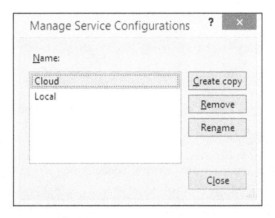

4. Select the new copy, click on **Rename**, and rename it Test, QA, or Prod (create one of each).

5. Next, select each setting in turn and fill out the settings for each environment (if you don't know what they are yet, you can change them at any time). Also, notice that we now have .cscfg files for each environment:

6. When we create a build, we'll be building all our environment packages in one go to save creating a build for each environment (you may prefer to have a build per environment depending on your circumstances). To do this, we need to modify the `.ccproj` file to tie the `TargetProfile` object to our build configuration. Unload the cloud service `.ccproj` and look for the following section in the XML:

```xml
<!-- Items for the project -->
  <ItemGroup>
    <ServiceDefinition Include="ServiceDefinition.csdef" />
    <ServiceConfiguration Include="ServiceConfiguration.Local.
      cscfg"
      />
    <ServiceConfiguration Include="ServiceConfiguration.Cloud.
      cscfg"
      />
  </ItemGroup>
```

7. Now, insert the following property group above it:

```xml
<!-- Tie TargetProfile to Configuration so we get the correct
  cscfg
  at build -->
<PropertyGroup>
  <TargetProfile Condition=" '$(TargetProfile)' == ''
    ">$(Configuration)</TargetProfile>
</PropertyGroup>
```

Building website deployment packages

Websites can be packaged into ZIP files and deployed to remote servers using `MSDeploy`; these packages can be used by system administrators or developers to deploy websites to the appropriate environment for testing or a live roll-out.

Manually publishing websites to the filesystem

We can manually build packages in Visual Studio, which, as I've said, is probably not a good idea for deployment packages (even if you're a lone developer with a limited budget, you can use the Visual Studio Online TFS build server, which gives you 60 minutes per month build time for free); however, it can actually be really useful to check that all the website content such as HTML pages, stylesheets, and scripts have been included, and that `Web.config` transforms have worked.

We'll look at manually creating a package in the following procedure:

1. Right-click on a web project and select **Publish**.

2. Click on the **Custom** button, and then enter a name in the **New Custom Profile** dialog (I've called mine `TestPackage`), and click on **OK**.

3. Now select **File System** from the **Publish method** picker and enter a directory to publish to in the **Target location** textbox, and click on **Next**.

4. Change the **Configuration** setting; I've selected **Delete all files prior to publish** so that the files are all deleted from the target folder before publish, and left all the other settings as they are (the **Precompile during publishing** option compiles the site to the target platform to make it start up faster, rather than it being JIT-compiled by the server, and **Exclude files from App_Data** is mainly for legacy ASP.NET applications).

5. Click on **Publish** to publish the site to the filesystem.

6. We'll now see our website published to the target directory so that we can verify that all the files are there and make sure our transforms have been applied.

7. We could also create a website in IIS with a virtual directory pointing to the publish directory to check whether the website runs.

Building web packages on a build server

We'll create a build definition to build all our websites in the sales solution (customer website, admin website, and mobile service) for each environment. Getting builds to work and produce what you want can be quite tricky; if you run MSBuild (which is what TFS uses to build solutions and projects) yourself, it's possible to build projects on their own quite easily rather than the whole solution; however, on the build server, when it gets a clean copy of the code, it doesn't have all the NuGet packages needed to build the project (if you've correctly left them out of the source control). The new build templates restore the packages before building a solution but not a project, so it's not easy to build a project without extra configuration (you can read more about NuGet and Team Foundation Build at http://docs.nuget.org/docs/reference/package-restore-with-team-build). Another issue is that working out the MSBuild parameter switches your need (here is a list of MSBuild properties: http://msdn.microsoft.com/en-us/library/bb629394.aspx and also a list of TF build environmental properties: http://msdn.microsoft.com/en-us/library/hh850448.aspx, which can be useful).

We'll create a build definition to create our packages in the following procedure:

1. In the **Team Explorer – Home** window, click on the **Builds** button:

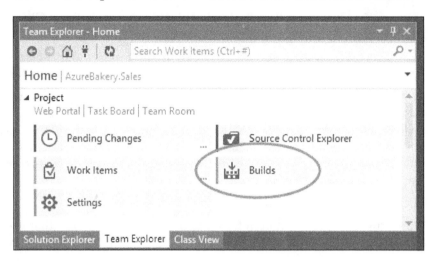

2. Click on the **New Build Definition** link to create a new build definition for our websites:

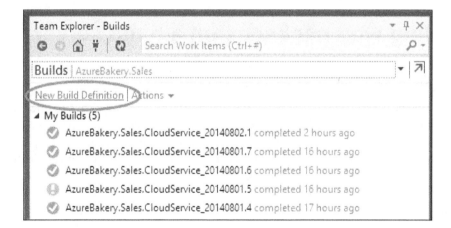

3. Change the **Build definition name** value in the **General** tab; it will default to the solution name.

4. You can change the **Trigger** setting if you like; I'm leaving mine as the default **Manual** setting.

5. The **Source** settings should be fine and should map the **Source Control** folder to the **Build Agent** folder automatically.

6. I've left the **Build Defaults** tab with the default setting of **Copy build output to the server**; this will copy the output to the **Drops** folder in the source control and allow us to download a `drops` ZIP for the build from the Visual Studio Online portal. You can change it to drop to a file share or a different source control location.

7. The **Process** tab is where we need to do most of the configuration.

8. First, select the **TfvcTemplate.12.xaml** template from the **Build process template** picker (these come from the `BuildProcessTemplates` folder created automatically at the root of our TFS project).

9. Pick the solution to build in the **Projects** picker under the **Build** section (it's possible to build multiple solutions and projects from here).

10. Click on the ellipsis button next to the **Configurations** textbox under the **Build** section, and add configurations for each environment in the **Configurations** dialog. You will need to manually type the names as they will not appear in the picker:

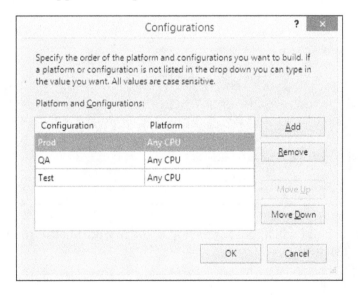

11. Change the **Output location** setting to **Per Project** so that all our builds are dropped into individual folders per project.

12. Now, under the **Advanced** section, enter the following parameters in the **MSBuild arguments** box; this will deploy the packages to the build destination with the project and environment structure intact:

```
/p:DeployOnBuild=true;DeployMethod=Package
```

13. I've left the **Retention Policy** setting with the default settings; feel free to change it to your own requirements.

14. Save the build definition, and we'll see it listed in the **Builds** tab. Build definitions are stored on the build server and not in the solution.

15. Right-click on the definition and select **Queue New Build**, and then review the details in the **Queue Build** dialog (at this point, we can actually modify the parameters so that we can potentially change the **MSBuild** arguments here, which will be useful if we weren't building all environments as we could insert /p:Configuration=OurEnv to select an environment). Click on **Queue New Build...** to build it:

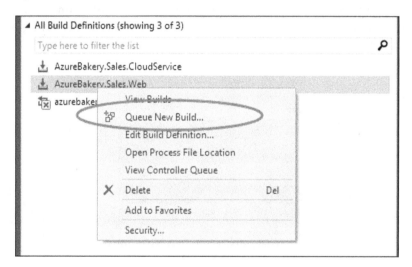

16. The new build will appear at the top of the **My Builds** list, showing its current status:

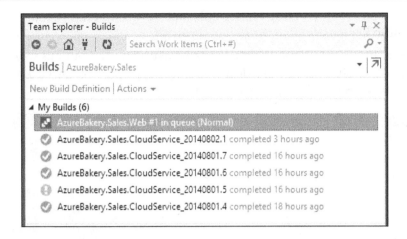

17. If we double-click on the build, the **Build Request** page will open, where we can see an overview of the build and also see the build details by clicking on the **View build details** link at the top.

18. Once the build has completed, we will see the results displayed automatically. If the build fails or there are warnings, we will see them in the **Summary** section, and we can see more details by clicking on the **View Log** link at the top of the page. When the build succeeds, we should see lots of green ticks and see the status of each configuration, and the build status will be updated in the **My Builds** list:

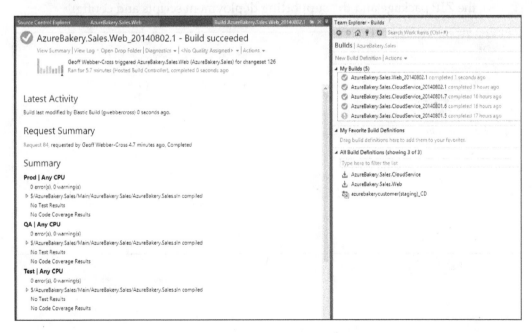

19. Click on the **Open Drop Folder** link, and we will be taken to our Visual Studio Online portal in the default browser.

20. From here, we will see exactly the same overview and options to view build logs, but we can also download the `drops` package by clicking on the **Download drop as zip** button:

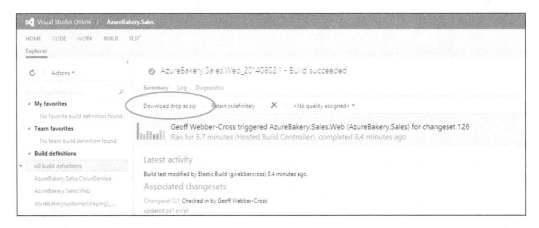

21. Download the `drops` package and take a look at the folder structure. We should see a folder for each environment, then under that folders for each website, which contain the same files we see when we do a manual publish, but also a website folder with a `_Package` suffix, which contains the ZIP package and the supporting deployment scripts and config:

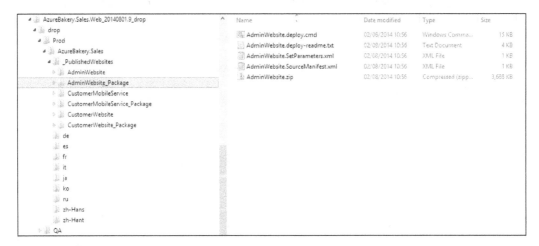

The publish process has extracted settings, which it thinks we may want to change, and put them in a `SetParameters.xml` file so that they can be changed easily during deployment. This gives us even more flexibility about how we choose to package our websites as not only can we have multiple environment configurations with transforms, but also we can use the `SetParameters.xml` files to further modify config settings just before publish. You can read more about this at `http://www.asp.net/web-forms/tutorials/deployment/web-deployment-in-the-enterprise/configuring-parameters-for-web-package-deployment`.

Building cloud service deployment packages

When we publish a cloud service to Azure through Visual Studio, we're creating a cloud service package (`.cspkg`) with an accompanying cloud service config (`.cscfg`—the same as in our solution) that is automatically deployed to Azure for us. We can create packages manually in Visual Studio or on a build server in a similar way to websites. This allows us to publish cloud services outside of Visual Studio from the portal or by using PowerShell.

Building cloud service deployment packages manually

As with manually publishing websites, it's not the best idea to publish cloud services built on a developer machine for the same reasons, but it can be a useful way of testing if our packages work as expected with the correct cloud configuration and application configuration transforms. We'll manually create a cloud package from Visual Studio in the following procedure:

1. Right-click on the cloud service project (not the role project) and select **Package**.

2. Select values for **Service configuration** (which cloud service config to use) and **Build configuration** (which .NET build config to use):

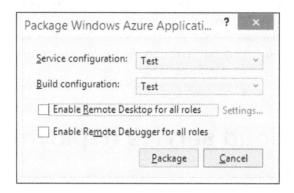

3. If you want to enable remote desktop, this can be done here. You can check the **Enable Remote Desktop for all roles** option or click on **Settings** to configure the user credentials for this.

4. Remote debugger can also be enabled from here, although remember, if we're not deploying a **Debug** version of code, this will not work, and we normally will not want to deploy debug code to production environments.

5. Click on **Package**, and Visual Studio will package our cloud service and open the **Windows Explorer** screen in the project's /bin/Config/app.package directory, where we will see our .cspkg and .cscfg files.

Cloud service packages are actually just zip files, so if we change the file extension to .zip, we can unzip it and see what's inside. There should be a .cssx file, which we can also change to .zip, which will unzip the file and show a directory structure.

Building cloud service deployment packages on a build server

We can build cloud service packages on a build server in pretty much the same way as websites, but with different MSBuild arguments, and an extra step is required to actually harvest the app.package folder with a post-build PowerShell script because it isn't automatically copied during the drops stage. To configure the **Process** tab, follow the same procedure to create a website build, but with the following differences:

1. Change the **Output location** setting under the **Builds** section to **AsConfigured**, which will allow us to control the copying of files to the drops destination.

---

2. Use this `MSBuild` argument if you have your target profile tied to build configuration:

   ```
   /t:Publish
   ```

3. Alternatively, you can use these arguments to manually select the profile without a tied target:

   ```
   /t:Publish /p:TargetProfile=Cloud
   ```

4. Copy the `GatherItemsForDrop.ps1` script from the TFS build extensions CodePlex site at `http://tfsbuildextensions.codeplex.com/SourceControl/latest#Scripts/GatherItemsForDrop.ps1`.

5. Save it to a new folder called `Scripts` under the `BuildProcessTemplates` directory at the root of the Visual Studio Online project (each project has one).

6. Locate the following section in the script:

   ```
   # This script copies the basic file types for managed code
   projects.
   # You can change this list to meet your needs.
   $FileTypes = $("*.exe","*.dll","*.exe.config","*.pdb")


   # Specify the sub-folders to include
   $SourceSubFolders = $("*bin*","*obj*")
   ```

7. Replace it with the following, which includes the `.cspkg` and `.cscfg` files and the `app.publish` directory:

   ```
   # This script copies the basic file types for managed code
   projects.
   # You can change this list to meet your needs.
   $FileTypes = $("*.cspkg","*.cscfg*")
   #$FileTypes =
       $("*.exe","*.dll","*.exe.config","*.pdb","*.cspkg","*.cscfg*")


   # Specify the sub-folders to include
   $SourceSubFolders = $("*bin*","*obj*","*app.publish*")
   ```

8. If you're building multiple environments simultaneously, like we have done in these examples, we need to modify the copy step so that the packages for the different environments are copied to individual folders and don't overwrite each other.

9. Locate the following section of the script right at the end:

```
# Copy the binaries
Write-Verbose "Ready to copy files."
if(-not $Disable)
{
  foreach ($file in $files)
  {
    Copy $file $Env:TF_BUILD_BINARIESDIRECTORY
  }
  Write-Verbose "Files copied."
}
```

10. Replace it with the following code:

```
# Copy the binaries
Write-Verbose "Ready to copy files."
if(-not $Disable)
{
  foreach ($file in $files)
  {
    $targetFile = $Env:TF_BUILD_BINARIESDIRECTORY +
      $file.FullName.SubString($Env:TF_BUILD_SOURCESDIRECTORY.
        Length);
        New-Item -ItemType File -Path $targetFile -Force;
        Copy-Item $file.FullName -destination $targetFile
  }
  Write-Verbose "Files copied."
}
```

11. Check in the script.

12. Back in the build definition, enter the path for the script in **Post-build script path** under the **Build | Advanced** section. It should be something like this:

```
$/AzureBakery.Sales/BuildProcessTemplates/Scripts/
GatherItemsForDrop.ps1
```

13. The build definition should now look like this:

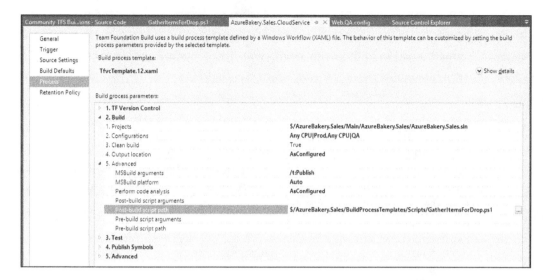

14. Now, when we build this package, we will get our `.cspkg` and `.cscfg` packages in the `drops` ZIP file.

Deploying web packages to Azure

Now that we've got a package built on the build server, we'll deploy it to Azure using the following procedure:

1. Create a website in the portal for one of the environments; I've called mine `http://azurebakery-test.azurewebsites.net/`.

2. Download the publish profile from the website's dashboard, and open it in Visual Studio (you can press *Ctrl + E, D* to quickly format it).

3. Unzip the `drop` package (make sure you unblock it first from the file properties) and copy the `MyWebsite_Package` folder to a temporary folder to make it easier to deploy.

4. Locate the following parameter in the `MyWebsite.SetParameters.xml` file:

```
<setParameter name="IIS Web Application Name" value="Default Web
   Site/CustomerWebsite_deploy" />
```

5. Change the value to the name of the website created in the portal, like this:

```
<setParameter name="IIS Web Application Name"
   value="azurebakery-test" />
```

6. Open a Visual Studio command prompt and change the directory to the `MyWebsite_Package` location (use `cd\` to change the directory to disk root, then `cd` and the path to change the directory to the desired path), and enter the following command with the website details taken from the publish profile to test (`/T`) the deploy (there are complete template help examples in the `Readme` file in the package, too):

```
CustomerWebsite.deploy.cmd /T /M:https://azurebakery-test.scm.
   azurewebsites.net:443/msdeploy.axd /U:$azurebakery-test
      /P:Sy4RBrTsrzwj2rpxia4Dc7Lg9R6u7Jt2bZ4RmC6zwXmXXXXXXXXXxxxxxxx
         xx /A:Basic
```

The `/T` parameter tests the deployment without actually deploying it (`MSDeploy -whatIf`), so we can check whether it's going to work. The `/M` parameter is the `MSDeploy` publish URL taken from the publish profile; you need to add `https://` to the start and add `/msdeploy.axd` at the end, which is the `MSDeploy` listener. `/U` is the username taken directly from the publish profile as is `/P` for password. We need to add `/A:Basic` for basic authorization.

7. When we run the `test` command, it outputs the script that the `deploy.cmd` script creates for us, which includes the details we entered in the command prompt, the package information, and the `parameter` file:

```
"C:\Program Files\IIS\Microsoft Web Deploy V3\msdeploy.exe"
   -source:package='C:\Temp\Package\CustomerWebsite_Package\
      CustomerWebsite.zip'
   -dest:auto,computerName="https://azurebakery-test.scm.
   azurewebsites.net:443/msdeploy.axd",userName="$azurebakery-
      test",
   password="Sy4RBrTsrzwj2rpxia4Dc7Lg9R6u7Jt2bZ4RmC6zwXmSkodQ36Rh8B
      eZx3mQ",
   authtype="Basic",includeAcls="False" -verb:sync
   -disableLink:AppPoolExtension -disableLink:ContentExtension -dis
      ableLink:CertificateExtension
   -setParamFile:"C:\Temp\Package\CustomerWebsite_Package\
   CustomerWebsite.SetParameters.xml" -whatif
```

8. Once we've got this working, change /T to /Y in order to deploy, and we'll see details about the files being copied.

9. Now, if we browse to the new site, the content should load correctly.

 If you have trouble getting this to work, it may be because the destination machine's details are incorrect, so it can help to publish the website from Visual Studio and look at the output window to see the destination machine's details.

Deploying cloud packages to Azure

Cloud packages can either be uploaded to a cloud service in the portal or published using PowerShell; what you choose comes down to personal preference, although using PowerShell allows us to automate deployments. There is a great reference for deploying cloud packages using PowerShell at http://azure.microsoft.com/en-us/documentation/articles/cloud-services-dotnet-continuous-delivery.

Uploading packages into a service through the portal is really straightforward; we'll see how in the following procedure:

1. Nearly every tab in the cloud services toolbar has an **UPLOAD** button that is used to upload packages to instances with no current package, or an **UPDATE** button for instances with a current package loaded, so click on any one button on the toolbar for the instance you want to update:

2. Enter a **DEPLOYMENT LABEL** value, which helps you to identify the deployment, and browse to the `.cspkg` package and the `.cscfg` configuration, which we built on the build server. The **Deploy even if one or more roles contain a single instance** option is basically steering you towards having at least two instances, so we don't have any downtime if one instance becomes unavailable due to maintenance or a failure; if your system can't be scaled (ideally, it should be designed to be stateless and scalable), you can check this option to stop the upload from failing. You can manually modify the `.cscfg` file to increase the number of instances before uploading:

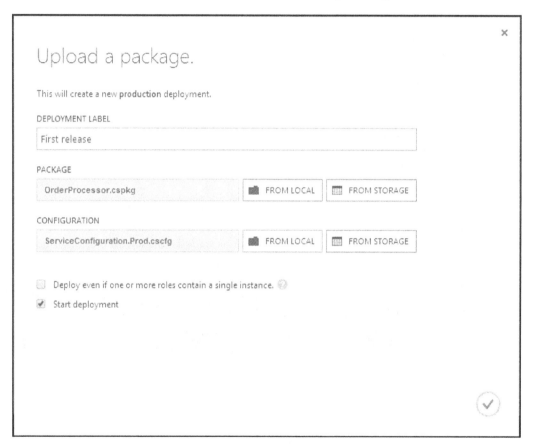

3. Click on the tick to start the upload, and we'll see the packages appear in the portal and then start.

Creating database scripts from Entity Framework Code First Migrations

We can easily create a T-SQL script from a database built with Code First Migrations by entering the following command in the **Package Manager console**:

```
Update-Database -Script -SourceMigration:$InitialDatabase
```

This command creates a T-SQL script for all migrations and opens it in Visual Studio. Unfortunately, scripts aren't created for the database seeding as this isn't part of Entity Framework migrations, so this has to be scripted separately.

Once we have these scripts, system administrators or database administrators can easily use them to build databases for our application environments without Code First Migrations. Once deployed, we can create more scripts to move to the next migration.

Of course, we can always manually create database schema scripts from SQL Server Management Studio. We can also use third-party tools such as Red Gate's SQL Compare product (http://www.red-gate.com/products/sql-development/sql-compare/) to create scripts.

The go-live checklist

This is a list of quick checks to perform when we're putting a system live to make sure we've not missed anything:

- The website and cloud service Web.config and app.config have correct connection strings, API keys, and so on, for publish
- Cloud service configs have correct connection strings, API keys, and so on, for publish
- The website and cloud services have config settings overridden in the portal if required
- **Logging level** has been set to **Verbose** initially (particularly for new systems and major changes) to quickly diagnose any problems, and changed to **Error** once the system is stable to save on the storage space
- The website and cloud services have the starting instance count configured correctly, and **auto-scale** has been set up
- Databases have the correct max size configured
- A database backup strategy has been implemented
- Databases have been updated with the latest migration scripts

Monitoring live services

Once we have systems live on Azure, we need to monitor their health so that if a system is failing, we are aware of it and can start fixing it as quickly as possible. There are a number of tools within Azure that we can use to help us monitor our service, and we'll take a look at these in this section.

The Microsoft Azure portal

The main dashboard in the portal is a great way of getting an overview of all the services (you may need to page through them) as we get a simple visual indicator for each service that shows us its state. The new preview portal also has a nice world map that shows the status of all the data centers. If there is a problem with a service, we can quickly navigate to it and get more information from its own dashboard, and then start diagnosing the issue.

Checking the portal is a good activity to perform daily in order to ensure the general health of the services, and for system administrators this can be added to their existing daily checks.

The Service Management REST API

If we have existing system-monitoring tools in place to monitor the health of our services, we can use the Service Management REST API to automatically monitor the health of our services. There is a good reference to the API at `http://msdn.microsoft.com/library/azure/ee460799.aspx`. All requests must be authenticated, and there is a good guide to doing this at `http://msdn.microsoft.com/en-US/library/azure/ee460782.aspx`.

Management services alerts

In the Management Service workspace in the portal, we can create e-mail alerts for various metrics when they pass a configurable threshold. Alerts are available for the following service types:

- Cloud services
- Mobile services
- SQL databases
- Storages
- Virtual machines
- Websites

It's possible to create 10 alerts per subscription, so if we have a lot of services (which the Azure Bakery system does), we need to select the most critical services to monitor. For the Azure Bakery system, the most critical services are as follows:

- For the sales customer website, the following services are critical:
    - **CPU Time** should be less than 900 ms so that we can see when an instance is working too hard and may have performance issues or need scaling up/out.
    - The **Http Server Error** value should be less than 1 per hour. This will catch any `5xx HTTP` errors and will alert us to any internal server issues.

- For the sales customer database, the following service is critical:
    - Storage must be less than 19,000 MB. This will alert us when we are getting close to our capacity of 20 GB, and will allow us to remove data or increase the max size limit of the database.

- For the production order processor worker role, the following service is critical:
    - **CPU** should be less than 90 percent so that we can see when an instance is working too hard and may have performance issues or need scaling up/out

- For the production database, the following service is critical:
    - Storage must be less than 19,000 MB. This will alert us when we are getting close to our capacity of 20 GB, and will allow us to remove data or increase the max size limit of the database.

- For the production Web API, the following services are critical:
    - **CPU Time** must be less than 900 ms so that we can see when an instance is working too hard and may have performance issues or need scaling up/out.
    - **Http Server Error** must be less than 1 per hour. This will catch any `5xx HTTP` errors and will alert us of any internal server issues.

- For the supply order processor worker role, the following service is critical:
    - **CPU** should be less than 90 percent so that we can see when an instance is working too hard and may have performance issues or need scaling up/out

- For the supply table storage, the following service is critical:
  - ° **Success** should be more than 95 percent. This will alert us if successful requests fall below 95 percent so that we can diagnose any problems.

- For the supply mobile service, the following service is critical:
  - ° **Uptime (endpoint/region)** should be more than 95 percent. This requires the mobile service to be in the **STANDARD** service tier with endpoint monitoring enabled, and will allow us to address any availability issues.

Azure PowerShell

We've used Azure PowerShell a number of times throughout this book, and it's an incredibly powerful tool that can be used to perform system administration and maintenance tasks. There is a full cmdlet reference at `http://msdn.microsoft.com/en-us/library/azure/jj554330.aspx`.

Azure daily service checks

This is a list of daily checks we should make for the Azure Bakery system once it is live:

- Check the portal dashboard for any service issues.
- Check error logs.
- Check the Service Bus queue and topic dead-letter queues (you will need to write a tool to do this).
- Check the **Management Services Operational Logs** for any live Azure issues that may affect services. You can also visit `http://azure.microsoft.com/en-us/status/`.

Azure periodic service activities

These are activities that should be performed periodically to ensure the health of the system:

- Check the individual monitoring dashboards for any high or unusual metric patterns so that any performance issues can be addressed.
- Check whether the database has sufficient capacity so that storage can be adjusted if required.

- Rebuild database table indexes (this could be done on a scheduled task as there is no SQL agent in SQL Azure). SQL Azure Databases, by default, are set to automatically recompute statistics, so this is not required.

- Archive and prune data that may no longer be needed to save on storage costs.

- Check whether the mobile service push notifications are receiving all broadcast notifications, and user-specific notifications are received by a test user.

- Touch-test application UIs to make sure there are no visual issues and everything is working as expected; problems may occur if there is an issue with some backend web services or storage.

- Evaluate service scaling to see if any services need scaling up (more CPU/memory/disk) or out (more instances) to meet continual loading or scaling out for variable loads; conversely, if services are under-loaded, they can probably be scaled down (less CPU/memory/disk) or in (fewer instances) to save cost.

- Check whether any services are not being used so that they can be switched off or even deleted to save cost.

Azure tool list

We've already used a large number of tools in this book, and there are a lot we haven't looked at, so here is a list of useful tools for development and maintenance activities:

- **The Azure portal**: This is the main port-of-call for most Azure-related activities (`https://manage.windowsazure.com` and `https://portal.azure.com`).

- **Visual Studio**: Visual Studio, with the Azure SDK, is the most powerful Azure development tool on the market, and we've already seen what it can do for us in this book (`http://www.visualstudio.com/`).

- **SQL Server Management Studio**: We've had a quick look at this, but not used it to its full capabilities with Azure. It's a really useful tool for administrative and maintenance tasks on SQL Azure Databases (`https://www.microsoft.com/en-us/server-cloud/products/sql-server/`).

- **Azure PowerShell**: This is an additional PowerShell module, an extremely powerful tool for administering Azure systems, and it is also useful for developers when the portal or Visual Studio doesn't have the capability to perform a certain activity (`http://azure.microsoft.com/en-us/documentation/articles/install-configure-powershell/`).

- **Azure AD PowerShell**: This is another additional PowerShell module for managing Azure AD. Again, we've only used a small number of its features (http://technet.microsoft.com/en-us/library/jj151815.aspx).

- **Red Gate's Windows and SQL Azure tools for .NET professionals**: These are a great set of tools for managing and maintaining Azure systems. This includes Cerebrata tools that Red Gate acquired (http://www.red-gate.com/products/azure-development/).

- **Red Gate's Developer Bundle**: There are some really useful tools in here for working with SQL databases, and these are particularly useful for doing database comparisons and creating scripts (http://www.red-gate.com/products/sql-development/sql-developer-bundle/).

- **New Relic**: This is a monitoring tool, which can be added to the Azure portal as an add-on, and requires agents to be stored into services via NuGet to provide monitoring data to the monitoring dashboard (http://newrelic.com/azure).

- **Zudio**: This is a cloud storage management tool with a browser, a desktop, and a mobile app client (zudio.co).

Summary

This is the end of this book; I hope you've enjoyed reading it as much as I've enjoyed writing it! Make sure you download the code samples as they have everything we've covered in this book and all the extra stuff I couldn't fit in.

This is by no means the end of learning about Microsoft Azure. The entire software industry moves at a rapid pace, and as developers and IT professionals, we have to work hard to keep up-to-date with what's going on. Azure is evolving and growing all the time; we've barely scratched the surface of what it can do now, and have more to learn as time goes on. In the 5 months it has taken to write this book, mobile services' .NET backend has become generally available, a whole new SQL Azure service model has been introduced, and a new preview portal was released, to name a few things, so we need to run fast to keep up!

Questions

1. Why is it important to use a build server to build deployment packages?

2. How can settings be set at publish time for web packages?

3. Why is it not a good idea to put certain connection strings and API keys in configs and transforms source control?

4. What issues do we have with config transforms in cloud services?

5. Why could it be helpful to deploy a website to the filesystem or publish a cloud service package locally?

6. What problem may we face while trying to build projects rather than solutions on the Visual Studio Online Team Foundation build server?

7. What extra step do we need to perform when building cloud service packages on the build server?

8. When we run a `deploy.cmd` script, what is the difference between the `/T` and `/Y` arguments?

9. What approach should we take to set logging levels when deploying a new system?

Answers

1. It ensures that packages are built from clean code straight from sources control without contamination from the development environment.

2. When web packages are built on the build server, a ZIP package is created with a set of accompanying scripts, including `SetParameters.xml`, which contains settings that can be configured before deployment.

3. It is a security risk because anyone with access to source control can obtain details of production systems, which can be misused.

4. Cloud services don't support transforms by default, so we have to manually add config transform files and edit the project to achieve this; alternatively, we can use the Slow Cheetah tool.

5. It can help us check whether all the required files are included and that config transforms have worked.

6. The build server restores NuGet packages before building solutions but not projects, which means if we haven't checked in our NuGet package binaries (which we shouldn't), the build will fail.

7.   We need to set the **Output location** setting to **AsConfigured** so that we get control over the copy to drops process, and add a custom post-build script to copy the `app.publish` folder and its contents to the drops target.

8.   `/T` tests the deployment with the `MSDeploy` `-whatIf` parameter, which shows what will happen and if it is likely to succeed. `/Y` runs `MSDeploy` for real.

9.   Initially set them to **Verbose**, allowing problems to be quickly diagnosed, then change to **Error**, so that we log important error information but save on storage costs.

Index

A

Access Control Service (ACS)
  about 34, 202
  authentication mechanisms 34
Active Directory (AD)
  about 34
  client application, adding 308-310
  configuring 151, 152
  features 34
Active Directory Federated
          Services (ADFS) 34
AD authentication
  Store app, configuring for 359, 360
add-migration command 106
AD manifest, Web API
  modifying 307, 308
administration system, small business
          system case study
  designing 44
  mobile application 44
  website 44
  Windows desktop application 44
administrative tasks, Microsoft Azure
          systems
  alerts 16
  billing 17
  data backup 16
  database maintenance 16
  domain names, renewing 17
  error logs 16
  OS updates 17
  password management 17
  release management 17
  SSL certificates, renewing 17
  training 16

admin sales website
  completing 163-165
admin website
  updating 351
alerts
  Build Alerts 89
  Checkin Alerts 89
  Code review Alerts 89
  setting, in Visual Studio Online 89-91
  Work Item Alerts 89
Apache Hadoop
  URL 31
application configuration
          transforms 370-372
Application Lifecycle
          Management (ALM) 77
application logging
  about 175
  blob storage, alternative to 184
  bug, diagnosing 185
  LOGGING LEVEL options 176
  table storage, alternative to 181
  tracing, implementing 177
application service principal
  modifying 158, 159
app services
  about 32
  AD 34
  BizTalk Services 33
  media services 32
  scheduler 33
  Service Bus 32, 33
  Visual Studio Online 33
authenticated user
  linking, to model 102

authentication base class
creating 313-315
authorization levels, mobile services
Admin/Only scripts and admins 326
Anonymous/Everyone 326
Application/Anybody with the
application key 326
User/Only authenticated users 326
AutoMapper
URL 327
automated exports 125-127
Azure
cloud packages, deploying to 387, 388
web packages, deploying to 385-387
Azure Active Directory
using 39
Azure AD auth
mobile service, configuring for 353, 354
AzureAdAuthorizeAttribute
implementing 159-163
Azure AD group authorization
AD group, creating 157
application service principal,
modifying 158, 159
AzureAdAuthorizeAttribute,
implementing 159-163
implementing 156
references 156
Azure AD PowerShell
URL 394
Azure AD single sign-on
AD, configuring 151, 152
adding, to website 151
MVC website, configuring for 152-154
used, for publishing website 154, 155
Azure daily service checks 392
Azure Fabric Controller 10
Azure management portal
used, for creating database 94-96
Azure mobile services
about 326
authorization levels 326
Azure Pack
URL, for installing 10
Azure periodic service activities 392, 393
Azure portal
URL 393

Azure PowerShell
about 392
cmdlet reference 392
URL 393
using 123, 124
Azure SQL Server
unsupported features 30
Azure storage diagnostics
configuring 271
Azure tool list
about 393
Azure AD PowerShell 394
Azure portal 393
Azure PowerShell 393
New Relic 394
SQL Server Management Studio 393
Visual Studio 393
Zudio 394
Azure websites
running locally 235, 236

B

backplane options, SignalR 293
Badge notification 33
batch processor tasks
adding 255
batch script
creating 284-286
Binary Large Objects (blobs) 29
BizTalk Services 33
blob storage
enabling 184, 185
used, for site diagnostic 189, 190
block blobs, storage 30
bottom toolbar, Microsoft
            Azure portal 25-27
bug
diagnosing 186, 187
Build Alerts 89
build definition, continuous deployment
examining 87-89
build server
cloud service deployment packages,
building on 382-385
web packages, building on 375-381

business infrastructure
  managing 12
Business Intelligence (BI) 31

C

cache 31
cache, tiers
  Basic 31
  Premium 31
  Standard 31
CER files
  creating 146, 147
Certificate Signing Request (CSR) 145
Checkin Alerts 89
client application
  adding, to AD 308-310
  authentication base class, creating 313-315
  building 310
  data service, creating 315, 316
  finishing 318
  SignalR service, creating 316-318
  testing 319
  WPF project, preparing 311, 312
cloud computing 9
cloud configuration 372-374
cloud deployment models
  community cloud 10
  hybrid cloud 10
  private cloud 10
  public cloud 10
cloud packages
  deploying, to Azure 387, 388
  reference link 387
cloud platform solution, factors
  cost 11
  infrastructure capabilities 11
cloud service deployment packages
  building 381
  building, manually 381, 382
  building, on build server 382-385
cloud service models
  IaaS 9
  PaaS 9
  SaaS 10
cloud services
  about 29, 229, 230

  characteristics 29
  diagnostics 267, 268
  examining 234
  idle cloud services, deleting 263
  scaling up 39
  web roles 230
  worker roles 230
cloud service staging environments
  using 63
code
  configuration changes, detecting 283, 284
Code review Alerts 89
commandLine attribute 287
common environment
  development/integration 60
  production environment 59
  QA environment 60
  test environment 60
common services, Enterprise system Azure
    Bakery case study
  authentication 54
  messaging 54
  selecting 54
Community Technical Preview (CTP) 11
compute emulator UI 236, 237
compute services
  about 27
  cloud services 29
  mobile services 28, 29
  virtual machines 28
  websites 27, 28
configuration changes
  in code, detecting 283, 284
configuration, continuous deployment 84-87
CONFIGURE tab
  about 224
  settings 224
connection string
  about 103
  configuring 253, 254
continuous deployment
  build definition, examining 87-89
  configuring 84-87
  setting up 80
  solution, adding to source control 80-83
controllers, Web API
  creating 298-301

cost, Microsoft Azure solution 13
Create, Read, Update, and Delete
    (CRUD) 327
critical services, Enterprise system
    Azure Bakery case study
  production database 53
  production management Web API 53
  production order processor 53
  sales customer website 53
  supply deliveries table 53
  supply mobile API 53
  supply process 53
custom domain name
  adding, to website 142-144
customer Azure mobile service
  creating 327
  mobile services project, creating 328
customer sales website
  completing 138
  final activities 141
  PayConfirm action 140
  user account panel, modifying 138, 139
customer website, small business system
    case study
  designing 42, 43

D

database
  automated exports 125
  backing up 125
  building, with EF Code First
    Migrations 96, 97
  creating, with Azure management
    portal 94-96
  managing, through Visual Studio 119-121
  managing, with SSMS 116-119
  restoring 125
database scripts
  creating, from Entity Framework Code First
    Migrations 389
data model
  creating 97-101
  managing, SSMS used 116

managing, through management
    portal 113, 114
managing, through Visual Studio 119
DataServiceBase class
  about 343, 344
  creating 361
DataService class 346
data services
  about 29
  cache 31
  creating 315, 316
  HDInsight 31
  recovery services 32
  SQL Server Database 30
  storage 30, 31
data services, Windows Phone application
  adding 343
  DataServiceBase class 343-345
  DataService class 346, 347
dead-letter queues 201
debugger
  stopping 275
decision flow diagrams, Microsoft
    Azure solution 14, 15
decoupling applications
  scaling out 39
  scaling up 39
dependency injection (DI) 138
development environment
  Microsoft Azure SDK 69
  mobile development 68
  preparing 67
  software, setting up 67, 68
diagnostics
  about 169
  Azure storage diagnostics, configuring 271
  configuring 267, 268
  enabling 170, 171
  files, accessing with FTP 175
  local diagnostics, adding 269, 270
  logfiles, viewing in Visual Studio 171
  logfiles, working with 171
  logs, downloading 174
  logs, streaming 172
Diagnostics.wadcfg function 234

E

EF Code First Migrations
  authenticated user, linking to model 102
  connection string 103
  database context, configuring 101, 102
  database, updating 104-108
  data model, creating 97-100
  enabling 104-108
  migrations, enabling 107
  used, for building database 96, 97
  used, for publishing 109-112
  Web.Config, modifying 103
Enterprise system Azure Bakery case study
  about 47
  conclusion 57-59
  critical services, identifying 53
  Microsoft Azure Services, selecting 54
  production requirements 49
  sales requirements 48
  sales system integration 52
  subsystems, identifying 49
  supply requirements 49
  system design 50
  system requirements 48
Entity Data Model (EDM) 96
Entity Framework (EF) 96
Entity Framework Code First Migrations
  database scripts, creating from 389
entity model, production order processor
  adding 242, 243
environmental variables 287, 288
error
  producing 187
  searching 187
example environments sets
  large business 62
  medium business 61
  small business 60, 61
executionContext attribute 287
external login
  modifying 133-135

F

files
  accessing, with FTP 175
FileZilla
  URL 175
FTP
  used, for accessing files 175

G

Git
  URL 327
Global Assembly Cache (GAC) 365
go-live checklist 389

H

HDInsight 31
HTTP Secure (HTTPS) endpoint 145
HTTP traffic
  redirecting, to HTTPS 150, 151
hub, SignalR
  creating 302-304

I

IaaS 9
idle cloud services
  deleting 263
Infrastructure as a Service. *See* **IaaS**
infrastructure capabilities, Microsoft
    Azure solution 12
IntelliTrace
  debugging with 276, 277
  URL 278
inversion-of-control (IoC) 138

J

JSON Web Token (JWT) 34

K

Kudu
  about 77, 190, 191
  references 190, 191

L

life cycle methods, worker roles
  OnStart method 234
  OnStop method 234
  Run method 234
line of business (LOB) systems 44
live services
  monitoring 390
load balancing methods
  failover 35
  performance 35
  round-robin 35
local debugging, Azure mobile services
  reference link 354
local diagnostics
  adding 269, 270
logfiles
  viewing, in Visual Studio 171, 172
  working with 171
LOGGING LEVEL options
  Error 176
  Information 176
  Off 176
  Verbose 176
  Warning 176
logs
  downloading 174
  streaming 172, 173
  stream logs, filtering 174

M

management portal
  database, managing through 113, 114
  features 115, 116
management services alerts 390-392
management tool
  selecting 124
media services 32
message partitioning
  reference link 205
messaging simulator
  about 212
  completing 220
  data service, creating 214, 215
  messaging service, creating 216-220

  project, setting up 213, 214
  running 220-222
Microsoft Azure
  overview 10, 11
  URL, for purchase options 18
  URL, for requesting invoiced payments 18
Microsoft Azure account
  creating 18-20
Microsoft Azure portal 390
Microsoft Azure SDK
  about 69
  URL, for installing 69
Microsoft Azure Service Bus 293
Microsoft Azure Services
  about 27, 93
  app services 32
  compute services 27
  data services 29
  network services 34
**Microsoft Azure Services, Enterprise
      system Azure Bakery case study**
  common services, selecting 54
  production services, selecting 56
  sales services, selecting 54, 55
  selecting 54
  supply services, selecting 57
Microsoft Azure solution
  decision flow diagrams 14, 15
  selecting 11
Microsoft Azure solution, factors
  cost 11-13
  infrastructure capabilities 12
  platform capabilities 11, 13
Microsoft Azure systems
  administration 16, 17
mobile development
  about 68
  requisites 68
  URL, for requisites 68
mobile service
  about 28, 29
  authentication, integrating with
      sales website 334, 335
  channel registration API controller,
      adding 336-338
  cleaning up 332, 333
  configuring, for Azure AD auth 353, 354

creating 328
development app settings, configuring 333
exploring 329, 330
integrating, with sales database 333
Mobile service DbContext 331
order controller, adding 338
publishing 339-341
sample data entity 331
sample scheduled job 331
sample table controller 330
scaling out 39
WebApiConfig 332
Mobile service DbContext 331
MONITOR tab 223
MVC website
configuring, for AD single sign-on 152-154
MVVM Light 214

N

network services
about 34
Virtual Network 34
New Relic
URL 394
Notification Hub 33
notifications debug, Windows
   Phone application 348
NuGet
URL 375

O

OAuth
URL 131
OAuth authentication
external login, modifying 133-135
implementing 131
providers, URLs 132
Twitter application, creating 132, 133
Twitter login, testing 136-138
object-relational mapper (ORM) 96
OnStart method 234
OnStop method 234
OpenSSL
references 148
used, for creating PFX certificate 148

options, for creating database
Code First approach 96
Code First (Reverse engineered) 96
Database-First technique 96
Model-First technique 96
OrderController class 356
order processor
updating 349, 350
OrderTopicProcessor
using, in worker role 248-250
OS upgrades
URL 279

P

PaaS 9
page blobs, storage 31
PayConfirm action 140
PeekLock mode 32
persistence 38
PFX certificate
creating, with OpenSSL 148
Plain Old CLR Object (POCO) 96
Platform as a Service. *See* **PaaS**
platform capabilities, Microsoft
   Azure solution 13
platform environments
cloud service staging environments,
   using 63
common environments 59, 60
designing 59
example environments sets 60, 61
website deployment slots, using 62, 63
Portable Class Library (PCL) 347
portal, Microsoft Azure
bottom toolbar 25, 26
exploring 22
side toolbar 25
top toolbar 22-24
URL 18
website, configuring 72-77
prerequisites, OpenSSL VC++ 2008
reference, for 32 bit 148
reference, for 64 bit 148
pricing calculator
URL 13

production order processor
building 241
entity model, adding 242, 243
multiple instances, testing 262, 263
OrderTopicProcessor, using in worker
role 248-250
Service Bus topic, preparing 243
single instance, testing 261
task, adding 244
testing 260
TopicProcessorBase, creating 244-246
TopicProcessorBase, implementing 247, 248
production services, Enterprise system
Azure Bakery case study
order processor 56
storage 57
Web API 56
production subsystems, Enterprise system
Azure Bakery case study
production management system 50
production order processor 50
project configurations, multiple
environments
about 365, 366
application configuration
transforms 370-372
build configurations, adding
to solution 367, 368
Cloud configuration 372-374
website configuration transforms 369
Push Notification Service (PNS) 33, 328
push notifications, Windows Phone
application
channel helper, adding 348
manifest, modifying 347
setting up 347

Q

queues, storage 31

R

Raw notification 33
RDP connection
establishing 280-282
ReceiveAndDelete mode 32
recovery services 32

Red Gate's Developer Bundle
about 394
URL 394
Red Gate's Windows
about 394
URL 394
Redis 293
remote debugging
about 272-275
debugger, stopping 275
drawbacks 195
initializing 192-194
using 195
working 276
remote desktop connection
about 279
establishing 280-282
firewall issues 282
Remote Desktop Protocol (RDP) file,
downloading 279, 280
Remote Desktop Protocol connection . *See*
RDP connection
Remote Desktop Protocol (RDP) file
downloading 279, 280
resilient system
designing 38, 39

S

SaaS 9
sales services, Enterprise system Azure
Bakery case study
admin website 55
customer website 54
mobile API 55
order processor 55
security 56
storage 56
sales subsystems, Enterprise system
Azure Bakery case study
sales administration system 49
sales customer phone app 50
sales customer website 49
sales order process system 50
scalable system
designing 38, 39
scale out 38

scale up 38
scheduled job
  creating 251, 252
scheduled queue
  creating 251, 252
scheduled work activity
  connection string, configuring 253, 254
  creating 250
  queue, creating 251, 252
  scheduled job, creating 251, 252
scheduler 33
Secure Socket Layer certificate.
    See **SSL certificate**
server logging
  using 169
Service Bus
  about 32, 200
  Notification Hub 33
  queue 32
  relay 33
  topic 33
Service Bus queues 200
Service Bus topic
  about 200
  creating 202-206
  order message life cycle 201
  website, connecting to 206
Service Bus topic, production order
      processor
  preparing 243
ServiceConfiguration.cloud function 234
ServiceConfiguration.local function 234
ServiceDefinition.csdef function 234
Service Management REST API
  about 390
  references 390
service, SignalR
  creating 317, 318
services, small business system case study
  applications 46
  messaging 47
  security 47
  storage 47
Shared Access Signature (SAS) 202
side toolbar, Microsoft Azure portal 25
SignalR
  about 293

backplane options 293
hub, creating 302, 304
service, creating 316
URL 291
Simple Web Token (SWT) 34
site diagnostics
  blob storage, using 189, 190
  filesystem settings 188, 189
site diagnostics, facilities
  DETAILED ERROR MESSAGES 188
  FAILED REQUEST TRACING 188
  WEB SERVER LOGGING 188
SlowCheetah
  about 370
  URL 370
small business system case study
  about 41
  business requirements 41, 42
  conclusion 47
  critical systems, identifying 46
  services, selecting 46
  subsystems, identifying 42
  system integration 45
Software as a Service. *See* **SaaS**
software, development environment
  setting up 67, 68
  Visual Studio Express 2013, for
      Windows 68
  Visual Studio Express 2013, for Web 67
  Visual Studio Express 2013, for Windows
      Desktop 68
SQL Azure Servers
  Azure PowerShell, using 123
  management tool, selecting 124
  managing 112
  managing, tools 112
SQL Azure tools 394
SQL Compare product
  reference link 389
SQL Server
  about 293
  URL, for downloading 68
SQL Server Database 30
SQL Server Database, tiers
  Business editions 30
  Premium edition 30
  Web 30

SQL Server Management Studio. *See* **SSMS**

SSL certificate
about 144, 145
CER files, creating 146, 147
HTTP traffic, redirecting to HTTPS 150, 151
implementing 144, 145
OpenSSL, used for creating PFX
    certificate 148
uploading 149, 150

SSMS
URL 393
used, for managing database 116-119

start-up tasks
about 284
adding 286
batch script, creating 284-286
environment variables 287

sticky session 38

storage
about 30
block blobs 30
page blobs and disks 31
queues 31
tables 31

storage emulator UI 237, 238

storage queue processor base
creating 255

StorageQueueProcessorBase
implementing 257, 258

stream logs
filtering 174

subscription
adding 20, 21
selecting 17, 18

SUBSCRIPTIONS tab
about 225
settings 225

subsystems, Enterprise system Azure
    Bakery case study
identifying 49
production 50
sales 49, 50
supply 50

subsystems, small business system
    case study
administration system 42

administration system, designing 44, 45
customer website 42
customer website, designing 42, 43

supply mobile service
barcode controller, creating 355
creating 352
order controller, creating 356

supply services, Enterprise system
    Azure Bakery case study
mobile API 57
order processor 57
storage 57

supply subsystems, Enterprise system
    Azure Bakery case study
supply processing system 50
supply tablet application 50

supply Windows Store application
configuring, for AD authentication 359, 360
creating 358
DataServiceBase class, creating 361

system, architecting
about 40, 41
critical systems, identifying 41
Microsoft Azure Services, selecting 41
requirements, gathering 41
subsystems, designing 41
subsystems, identifying 41
subsystems, integrating 41

system design, Enterprise system Azure
    Bakery case study
sales customer phone app 51, 52
sales order processor 52

System.Diagnostics.Trace methods
TraceError(string) 176
TraceError(string, object[]) 176
TraceInformation(string) 176
TraceInformation (string, object[]) 177
TraceWarning(string) 177
TraceWarning (string, object[]) 177
WriteLine(string) 177

T

table data
querying 183

table designer
using 122

table storage
  about 31
  advantages 181
  scaling 39
  setting up 181-183
  table data, querying 183
Tabular Data Stream (TDS) 30
taskType attribute
  background 287
  foreground 287
  simple 287
Team Foundation Build
  URL 375
Team Foundation Server (TFS) 70, 77
TF build environmental properties
  reference link 375
TFS build extensions
  reference link 383
Tile notification 33
Time to live (TTL) 201
Toast notification 33
TopicClient object
  reference link 209
TopicProcessorBase
  creating 244-246
  implementing 247, 248
topic workspace
  CONFIGURE tab 224
  exploring 222
  MONITOR tab 223
  SUBSCRIPTIONS tab 225
top toolbar, Microsoft Azure portal
  about 22-24
  credit status flyout 23
  home button 22
  language menu 24
  main menu 24
  subscriptions menu 23
  top menu 22
Trace object methods
  URL 177
tracing
  implementing, in application 177-180
Traffic Manager 35
Transact-SQL (TSQL) 30
Twitter application
  creating 132

URL 132
Twitter login
  testing 136-138

U

unit of work (UoW) pattern 138
user account panel
  modifying 138, 139

V

virtual machines 28
Virtual Network 34
Visual Studio
  database, managing through 119-121
  logfiles, viewing in 171, 172
  table designer, using 122
  updates, checking 69, 70
  URL 393
Visual Studio Express 2013
  for Web 67
  for Windows 68
  for Windows Desktop 68
Visual Studio Online
  about 33, 77
  account, creating 78
  alerts, setting up 89-91
  project, creating 77-79
  URL 77

W

Web API
  about 292
  AD manifest, modifying 307, 308
  publishing 305, 306
WebApiConfig 332
Web API service
  building 293
  controllers, creating 298-301
  project, creating 294-297
Web.Config
  modifying 103
web packages
  building, on build server 375-381
  deploying, to Azure 385-387
  reference link 381

web roles 230
website
  about 27, 28
  Azure AD single sign-on, adding to 151
  configuring, in Microsoft Azure
      portal 72-77
  creating 70, 72
  custom domain name, adding to 142-144
  publishing manually, to filesystem 374, 375
  publishing, with AD single sign-on 154, 155
  scaling out 38
  setting up 186
website configuration transforms 369
website, connecting to Service Bus topic
  about 206
  message, sending from controller 211, 212
  messaging logic, creating 208, 209
  website, creating 207
website deployment packages
  building 374
website deployment slots
  using 62, 63
WebSockets
  URL 293
Windows Identity Foundation (WIF) 34
Windows Phone application
  completing 349
  creating 342, 343
  data services, creating 343
  notifications debug 348
  push notifications, setting up 347
worker roles
  about 230
  creating 230-232
  examining 233
  finishing 258-260
  life cycle methods 234
  OrderTopicProcessor, using 248-250
  publishing 238-241
Work Item Alerts 89
WPF project
  preparing 311, 312

X

xPath variable
  URL 288

Z

Zudio
  URL 394

Thank you for buying
Learning Microsoft Azure

About Packt Publishing

Packt, pronounced 'packed', published its first book "Mastering phpMyAdmin for Effective MySQL Management" in April 2004 and subsequently continued to specialize in publishing highly focused books on specific technologies and solutions.

Our books and publications share the experiences of your fellow IT professionals in adapting and customizing today's systems, applications, and frameworks. Our solution based books give you the knowledge and power to customize the software and technologies you're using to get the job done. Packt books are more specific and less general than the IT books you have seen in the past. Our unique business model allows us to bring you more focused information, giving you more of what you need to know, and less of what you don't.

Packt is a modern, yet unique publishing company, which focuses on producing quality, cutting-edge books for communities of developers, administrators, and newbies alike. For more information, please visit our website: www.packtpub.com.

About Packt Enterprise

In 2010, Packt launched two new brands, Packt Enterprise and Packt Open Source, in order to continue its focus on specialization. This book is part of the Packt Enterprise brand, home to books published on enterprise software – software created by major vendors, including (but not limited to) IBM, Microsoft and Oracle, often for use in other corporations. Its titles will offer information relevant to a range of users of this software, including administrators, developers, architects, and end users.

Writing for Packt

We welcome all inquiries from people who are interested in authoring. Book proposals should be sent to author@packtpub.com. If your book idea is still at an early stage and you would like to discuss it first before writing a formal book proposal, contact us; one of our commissioning editors will get in touch with you.

We're not just looking for published authors; if you have strong technical skills but no writing experience, our experienced editors can help you develop a writing career, or simply get some additional reward for your expertise.

Learning Windows Azure Mobile Services for Windows 8 and Windows Phone 8

ISBN: 978-1-78217-192-8   Paperback: 124 pages

A short, fast and focused guide to enhance your Windows 8 applications by leveraging the power of Windows Azure Mobile Services

1. Dive deep into Azure Mobile Services with a practical XAML-based case study game.

2. Enhance your applications with push notifications and notifications hub.

3. Follow step-by-step instructions for result-oriented examples.

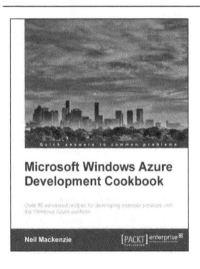

Microsoft Windows Azure Development Cookbook

ISBN: 978-1-84968-222-0   Paperback: 392 pages

Over 80 advanced recipes for developing scalable services with the Windows Azure platform

1. Packed with practical, hands-on cookbook recipes for building advanced, scalable cloud-based services on the Windows Azure platform explained in detail to maximize your learning.

2. Extensive code samples showing how to use advanced features of Windows Azure blobs, tables, and queues.

3. Understand remote management of Azure services using the Windows Azure Service Management REST API.

Please check **www.PacktPub.com** for information on our titles

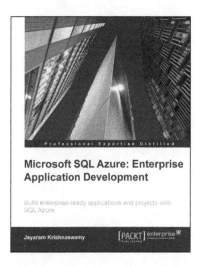

Microsoft SQL Azure: Enterprise Application Development

ISBN: 978-1-84968-080-6   Paperback: 420 pages

Build enterprise-ready applications and projects with SQL Azure

1. Develop large-scale enterprise applications using Microsoft SQL Azure.

2. Understand how to use the various third-party programs such as DB Artisan, RedGate, and ToadSoft developed for SQL Azure.

3. Master the exhaustive data migration and data synchronization aspects of SQL Azure.

4. Includes SQL Azure projects in incubation and more recent developments including all 2010 updates.

Windows Azure Programming Patterns for Start-ups

ISBN: 978-1-84968-560-3   Paperback: 292 pages

A step-by-step guide to create easy solutions to build your business using Windows Azure services

1. Explore the different features of Windows Azure and its unique concepts.

2. Get to know the Windows Azure platform by code snippets and samples by a single start-up scenario throughout the book.

3. A clean example scenario demonstrates the different Windows Azure features.

Please check **www.PacktPub.com** for information on our titles

www.ingramcontent.com/pod-product-compliance
Lightning Source LLC
Chambersburg PA
CBHW081501050326
40690CB00015B/2878